Who Runs Georgia?

Calvin Kytle and James A. Mackay

Who Runs Georgia?

Foreword by Dan T. Carter

THE UNIVERSITY OF GEORGIA PRESS

ATHENS AND LONDON

Published by the University of Georgia Press
Athens, Georgia 30602
© 1998 by Calvin Kytle and James A. Mackay
Foreword © 1998 by the University of Georgia Press
All rights reserved
Designed by Erin Kirk New
Set in Palatino by G&S Typesetters
Printed and bound by Maple-Vail, Inc.
The paper in this book meets the guidelines for
permanence and durability of the Committee on
Production Guidelines for Book Longevity of the
Council on Library Resources.

Printed in the United States of America

02 01 00 99 98   C   5 4 3 2 1

Library of Congress Cataloging in Publication Data

Kytle, Calvin.
Who runs Georgia? / Calvin Kytle and James A. Mackay ;
foreword by Dan T. Carter.
p.   cm.
Includes bibliographical references and index.
ISBN 0-8203-1986-4 (alk. paper).
— ISBN 0-8203-2075-7 (pbk. : alk. paper)
1. Georgia—Politics and government—1865–1950.
2. Elite (Social sciences)—Georgia—Interviews.
I. Mackay, James A. (James Armstrong), 1919–   . II. Title.
JK4316.K97 1998
306.2'09758—dc21   98-13240

British Library Cataloging in Publication Data available

To the memory of Cullen Gosnell, John A. Griffin,

Grace Towns Hamilton, George Mitchell,

and Josephine Wilkins.

Contents

Foreword

Dan T. Carter

I first read this manuscript well over a decade ago, and I can still remember that mixture of surprise and pleasure I felt as I turned the pages. In the years that followed, a number of historians and journalists have begun to explore the interplay of racial, social, and economic forces in the history of the postwar South, but *Who Runs Georgia?* remains as insightful today as it was when I first read it in 1982.[1]

Above all, it offers us the advantage of immediacy in recapturing both the substance and the texture of political life in the American South poised between the end of one era and the beginning of another. The collapse of the cotton economy during the Great Depression undermined the foundations of the old order, a process subtly reinforced by Roosevelt's New Deal and the upheavals of wartime mobilization. At the same time, the Supreme Court's 1944 decision (*Smith v. Allwright*) outlawing the white Democratic primary challenged the very linchpin on which the old order had rested: white supremacy and black disfranchisement.

Southern progressives were by no means united on a reform agenda. Some were far more interested in traditional "good government" goals than in taking on such controversial issues as Georgia's infamously undemocratic county unit system, the abuse of corporate power, the rights of the fledgling labor movement, or the ongoing pattern of discrimination against African Americans.

Of these issues, race was easily the most contentious. A handful—a very small handful—like novelist Lillian Smith, were willing to challenge the system head on. Most other whites who saw themselves as moderates or even liberals on the race question were content to work within the existing segregated social order, defending the right of black Georgians to vote and be free from the more brutal forms of white oppression. In a sense, this was a generation of liber-

als caught between the end of the class-oriented politics of
the New Deal era, which downplayed race, and the begin-
nings of the new-style liberalism of the 1950s and 1960s,
which emphasized individualism, personal rights, and the
corrosive impact of racism.

Still, there was a vague overlapping consensus: the New
Deal had saved the region from economic collapse, the war
had generated an economic boom that brought opportunity
to millions of southerners, and the next stage was to institute reforms that would bring about the "democratization"
of the region and the end of rule by self-serving economic
elites and racist demagogues. If conservatives remained in
the driver's seat in most states, postwar reform candidates
like Arkansas's Sid McMath, North Carolina's Kerr Scott,
and Alabama's Big Jim Folsom suggested the possibility of
better days ahead for southern reformers.

Nor were such voter rebellions limited to statewide political movements. The interviews that Calvin Kytle and James
Mackay conducted in Augusta, for example, give the reader
a vivid portrait of the clash between reform-minded return-
ing veterans and Roy Harris's Cracker Party, a quintessential
example of the state's entrenched and often corrupt local political machines.

For Georgia's conservative leaders—like their counterparts across the South—the political upheavals of the postwar era threatened their survival. As historian-journalist
John Egerton so aptly summarized the credo of the large-
scale landowners, small-town elites, corporate leaders, and
utility executives who had dominated the politics of the
region, the only South worth defending was one of "low
taxes, low wages, high profits, and balanced budgets; states'
rights, limited government, and selective federal aid without interference from Washington; a cheap, plentiful labor
force without unions; and always, unfailingly, an abiding
devotion to segregation and white supremacy."[2]

For Egerton, no state more aptly symbolized the conflict

between the past and the future than the Georgia of the late 1940s. In some respects, progressives in that state labored under peculiar disadvantages. An archaic form of political representation—the county unit system—meant that voters in the rural countryside had far greater power than their urban counterparts. It was a system that strengthened the hand of reactionaries like Eugene Talmadge, who made it to the governor's mansion repeatedly by offering voters a witch's brew of racism, pseudopopulism, and economically reactionary policies. Because of the county unit system, he was able to combine these reactionary policies with an open contempt for the state's urban voters, boasting with only mild exaggeration that he had never campaigned in a county that had a streetcar. (In conversations with his male cronies around the state, he was more explicit: "Come see me at the mansion. We'll sit on the front porch and piss over the rail on those city bastards.")[3]

In spite of this undemocratic electoral system, Georgia voters elected two moderately progressive governors, Ed Rivers and Ellis Arnall, and the state boasted an articulate minority of white reformers willing to speak out against poverty, racism, and the rule of reactionary political elites. In the wake of *Smith v. Allwright,* these embattled white reformers gained important political strength when more than one hundred thousand black Georgians registered and voted solidly against Eugene Talmadge when he made his third bid for the governorship. At the same time, the Congress of Industrial Organizations had launched its "Operation Dixie" with the goal of bringing a million southern workers—black and white—into a dynamic political labor movement, and Georgia was one of the target states.

Leaders of the old regime, well aware that the white majority was uneasy in the wake of a generation of uncertainty and upheaval, moved quickly to manipulate these fears in order to maintain their privileged racial and economic position.

Race as always proved the flash point. The year had scarcely begun before "unknown persons" murdered a south Georgia veteran who had become the first registered black in his black belt county, and it reached a bloody climax that summer when a Walton County mob—unmasked and operating in broad daylight—calmly lynched two black tenant farmers and their wives in the wake of a dispute with the landlord. The Walton County sheriff expressed little interest in investigating the incident, although he did concede that the mob overreacted. "They hadn't ought to killed the two women," he apologetically explained to a visiting reporter.[4]

Thus, even though newly registered black voters made it possible for moderate candidate James V. Carmichael to gain a popular majority in the 1946 Democratic primary, Georgia's county unit system allowed the dying Eugene Talmadge to capture a majority of the all-important county unit votes. After his father's death between the primary election and the swearing-in ceremony, Herman Talmadge failed in his bizarre effort to seize the state governorship. But only two years later, riding a tide of political reaction and white supremacy, he won in a special election.

By the early 1950s, the postwar hopes of southern liberals had been dashed. Nothing more fully illustrated the changed political terrain than the smear campaign used to defeat Senator Frank Porter Graham, the much respected southern liberal and longtime president of the University of North Carolina.

In 1949, North Carolina governor Kerr Scott had appointed Graham to fill an interim vacancy in the United States Senate. When Graham ran for reelection the following year, his conservative opponent, Willis Smith—a prominent Raleigh lawyer and former president of the American Bar Association—introduced the new twin themes of southern politics: red-baiting and racism. With the effective assistance of reactionary advisers, notably a twenty-eight-year-old radio newsman named Jesse Helms, Smith's campaign blanketed the state with scurrilous flyers and ads depicting Graham and other southern liberals as communist fellow travelers intent on destroying the South through encouraging racial amalgamation. ("Do you want Negroes working beside you and your wife and daughters . . . eating beside you . . . using your toilet facilities?")[5]

That same year, using similar smear tactics, Florida's conservative congressman George Smathers unseated the veteran New Deal senator Claude Pepper (or the "Red Pepper" as Smathers and his followers labeled him).

In Georgia, the war seemed over without a battle. After gaining election in 1948 to the last two years of what would have been his father's third term, young Herman Talmadge had skillfully adapted the new mantra of southern politics: liberalism equals communism equals mongrelization of the races. Ellis Arnall, the one-time white knight of Georgia liberals, refused to run and later justified his decision: "Herman had pulled everybody so far to the right that there was no way I could have won."[6]

Insofar as the emotional issues of race and radicalism were concerned, Arnall's characterization of Georgia politics was on the mark. In that state and throughout the region, conservatives like Talmadge—using an artful blend of racism, anticommunism, and a traditional fear of "outside agitators"—had successfully turned back the struggling efforts of progressive southerners and their white supporters to break the deadlock of the past. By the early 1950s, the labor movement's effort to organize the South had collapsed under the fierce assault of conservative business leaders and their political supporters. At the same time, racist politicians across the region had mobilized the power of the state to intimidate black citizens in a futile effort to return to the days of unquestioned white supremacy. It would take another fifteen years of bitter struggle before the combined forces of the civil rights movement and the intervention of all three branches of the federal government finally forced white southerners to abandon segregation and the cruel trappings of white supremacy.

Herman Talmadge played the race card as well as his father, but the old-style racism of the pre–World War II South was living on borrowed time. Try as they might, postwar conservatives could not return to the past. The continuing decline in the influence of rural and small-town Georgia, the rise of suburbia, and the growing influence of Atlanta's corporate and business interests had reshaped the state's economy and political structure. Like Humpty Dumpty, the old regime could not be put together again. Thus, for example, the younger Talmadge moved deftly to absorb some elements of postwar reformers, emphasizing the importance of good schools, improved transportation, and more efficient public administration, even if it was to be financed primarily by regressive sales taxes.

Of course Calvin Kytle and James Mackay did not have the advantage of hindsight when they began traveling around Georgia in the spring and summer of 1947.

It makes it all the more astonishing that this document remains, in many ways, as fresh and relevant as it was a half century ago. Bound neither by a preconceived set of questions nor a rigid methodology, they often let the conversation take its own heading. As a result, we have the sense that we are hearing—unimpeded—the voice of a generation.

After reading this book, who could ever forget the voices of this colorful cast of scoundrels, cynics, and occasional heroes? On every page, there are also insightful observations by the authors based on their close observation of local politics. At a time when scholars' interest in the role of gender lay far in the future, for example, Kytle and Mackay point to the critical role that black women played in the emergence of local black political participation. Anyone interested in the early stages of the civil rights movement—and in the white ambivalent response—will find *Who Runs Georgia?* essential reading.

In my view, however, the greatest strength of this book lies in its relentless probing of the intersection between economic and political interests. Historians often speak of the advantage of hindsight, but the authors of *Who Runs Georgia?* may have been greater beneficiaries of their immediate past, for they were part of a generation shaped by the economic crisis of the 1930s, a generation that had been forced to ask the kind of fundamental question that is timeless: What is at the intersection of economic interests and political power? In this case, who *really* ran the state of Georgia?

Scholars have long known about this manuscript. Now, thanks to the University of Georgia Press, another generation can have the pleasure and reward of learning what Kytle and Mackay learned fifty years ago about a critical moment in the history of their state and region.

NOTES

1. It would be impossible to mention all the many autobiographies and memoirs that have appeared or to include all the accounts of the immediate postwar South, but any list of essential reading would certainly include John Egerton's *Speak Now Against the Day: The Generation before the Civil Rights Movement* (New York: Alfred A. Knopf, 1994), Patricia Sullivan's *Days of Hope: Race and Democracy in the New Deal Era* (Chapel Hill: University of North Carolina Press, 1966), and Numan Bartley's *The New South, 1945–1980* (Baton Rouge: Louisiana State University Press, 1995).

2. Egerton, *Speak Now Against the Day*, 330.

3. Numan V. Bartley, *The Creation of Modern Georgia* (Athens: University of Georgia Press, 1983), 175.

4. William Anderson, *The Wild Man from Sugar Creek: The Political Career of Eugene Talmadge* (Baton Rouge: Louisiana State University Press, 1975), 233.

5. Augustus Burns and Julian Pleasants, *Frank Porter Graham and the 1950 Senate Race in North Carolina* (Chapel Hill: University of North Carolina Press, 1990), 223.

6. Egerton, *Speak Now Against the Day*, 521.

Authors' Preface

I

Of all the Georgians shocked by the turn of political events after the 1946 Democratic primary, none were more confounded, disappointed, and outraged than the six who commissioned the study on which this book is based: George Mitchell, of the Southern Regional Council; Grace Hamilton, of the Atlanta Urban League; Alexander Miller, of the Anti-Defamation League; Josephine Wilkins, of the Citizens' Fact-Finding Movement; A. T. Walden, of the all-Negro Georgia Association of Citizen Democratic Clubs; and Frank McCallister, of the Georgia Workers' Education Service.

I think it accurate to say that this group constituted the Atlanta nucleus of a new class of southern rebels, one whose common cause would later redefine the regional culture. In 1947, however, its members were united as much by frustration as by their internalized and institutionalized hostility toward the flourishing injustices of the status quo. To one degree or another, each had carried a heavy emotional investment in Ellis Arnall's reform program; Arnall himself had credited Josephine Wilkins and her Fact-Finding Movement for the rationale and much of the content of the new state constitution, a major accomplishment of his administration. Now, their hopes shattered by the return of the Talmadges, they wanted to know what had happened, who and what social forces had caused it to happen, and what they and the organizations they led might do to make sure it did not happen again. George Mitchell served as the group's coordinator, and it was he who got a grant from the Julius Rosenwald Foundation—as I recall, for five thousand dollars—to hire Jamie Mackay and me in an effort to find out.

At the time, Jamie and I were only a year back from service in World War II. Jamie had just passed the Georgia bar. I had just lost my job on the planning staff of what was to have been a regional newsmagazine but which had made it only through a prototypical issue before running out of capital. The two of us were known personally to some members of the group, notably Miss Wilkins and Dr. Mitchell. The others were inclined to think well of us, I believe, for having earlier shown a willingness to stick our necks out; we had been chairman and treasurer, respectively, of the Georgia Veterans for Majority Rule, an ad hoc committee organized to raise money for the first court assault on the county unit system. So much for credentials.

When we began our assignment, Herman Talmadge's election to the governorship by the legislature was being challenged by M. E. Thompson, the lieutenant governor nominate. Arnall, who as incumbent governor had refused to vacate until a legitimate governor had been seated, had now stepped aside, awaiting a decision from the state supreme court. The decision in Thompson's favor came down a month before adjournment of the General Assembly, which we had been monitoring. Shortly thereafter, Jamie and I took off in a '42 Plymouth on a trip that yielded, all told, more than a hundred interviews, sixty-four of which are included in these pages as Part 2.

It was a suspenseful summer. The Talmadge and Thompson factions were regrouping nervously for the 1948 special election, in which the Negro's right to vote was expected once again to be the dominant campaign theme. In South Carolina the state supreme court was debating the constitutionality of an act of the legislature that would preserve the white primary by removing all references to it from the statute books. The anticipated decision was a worry to the Talmadge forces, for they had proposed a similar strategy as a way to keep Georgia's own white primary.

What Jamie and I did, I suppose, would nowadays be called anecdotal research. Dr. Mitchell, himself a scholar of considerable stature, clearly was not asking for a product of footnoted scholarship. Blessedly, he never once talked of "methodology." He helped us work up a list of basic interview questions—the essential one being "Who runs Georgia?"—but cautioned us to use the questions mainly as points of departure. "Let your subjects roam," he said. "This isn't a crop survey, and nuance is all important." He told us to talk with anybody of political consequence that we could get to talk. Whenever we had something worth reporting, he said, or if ever we felt in need of direction, he would call a meeting of the group. Otherwise, he and the others would await our written summary. He advised us to write with no intent of publication. The committee's members wanted the truth as we saw it; we should write for them as our only readers. This was the sum of our instructions.

A mutual friend volunteered advice, mostly about how to get members of the enemy camp "to open up." Offering a man a cigarette was a good way to put a stranger at ease, he said, and smoking would also help us appear more relaxed. (Remember, this was thirty-five years before the surgeon general's report.) More constructively, he warned us that note taking could be "distracting and even intimidating." As a consequence, with few exceptions, Jamie or I took notes only when it was important to record numbers. We developed a skill that neither of us has retained, that of memorizing long and often circumlocutory conversations. (The portable tape recorder was yet to be invented.) So, to ensure accuracy, as soon as an interview closed, we would dash to the nearest convenient flat surface (which sometimes meant a picnic table in a public park) and get out my Royal portable, and I would type up a report while everything was fresh on our minds.

We found most of our subjects easy to talk with. Jamie would introduce himself as a young lawyer who was thinking about going into politics. I would say, truthfully, that I was collecting material for what I planned to be a political novel. If we dissembled at all, it was to say nothing about the Atlanta group that was paying us subsistence money while we toured the state. Perhaps because we were young, open, and harmless looking, we found people, including the most tough minded of the politicians, almost invariably eager to talk, even when they were telling us things that should have embarrassed them. Why this is so is something perhaps best left to a psychiatrist, but I suspect the explanation may lie in the same psychology that leads men conditioned to keep their mouths shut at home to confide readily in strangers. A few of the persons on our list agreed to talk with us only on condition of nonattribution, and this is why, for example, you will find here no record of our talks with Ellis Arnall or Philip Weltner, although we drew liberally on their views in developing our narrative summary (Part 1).

As it turned out, we met informally with the committee about a half dozen times over the course of the year. Sometimes we were joined by others in what the Talmadges routinely called "that crowd of Atlanta liberals" (some "crowd"), among them Dorothy Tilly of the Georgia Methodist Churchwomen, one of the two southerners appointed by President Truman to the U.S. Committee on Civil Rights. Jamie and I were together responsible for the content and structure of our reports. The prose, however, was mine. The summaries went through several working titles (in some libraries you can find one of them cataloged as *We Pass*). The full report went through enough versions that when I went into the files earlier this year and set about preparing it, at last, for publication as a book, I had trouble identifying the final draft.

Though our report never got beyond manuscript form, it acquired a currency that gave it a surreptitious readership of some influence. It also gave Jamie and me a short-lived notoriety. When our project was done, copies were given to members of the committee for discreet distribution. Some-

how, one got into the hands of W. O. "Bee" Brooks, editor of
the Talmadge newspaper, the *Statesman*, who over several
issues ran excerpts out of context, ostensibly to prove that
there were "sinister" forces at work in Atlanta backed by
Yankee money. Jamie he described as "the misguided son of
a prominent Methodist minister." About me he could report
only that I was "without visible means of support." When
Jamie subsequently ran for the state legislature and later for
a seat in the U.S. Congress, quotes from the report were
regularly used by his opposition in efforts to discredit him—
unsuccessfully, I'm happy to say. I drew on our findings for
several newspaper and magazine articles during the forties,
and over the years what appears here as Part 1 was deposited in special collections at several universities, where more
than one doctoral candidate has apparently found it useful.

Publication of *Who Runs Georgia?*, however, is the first
time that the complete report has been made generally available, and it is in every important detail exactly as we submitted it to our committee more than fifty years ago. Going
through it for errors in spelling and syntax, I have found it a
youthful work written in a style that sometimes makes me
wince, and I have wished many times to rewrite. Honesty
required me to resist every time. It is also a work of a particular time and place, when both races used "Negro" as
the polite word for African American; when public figures
spoke of "the people" meaning *white* people; when Georgia
was still a one-party state and political campaigns were
conducted through long speeches on the stump rather than
ten-second television bites. The text remains faithful to the
period. Wherever I felt a contemporary reference might be
incomprehensible to today's readers, I have written an end
note, sometimes a rather long one. I have taken only one liberty within the body of the manuscript; I have cut words
and phrases and sometimes paragraphs wherever I found
I'd repeated myself.

Once, after reading one of the drafts, George Mitchell said

to me gently, "My, Calvin, you *do* have a tendency to curl pigtails." What he meant was that I was not always content to let a fact speak for itself. He was right, and this time I have tried earnestly to get rid of the last curl.

                                            CALVIN KYTLE

II

In September 1948 *Harper's* magazine carried Calvin's prophetic piece *A Long Dark Night for Georgia?* The night came, and it lasted for eighteen years, most of which I spent as a member of the lower house of the Georgia legislature.

I had long been interested in legislative politics as well as private practice, and I venture to say that what has characterized my life—and Calvin's as well—is the same point of view, and some of the same passion, that come through between the lines of this book.

For an important part of this point of view I credit the then head of Emory University's department of political science, Dr. Cullen Gosnell, a true "tiger in the ivy." In 1917, the primary election rules prescribing the county unit system were enacted into law. Dr. Gosnell was one of the few to protest the resulting malapportionment of political power. With courage and tenacity, he argued that the system frustrated and confounded the will of the people, and he spent his life fighting for its abolition. Calvin and I were among the students who joined his crusade.

So, when in the spring of 1950 a seat became vacant in the DeKalb delegation to the state House of Representatives, I thought I saw a small opportunity to help advance the cause. I campaigned, and won, on a promise to support funding of the Minimum Foundation for Education (later accomplished with passage of a 3 percent general sales tax) and to work for a fair and effective ballot.

I served for six terms, all told, and for me it was an exciting and instructive time. I made some good friends, became a reasonably good and temperate negotiator, and learned much about human behavior that both cheered and depressed me. But for most purposes of general welfare the General Assembly was stagnant. From where I sat on the House floor I heard *every* gross appeal to ignorance and fear, as well as to racial, religious, and sectional prejudice. These same appeals were carried regularly in the Talmadge organ, the *Statesman*; Tom Linder's *Market Bulletin*; and the most virulent of all, Roy Harris's *Augusta Courier*, which circulated in every one of the 159 counties. The political rhetoric of that era was lethal. Discouragingly, too, all our attempts to reform election procedures, which the DeKalb delegation faithfully pursued, were fruitless.

In those days, it was axiomatic that no one need apply for the office of governor or U.S. senator if he lived in any one of the six big urban counties. All my constituents lived in DeKalb, the second most populous county in the state. Because of the unit system, they were effectively disfranchised. It was impossible to get the system abolished by act of the assembly, for to ask support from the rural legislators who dominated it was to ask them to vote themselves out of office. Moreover, these entrenched rural legislators would gleefully assure us "complainers" that we would never obtain relief from the other two branches of government either, because governors and judges gained power under the same system. They were more right than wrong; the petitions from our delegation to successive governors never even got the courtesy of replies.

Yet the times were changing. The economy was growing, new people were flocking to Georgia, and blacks were voting in increasing numbers. Perhaps most promising of all, public-spirited citizens were continuing to seek redress through the federal courts despite Justice Felix Frankfurter's determination to keep the courts out of "the political thicket." What's more, the fight for electoral equity was no longer confined to Georgia. In fact, the breakthrough came in 1962 when the Supreme Court, overriding Frankfurter's objection, heard a Tennessee case, *Baker v. Carr*, and in effect ruled that to give disproportionate value to votes according to citizens' place of residence violated the equal-protection clause of the Fourteenth Amendment. Armed with this decision, Morris Abram, a brilliant and indefatigable lawyer who had argued several earlier suits, immediately filed *Sanders v. Gray* and won. On March 18, 1963, the U.S. Supreme Court ruled that "within a given constituency there can be no room for but one constitutional rule—one voter, one vote." A splendid young state senator, James P. Wesberry Jr., then won a suit seeking equitable congressional apportionment. With that, the unit system was doomed. The long dark night was almost over.

So much for judicial relief. What about Congress?

In 1964, shortly after passage of the most comprehensive civil rights act in the nation's history, I ran for Congress from the new Fourth District and defeated the Republican nominee in the general election. I took office with an old associate, Charles Weltner, who had been reelected from the remainder of the old Fifth. We had hardly been sworn in when President Lyndon Johnson proposed legislation to guarantee minorities free and nondiscriminatory access to the polls. Charlie and I voted for the Voting Rights Act of 1965 and felt no backlash; after all, our constituents had known all about discrimination at the ballot box for decades.

The conclusions that Calvin and I came to in 1947 have stood the test of time fairly well. Georgia, and the dialogue of state politics, changed radically, as we had hoped they would, with an end to the county unit, one-party system, and time has proved that people historically banned from the processes of democracy can be educated to the demands of self-government. Current events in Washington, though, may imply something different. Unhappily, one can read the pages that follow and listen to the evening news (I did both yesterday) and conclude that what stamped Georgia politics in the late forties has been enlarged and exported. The name-calling, the negative campaigning, the unregulated solicitation and misuse of campaign funds, the crushing weight of corporate power, the civic passivity and low voter turnout—all have come to typify our national political behavior. It's as if the gallus-snapping, shirt-sleeved demagogues of Georgia's yesterday have merely moved north, acquired Armani suits and new accents, and gone on network television.

I live now on the Georgia side of Lookout Mountain, in what is surely one of the loveliest spots on earth. It may be that my years and the natural beauties of this place combine to make me unusually prone to reflection, certainly more so than my younger friends, preoccupied as they are with the pressures of their days. Nevertheless, I cannot help hoping that this half-century-old study of ours will find some readers among the present generation and perhaps move them to think about our findings in the context of today's messy political environment.

JAMES A. MACKAY

PART 1

The Way It Is

Prologue

It was early February 1947, and we had come to this man first, knowing we would get an honest answer. He was Secretary of State Ben Fortson, a man of rare distinction: after fifteen years in state politics, he still commanded the respect of both factions.

Our question depressed him. He repeated it, shifting his cigar from one corner of his mouth to the other as he spoke. "Who runs Georgia?" And he sighed. "The corporations. The corporations run Georgia. That's why it won't make any difference, really, who the court decides for. The same old people will run things. It'll just cost 'em a bit more if the court decides for M. E."

Since then we have interviewed several hundred other Georgians. We sat through most of the 1947 session of the General Assembly, and during the summer we took a swing through the state by car. We talked with legislators, lobbyists, merchants, bankers, county and state officials, newspaper reporters and editors, doctors, preachers, teachers, farmers, hotel keepers, clerks, factory workers, filling station operators—people who see politics variously as a business, a sport, a civic obligation, or a morality play.

We were prepared for the platitudes and the glorified cynicism we got from politicians. We knew enough to expect innocence, indifference, or ignorance from people who had no direct interest, either personal or academic, in politics. But what got us—in the heart and sometimes in the stomach—were the responses from men of acknowledged leadership, men who had tried for most of their lives to make government meet the needs of the people.

Each had a different experience to describe, but they all seemed to be of the same mind. They talked sorrowfully, and almost without exception somewhere during the interview there would come the note of despair, followed by a pause and the gesture of resignation—a shake of the head, a long sigh, a shrug, an upturned palm.

"There are forty counties in the state that can be bought up till the day of election," a famous newspaper editor told us. "There are forty more—you might call them venal. The venal ones won't sell for cash, but they can be had. An expert bargaining agent who knows the key men to bargain with can swing them to almost any candidate."

"What's important in Georgia politics," said a veteran legislator, "is not how the people vote but how the votes are counted."

"We've never had an honest vote in Georgia," a former governor said matter-of-factly. "Why, there are Lord knows how many counties that hold up their returns till the last minute, then come out for the man they know will win. If that means they have to change the returns—okay, they change the returns."

"We'll never have honest elections in Georgia till we have a mandatory secret ballot in every county, and maybe not until we require voting machines in every militia district," a country editor and a former state senator said. "That business in the general election in Telfair last year? I think maybe our primaries have been even worse."

"By golly," said a former commissioner of revenue, "what we need is a thorough overhaul of the tax structure. We ought to get some real experts down here—say, a team from the Brookings Institute—and have them do an objective study and offer some recommendations. But do you think our legislature would stand for that? They don't exactly welcome experts from Georgia, and it's for sure they're not gonna listen to any from anywhere else." He reflected a moment. "They're afraid that any recommendation for a change in the tax system is going to lead to new taxes—which of course it should—and to their way of thinking new taxes automatically mean higher taxes. Before we can do much of anything, we've got to educate the legislature."

"The people aren't interested in issues," said another newspaperman. "All they want is a show—some good stump talk and barbecue. Maybe they want good roads and three-dollar license plates. A few of them talk about the need for good schools. But beyond that, if they want anything out of the state, they sure haven't shown it."

"The people?" said a welfare worker. "They want everything Ed Rivers gave them without having to pay for any of it."

"We're stuck," said an experienced legislator from a four-unit county. "The county unit system makes it possible for a few Atlanta corporations to control the state, and yet the people cling to the county unit system, thinking that without it we'd be run by city machines. Where's the sense to that?"

"You can't get elected in Georgia without money," said a sixty-five-year-old lawyer, "and you can't get money except from the wrong people."

"I'm glad now I wasn't elected," said a defeated candidate for governor. "I'd hate to have to try to stand up against all the pressures from the special interest groups who supported me. You add up everything it takes to run a campaign—radio time, newspaper ads, workers to put up posters all over the state, automobiles, all that—and I'd say it takes a quarter of a million dollars to run anybody's campaign. The thing is, the Big Boys don't give that kind of money for nothing, and you can't get it from preachers."

Such talk wasn't confined to the older men. We heard it from a few our own age, World War II veterans serving their first terms in the General Assembly. "They'll never get me to run again," one of said. "I've learned you can't stay a decent human being and play practical politics." Another one, deploring the complacency of his home folks, said sourly, "The people of Georgia are getting just the kind of government they deserve."

We keep thinking of these people, and of the political realities that have sickened them. Now, every time we pick up a newspaper, things they had to say appear between the headlines, like editorial asides. They are the explanatory notes to the election of Herman Talmadge by the legislature, the year-long battle for control of the Democratic Party, the election frauds in Telfair County, the vote auction in Dodge, the clerical error that may invalidate 350 local bills, the illegal efforts to purge the voter registration lists, and—oh yes—the reports of serious deficiencies in the departments of health, welfare, and education. We read these things and recall their voices, and we ask ourselves, "What, in the name of democracy, is happening to Georgia?"

The Men in the Wings

It's not quite true to say that the corporations run Georgia. What's more nearly accurate is that a few executives in a few corporations, together with a few skilled politicians, run Georgia.

You can name on no more than ten fingers the economic groups that dominate the state government: the gas and electric utilities, the railroads, the pipelines, and the trucking companies, all of which seek favorable representation before the Public Service Commission; the liquor dealers, who fight a perennial battle against the threat of new dry laws; the Coca-Cola and Nehi bottlers, ever fearful of a soft drinks tax; the insurance companies and independent contractors that do business with the state; the textile mills, whose owners have found that the best way to fight unionization is through prohibitive legislation; and the banks, which in one way or another are invested in all the corporations. That's just about the crop.

It's our judgment that the policy makers for these industries have no doctrinal interest in politics. They simply want to be as free of taxation as possible, to protect themselves against government regulation, and to get special favors from time to time. But to get what they want, and to avoid what they don't want, requires that they keep an "in" with the executive division by donating vast sums of money to campaign coffers. It requires, further, that they maintain a favored position with the assembly, not only by backing individual legislators but also by pressure and negotiation through lobbyists and trade associations. While their stated purpose is to prevent undue interference from government, their impulse is to seek absolute security through absolute control.

We don't think, either, that the corporations have a special, enduring devotion for any one politician. With the possible exception of Ellis Arnall, whom they often considered "unreasonable," they have shown a disposition and the adaptability to work with them all. Few men offering for public office are so bold or so imprudent as to differ with them on principle.

For their purposes, corporation executives need a political personality who can reconcile their special demands with the conflicting demands of the public, a man who, as Emory University professor Cullen Gosnell once put it, "can pull the wool hat over our eyes." There are some among them who deplore a demagogic stump appeal and who would like to see a bit more dignity around the capitol. Sometimes they'll put the heavy money behind a man in a business suit—say, Richard Russell—who neither chews tobacco nor wears red suspenders and string ties nor affects a drawl and bad grammar. On occasion they quarrel among themselves, as the railroads and pipelines did in 1941, at which times the more influential politicians are pressed to take sides, and civil servants, cloaking themselves in neutrality, take on the look of bewildered children caught in a custody fight.

But the corporation agents never let a quarrel so offend a strong politician that, should that politician get in power, they can't buy their way back in. Usually, though they may

give their main support to a preferred candidate, the men
with money are careful to make respectable contributions to
all contenders, just in case. Whoever wins is their man. If
revenue must be raised, they have the tacit promise that it
will not come from their pockets. They can be sure that there
will be none of this hated planning in Georgia, none of this
nonsense about enlarging and integrating government services into a costly program for the general welfare. Thus,
instead of tackling basic problems, we will continue to wage
Pyrrhic war against the Negro. Our children will continue
to suffer from substandard schools, our sick from inade-
quate medical facilities, and most of our people from insuf-
ficient incomes.[1]

We don't mean to imply by this that corporate control is
new or that it is unique to Georgia. We know from our high
school history that the banks of Wall Street and the manufacturers of New England took over in the South about the
same time they came to power in America—that is, after the
collapse of Populism in 1896. Nor do we mean to say that
corporations have no right to concern themselves with government. Corporations exist only by virtue of special or
general acts of the legislature; their very lives depend on
the state. The power to tax being the power to destroy,
an unfriendly assembly could move an entire industry to
the edge of bankruptcy. What's more, most corporations to
some degree are always vulnerable to shakedowns from political hacks who either threaten to introduce a damaging
bill unless they pay through the nose or who, for a price,
arrange to have a pending bill withdrawn. If they intend to
stay in business, corporations have to interest themselves in
government.

What we do mean is that the influence of the corporations
has been peculiarly virulent in Georgia, as in most southern states, because our resistance has been peculiarly low.
Our impoverishment after the War Between the States left
us helpless against economic penetration from the North.

("The great question," said Robert Toombs sixty years ago, "is shall Georgia govern the corporations or the corporations govern Georgia.")[2] For a wild, brief moment we rallied behind Tom Watson,[3] hoping through him to join our strength with that of the West and break the bonds of eastern finance. When that failed, our only alternative seemed to be to deal with the Yankee on his terms. Our romantic cultural tradition, our violent paroxysms of race prejudice, and the absence of a strong and vocal labor movement tended to obscure what was happening to us, to make it easier for the industrialists and financiers to establish an invisible tyranny. The result was that Georgia has been reduced to the status of a colony where, by continued infestation of the state government and through the artful work of modern-day Scalawags, the agents for northern capital have been able to keep her.

Playing as they do such a vital role in our economy, capitalists have every right to fair representation in government. But when they begin to dominate the forces of government to the exclusion of other equally contributive groups, government becomes less and less *for* the people. And if circumstances should conspire so that businessmen with money support politicians of excessive ambition, and the result is tight control of the election machinery by a favored few, then government *by* the people is through.

We think that day almost came in Georgia last year. We think that is our crisis today.

The County Unit System and Whom It Serves

One of our proud delusions is that we in Georgia are blessedly free of machine politics.

Another is that, since political power is vested in the small rural counties, the state operates primarily for the benefit of our country folks.

If the two of us can believe what we have seen and heard, the truth is something quite different. The evidence is that there is not one political machine in Georgia but a score or more machines, the so-called courthouse rings, and that these sundry and independent county machines constitute the gears in a larger statewide machine. Largely because of this, the state has functioned primarily for the benefit of a privileged minority. No state administration has ever done more than to touch very tentatively the basic wants and needs of the majority, either country or city.

True, Georgia has no Boss Crump. It has no city machine comparable to that of the Pendergasts in Kansas City or Mayor Curley in Boston, with power enough to make a whole state beholden. The Georgia political machine has no common leader and no central discipline. It needs neither, for the very things that perpetuate it are supported by law and public opinion.

These things are the county unit system and the large number of small counties.[4]

A determining factor in the Democratic state primary, the county unit system is a cumbersome, costly, grossly unfair process for electing state officials, and most politicians and practically all urban middle-class Georgians know it. Political careerists, however, dismiss with a smile any suggestion that it be abandoned or revised. "It's mighty good for us country boys."

Georgia's rural population has been sold so thoroughly on the merits of the county unit system that they defend it reflexively. They say stoutly that the system is their only defense against the cities (meaning Atlanta, the root of all evil); without it, they say, farmers would have no voice in state government. Some of them recognize it as an insult to democratic principle yet say that even though undemocratic it's best for Georgia. Some will admit to the existence of county machines, or to the fact that the state is run by big Atlanta interests anyway, but few will say that to do away with the system might destroy all machines. Others say simply that they're for the system and offer no reasons at all. In their minds the system is as deeply entrenched as their prejudice toward the Negro. In fact, the system endures because of another kind of prejudice—the prejudice toward city people and city ways.

And yet we are convinced that this treasured system, under which state officers are elected by 159 counties rather than the votes of seven hundred thousand people, has made for continued machine rule. Here's how:

Because county unit votes are not figured accurately in ratio to a county's population, and because only a plurality of unit votes is needed, the important factor for election is not the will of the most people but the will of the people in the curiously strategic small counties. To be elected governor, for instance, a man must have 296 of the 410 county unit votes. Conceivably, he could get them without ever stepping foot in Atlanta, Macon, LaGrange, Augusta, Savannah, Albany, Rome, or Columbus. All he would need would be the unit votes from 103 of the 121 two-unit counties. In 1946 he could have been elected governor even though every ballot cast in the 56 larger counties went to his opponent.

By thus disfranchising the people in the large population centers, the county unit system reduces the electorate to a number that can be easily influenced and manipulated.

Under this system, we do not have one race in the Georgia primary but 159 different races, one for each county, whose unit votes must be obtained for victory within that county. This raises to disproportionate value the bargaining power of persons of local political influence and enormously increases the importance of the county rings, especially in counties where the people are about evenly divided between the traditional factions.

The prerequisite to winning a state election, therefore, is the ability to know and deal with the political leaders in those counties whose combined unit vote is sufficient to

ensure a plurality. This ability comes only after long experience, and its successful application requires an amoral attitude, a mind for details, a gift for organizing, and a salesman's personality. Few men in the state qualify, and yet
these are the indispensable men in any campaign.

In 1906 Tom Watson argued for the county unit system,
saying that without it the state would be run by a few city
bosses using "corporation influences, the job lash, money,
whiskey, and log rolling." As it's turned out, the system has
encouraged the very evils he said it would prevent. Under
the county unit system the balance of power rests with the
people least prepared to resist "corporation influences"—
that is, the people whose haunting need for money makes
them prey to the "job lash" and whose lack of schooling
makes them suckers for the deceptive talk of demagogues.
Tom Watson thought the system fine for Populists in 1906
because "we hold the balance of power in the country counties, and the country counties rule the state." The same
system is fine for the corporations in 1948 because they control the men who hold the balance of power in the country
counties.

This domination by corporations derives from two simple
circumstances: (1) It takes a lot of money to run campaigns;
and (2) corporation leaders have come to accept the need to
play politics as a matter of survival and to regard political
action as a normal cost of doing business.

The men who finance campaigns have grown understandably fond of Georgia's election procedure. It materially
reduces the expense of electioneering. (Why, for instance,
try at all for the six unit votes in Fulton County? A precinct-
by-precinct campaign among Fulton's ninety-three thousand voters, such as was conducted in 1946 by candidates
for Congress from the Fifth District, would cost at least
twenty-five thousand dollars. The same amount spent in a
dozen two-unit counties might very easily bring in as many
as twenty unit votes.) Equally as important, the unit system

has proved to be an almost impregnable defense against any serious threat to the status quo, such as the threat posed by the Weltner-Fortson movement in 1936.[5] Its divisive influence keeps dissident elements throughout the state from getting together and organizing. And, as an inherent factor in the preservation of the 159 distinct county governments, only the richest of which have resources enough to provide minimal public services, it helps sustain the ignorance and poverty from which the corporations' power derives.

What all this adds up to is a statewide political machine that is the product not of invention but of historical cause and effect. It operates naturally, almost inevitably, without any necessity for conspiracy. The money of corporation executives, the practiced skills of a few state politicians, and the exaggerated influence of leaders in the small, underpopulated counties constitute a machine that is as vicious and as durable as any of the most tightly entrenched city machines anywhere in the country.

For this unsavory situation corporation leaders must assume most of the responsibility. It so happens that in politics, where money is the essential ingredient, their freedom to put money behind one candidate and to keep it from another constitutes the final and most tenacious force for control.

You Pay the Bills, You Can Call the Tune

It's awfully hard to put your finger on the source and amount of campaign funds. No faction ever publishes a complete and accurate accounting, and all you get from workers in the several campaign headquarters is evasion and contradiction.

About the only thing for sure is that campaigns cost plenty. As a very simple gauge, take the standard rates for radio and newspaper advertising. It costs $1,100 to run a single ten-inch ad in all the papers in Georgia, something that's done many times during a campaign by all leading contestants. Fifteen minutes during a peak listening period on WSB alone costs $162.

Probably not even the managers themselves know exactly how much is spent on a candidate, and it's certain that the candidates don't. The money put out through state campaign headquarters is only a part of the total expense. Additional money, of which there is no permanent record, is raised by local committees and spent within the county. Large amounts also are spent independently by special interest groups. It's of some help to a candidate's conscience if he does not know the amount of money being spent on him, for the law that limits campaign expenses to twenty-five thousand dollars requires only that the candidate report what *he* has spent or caused to be spent.

A worker in one headquarters is inclined to understate the campaign expenses of his candidate and to exaggerate those of the opposition. A Carmichael man told us, "They were so desperate they spent four hundred thousand dollars to elect Gene Talmadge." A Talmadge man insisted that "Ellis Arnall, Jim Cox, and the Coca-Cola Company" spent a similarly staggering sum on Carmichael. Significantly, however, both estimated the costs of their own campaigns at one hundred thousand dollars.

Four hundred thousand seems to be a bit out of bounds for even an extravagant candidate. One person whom we consider reliable said the most expensive race in Georgia was the one conducted by Senator Walter George in 1938, and that amounted to only $300,000. The next most expensive was Ellis Arnall's for governor in 1942: $250,000. The three leading contenders for governor in 1946 undoubtedly spent between $100,000 and $150,000 through their state headquarters; what was spent on their behalf at the county level and by trade associations and ad hoc issue groups might have raised the total outlay to twice that.

We would judge, then, that any candidate for governor who intends to run better than a sack race must be backed by one hundred thousand dollars at a minimum.

Some of this money comes unsolicited in small amounts from individuals. Most of it, however, comes from corporations. The politicians don't deny this. Though they get tongue-tied when asked about corporate contributions to their own campaigns, they're astonishingly quick to tell of the Big Money given their opponents.

Corporations don't give money as corporations. There's a law against that. What happens is that corporation directors, officers, and their paid consultants give the money in their capacity as free, private American citizens. Except for the independently wealthy among them, they rarely dip into their own pockets or bank accounts for political donations. The money is passed to them, and noted in the company books, as "bonuses," salary increases, or professional fees— either by action of the corporate board or under the discretionary authority of the chief executive officer—with the tacit understanding that it is to be discreetly transferred to the candidate or candidates of choice. The donations, we're told, are usually made in cash, in sums of one thousand and five thousand dollars.

Winning Votes Is For Politicians

To the candidates, the corporations are important for one reason: they pay the bills. No corporation is able to deliver enough votes to matter. The one exception is said to be the Georgia Power Company, whose business extends into 138 counties and which keeps a full-time agent in each. But even the influence of the Power Company has waned since the thirties. Its representatives no longer openly endorse candidates, as they used to do almost in the spirit of public service. The day has passed when Preston Arkwright, its president, would "encourage" employees, by way of prominent messages on bulletin boards and insertions in pay envelopes, to vote for the candidate most sympathetic to the "needs of the utility industry." Some mill owners, of course, are either so respected or so feared that a word from them may swing the votes of their employees; a few wealthy landowners may still be able to sway or bully their tenants. But this is not generally true. Georgians do not take to coercion, and we've found few workers who so love their bosses that they'll vote after his mere example. Workers in the big textile mills haven't listened to their bosses with much affection since the black days of 1934 when the owners broke up strikes by getting Gene Talmadge to call out the state guard. In recent years, too, as more and more Georgia industries have been organized, the political authority once belonging to the boss has tended increasingly to be transferred to the union leader. By and large, Georgia voters don't like corporations any more than they like Yankees, the PAC, or "niggers."

But in the present scheme of things it's not necessary for corporation officials to busy themselves getting votes. It's only necessary that they have an understanding with the politicians. Getting the votes is the politician's job.

To get the votes that count—that is, the farm vote that determines the county unit vote—it is not enough to have a candidate who can sell himself to the people and plenty of money to campaign with. Every bit as essential, and an essential that gives Georgia politics its unique character, is an intimate knowledge of, and an ability to bargain with, the leadership in the rural counties.

Georgia counties vary in the nature of their political leadership about as much as they do in history and geography. In many counties the person of most influence is likely to be the head of an old and prominent family, whose advice is followed and opinions esteemed because the people have been conditioned to accept the authority of a cultivated aristocracy. In other counties he may be a banker or a landowner, or a dealer in farm equipment, or almost anybody to whom large numbers of people owe money or their livelihoods and who for that reason can exert a constant, if only implied, threat of economic reprisal. Or he might be a doctor, a lawyer, a judge, a newspaper editor, or a preacher— someone who at one time or another has done some service for almost everybody in the county and is popular besides. In many counties, too, there is no one leader, nor a group of leaders of common mind, but two or more rival factions of almost equal strength, divided over strictly local issues and personalities. Sometimes these leaders hold the key elective offices in the county—commissioner, ordinary, sheriff, tax collector. Sometimes they have only an "in" with the men who do. Either way, they are the men who not only determine for whom a county goes but in many instances control the details of the election procedure—where the polls are located and who manages them, how and when the registration list is purged, and on occasion what kind of ballot is used. Time and time again, in our conversations throughout the state, we were told that about two hundred such strategically positioned men decide who will be elected governor of Georgia.

From county to county these leaders also differ in their motives. Some concern themselves with politics exclusively for reasons of personal vanity; they like to be able to call a governor by his first name, to walk into his office without an appointment, to "fix" things for a friend. Many are moved by the more tangible incentives—patronage, roads, county benefits, and state business—but probably only a small minority are in it entirely for the money.

For the past seventeen years Georgia has had only two political organizations, one identified with Eugene Talmadge, the other with Ed Rivers. Some county leaders are constant in their allegiance to Talmadge, others to Rivers. Still others are constant only in their opposition to Talmadge. Moreover, a lot of these county ringmasters (how many we do not venture to guess) seem to be loyal to no faction but reserve their support for the candidate who seems most likely to win and who promises them or their county the most rewards.

In the race for governor, therefore, the most valuable man in any camp is the one who knows how to negotiate with the county leaders. Whoever does it has an intricate job on his hands. He's got to know all the local leaders by name, and to know enough about the social and economic environment of each county to be able to tell the true leaders from the false. More than that, he must know their strengths and weaknesses, their public records and private indiscretions; he must know enough about them to make irresistible appeals. He's got to know who among them will resent an offer of money from state headquarters to pay for local campaign expenses and who among them won't turn a hand until money is received. He must be a good trader and a man of more than average charm and persuasion; one of his hardest jobs is to convince them that his man will win.

By all odds the most conspicuous and most expert of such men is Roy Harris, leader of Augusta's Cracker Party and former Speaker of the House.

At one time or another Mr. Harris has labored in the vineyards for every successful candidate for governor since Richard Russell. He managed three campaigns for Ed Rivers: 1928 (lost), 1936 (won), and 1938 (won). With Rivers's approval, he managed Ellis Arnall in 1942. Then, vindictive toward both Rivers and Arnall, he worked long and hard for Talmadge in 1946. He is the man who put Herman Talmadge in the governor's chair for three months last year.

In twenty-seven years of active participation in state politics, surviving one factional brawl after another, Harris probably has learned more about the functions of government on every level than any other man in the state. He knows as much about the Georgia of textbooks as their authors, and he knows considerably more about the Georgia people and the behavior of the courthouse rings than anyone has ever dared put on paper. His files on Georgia personalities are reputedly worth a fortune.

Some of Harris's successes have so awed the politically uninitiated that there has developed a legend around him for omniscience. It's a persistent legend, despite all his attempts to explode it. "Only difference between me and the guy on the other side," he likes to say, "is I get up earlier and stay up later."

In our interview with him, he elaborated: "There's no mystery to Georgia politics. To win in Georgia you've got to be a smart organizer and work hard. That's all. You've got to know the counties. You've got to know who the leaders are, and how the people think and what they want. You've got to know how the counties line up—what counties are in the bag, what counties to work on, and what counties to forget about.

"Last spring (1946), right after everybody announced, I wrote letters to six friends in every county in the state. I asked them which of the three candidates—Rivers, Talmadge, or Carmichael—was likely to carry the county. When I got my answers, I studied them for a while and then told Gene he had seventy-five counties guaranteed. We then decided on twenty-five or so counties where we thought we had an even chance or better and started concentrating on them. We let our local people handle the seventy-five sure counties and, except for routine publicity, forgot about the rest, considering them lost. We put practically all our time and attention on those twenty-five crucial counties."

That, insists Roy Harris, is the secret. "You've got to be a smart organizer and work hard."

Corporate Members of the Cast

Fear ran the campaign that elected Eugene Talmadge last summer. Fear wrote the legislative program after his death.

With corporations it was fear of labor. With the Talmadge forces it was fear of an electorate that had been suddenly enlarged to include more than one hundred thousand Negroes. Behind both fears was the fear of change.

Much had happened during the past four years to increase these fears. For one thing, Ellis Arnall hadn't played ball.[6] The gentlemen who made up his campaign chest in 1942 had not made any vulgar demands. They had merely assumed that out of gratitude he would hear their cases sympathetically if they ever had to state them and that he would do them the courtesy of soliciting their advice before making any major decisions. To their annoyance, Arnall had seemed outrageously independent. Not only did he make his own decisions; one of those decisions was to endorse Henry Wallace for vice president. Besides that, he had attacked the Georgia Power Company publicly and had charged the bus and trucking interests with trying to set up a state monopoly. By 1946 most of the corporations had their fill of Ellis Arnall and were inclined to regard with suspicion any man bearing the Arnall label, even as reasonable and as personable a man as Jimmy Carmichael.

The way it looked to corporation executives and long-incumbent officeholders, Arnall had undermined the system from which their power derived. Preservation of the status quo had always depended on a diluted, small electorate. Now the electorate was beginning to slip out of hand—first with abolition of the poll tax, then with enfranchisement of eighteen-year-olds, next with the federal court mandate that Negroes be given the right of ballot. All this, plus some vigorous crusading by statewide civic groups, had caused a rise in voter registration from scarcely five hundred thousand in 1942 to well over a million in 1946. To top it all, the CIO with its hated PAC had come south, not only on the make for Georgia's virginal industries but also determined to organize a political opposition. About the only prop left untouched—but that being the most important prop of all—was the county unit system. "Thank God," the Big Boys could say in 1946. "Thank God for the county unit system."

The 1946 election returns showed exactly how important the system is. Because of it, Eugene Talmadge won the primary, although his chief opponent, James V. Carmichael, beat him by 16,000 popular votes. Talmadge got 297,245 popular votes; in all, more than 394,000 votes were cast against him. He won the race by 96 unit votes, having polled 242 to Carmichael's 146.

It was an unprecedented thing. For the first time the county unit system was exposed in its bare utility. Gene Talmadge had laughed, popped his galluses, and said the system had saved Georgia from the Negro; those sixteen thousand votes by which Carmichael led him—those and eighty-five thousand more—were all "nigger" votes. Nevertheless, cries of indignation came from city people all over the state; in Atlanta two suits were brought in the federal courts that sought to have the electoral process declared unconstitutional. Even after the U.S. Supreme Court declined to rule on the issue, Talmadge backers were troubled. The margin of victory had been uncomfortably close. They began to think that maybe the county unit system wasn't enough, that maybe something more was needed to keep voters in line. But Talmadge assured them they had nothing to worry about. "Just leave it to Gene," he told them. They relaxed, momentarily confident that Ole Gene would handle things.[7]

As it happened, Eugene Talmadge did not live to handle things. After his death on December 21, Georgia entered a period of chaos and uncertainty. Herman Talmadge persuaded the legislature to elect him to replace his father, thus raising the curtain on a comic opera that ran for eighty-nine days, when the state supreme court ruled his election illegal and in effect named M. E. Thompson, the lieutenant governor nominate, the legitimate governor.

In the beginning few people seemed to see much aspect of principle in the quarrel between M. E. Thompson and Herman. The popular view was that it was just another squabble between politicians. Thompson's following was small and less than aggressive, and the people who did recognize the principle at stake, perhaps out of false confidence that it would be defended by the legislature, were mostly inarticulate. Talmadge people, on the other hand, were unencumbered by any idea of principle. They wanted Herman for governor, and they made plenty of noise about it. In all the confusion it was easy for the northern press, and for some Georgia columnists who ought to have known better, to assume them to be the people of Georgia.

It was this thunderous demonstration of loyalty to the Talmadge name, along with skillful behind-the-scenes maneuvering by Roy Harris, that caused the legislature to elect Herman.[8] It might be that these same things caused corporation leaders to support him. We doubt this, however. We rather think that their support was more voluntary, that in the scheme that put Herman in office they were the hand to Roy Harris's glove.

As described to us by one company executive, the position of the Big Boys was something like this:

They supported Herman Talmadge not because they were opposed to M. E. Thompson but because Herman looked like a sure winner and because they knew from experience that he could be trusted. They didn't desert Thompson. To keep their collective foot in the door, they made respectable contributions to his campaign. But Thompson was, at best, an indefinite quantity. Colorless, always the schoolteacher, he had carried on a very dull race for lieutenant governor, saying simply that he was standing on his record as a public servant and that if elected he would back to the hilt whatever programs the Democratic Party might draft at its Macon convention. Particularly damaging in their eyes was his relationship to Ellis Arnall and Ed Rivers. As an Arnall man he had backed Henry Wallace at the 1944 convention; as a friend of Rivers's he was associated in the public mind with a man believed to be incorrigibly corrupt.

Herman's merits could almost be codified. He was the heir to the only intact political organization left in the state. In the *Statesman* he had the only political organ with a reliable and responsive readership. The magic of his name alone would conjure up a hundred thousand votes. He had learned Georgia politics at his father's knee, had managed his father's last campaign, and during his father's terminal illness had spoken for him. Having accepted some favors of his own, including an office suite in Atlanta's C&S Bank Building, he was thoroughly appreciative of the corporation viewpoint. Besides, if Herman was elected, he would be in office for four years, whereas Thompson's term as acting governor would be for only two. The corporations would like to have avoided the additional expense of an off-year election in 1948.

The lay of corporation sympathies was mutely acknowledged during the court battles between Talmadge and Thompson. Herman's lawyers were B. D. Murphy, counsel for the Central of Georgia Railway, and C. Baxter Jones Sr., counsel for the Bibb Manufacturing Company and the Macon banks. As best we can tell, the corporations supported Herman with something of the desperation of a man losing to a slot machine; the only way they knew to get back the money they'd already invested was to put in more money and hope for the jackpot. Their psychology even infected one of the men who'd financed the Carmichael campaign; he turned to Herman with the hope of retrieving part of a deficit that had originally amounted to about sixty-five thousand dollars.

The corporations may not have liked the means Herman used to get himself in office. They probably had nothing to do specifically with the legislative strategy to keep him there. Without question, some of them were shocked by the extreme measures he proposed to keep himself in power: the white primary bill, which would give the Talmadge leadership custody of all primary laws; two bills that would cancel all existing registration lists, institute a one-dollar poll tax, and make it a felony to challenge the act of a registrar; and a constitutional amendment that would extend the county unit system into the general election.

Whether they knew it or not, whether they cared or not, their position at this crucial time was almost exactly the position that certain German industrialists had occupied just before Adolf Hitler took over the chancellorship in 1934. As much as anybody in Georgia, they had cause to be glad that Herman Talmadge could not control the state supreme court.

The General Disassembly

The 1947 session of the General Assembly has been called the noisiest, the most fractious, the most unproductive session in Georgia's history. Here's what it accomplished:

A total of 679 bills were introduced, 132 in the Senate and 547 in the House. Of these, 391 passed both houses and were signed by Acting Governor Thompson. Two bills were vetoed. None received a pocket veto.

Of the 679 introduced, 368, or 54 percent, were for exclusively local application and 311, or 46 percent, were of general interest. Of the 381 signed by the governor, 301 were local bills and 90 were general bills, or general bills of local application.

Of the 90 general bills to pass, 33 were of special interest to private corporations.

However costly and frustrating the session may have been for the people of Georgia, it was not at all unprofitable for the corporations. They got most of the things they wanted and absolutely nothing they didn't want. For example:

Tax measures. Of the five tax bills to pass, only one authorizes new taxes; the other four grant exemptions. Even the one new tax law is a revenue measure in name only, its real purpose being to prohibit fortune-telling by permitting counties to charge exorbitant license fees (up to one thousand dollars). Some thirty other tax measures died along the way. A sales tax nearly passed. An increased income tax was proposed but never seriously considered. Other bills would have taxed documents, motor vehicles, soft drinks, aviation gas, premium receipts, admissions, liquor, horse racing, slot machines, wild lands, and the ballot.

Regulation of business or professions. Legislation in this category breaks down like this:

Labor. Two bills affecting the rights of labor cleared both houses (the Senate unanimously) and were signed into law with little public protest. Together they ban the closed shop and union shop, the involuntary checkoff, and mass picketing. More about them later.

Banks and Banking. Eighty percent of the bills affecting banking passed, all designed to give banks more freedom of action. Specifically, the new acts authorize directors to elect executive committees to carry on the work of the boards; permit directors to fill board vacancies; remove the ceiling on the amount of federal securities a bank can hold; increase the items a mortgage may embrace; and reduce the workweek to five days by permitting banks to close on Saturdays.

Insurance. One act authorizes insurance companies to acquire property for leasing purposes in value up to 5 percent of the company's total assets, thereby virtually removing the ceiling for larger companies. Another removes the limit of fifteen directors, authorizing a company to have as many directors as it chooses to specify in its bylaws. Two lengthy bills were passed amending the rate-fixing procedures for casualty, fire, marine, and inland marine insurance. These same bills create a rating organization to which all companies are bound. In effect, by preventing rate wars, they outlaw price competition and practically guarantee maintenance of the maximum rates approved by the state insurance commissioner.

Corporations. Two acts apply to private corporations in general. One provides exemption from taxation upon liquidation of subsidiaries. The other simplifies the procedure for changing the home office location of a domestic corporation.

Railroads and Public Utilities. The only act explicitly to do with railroads changes the method for sounding train whistles at grade crossings. Another one, S.R. 21, is an enabling act permitting the disposal of transportation lines by electric power companies. It merely carries out the terms of an order issued by the Public Service Commission.

Real Estate. Landlords who have been unable to evict tenants now can get some compensation. By court order they may collect double rent from the time the tenant was legally obligated to vacate until the time he actually vacates.

Acknowledging the need for additional state revenue, corporation lobbies put their weight behind the sales tax as the least offensive of all the proposed money-raising measures. They weren't displeased that it was killed; its passage would have placed 65 percent of the tax load on persons who earn 15 percent of the state's wealth.

The sales tax proposal, incidentally, was in the same class with the antilabor bills in that neither had been an issue of the primary campaign and neither drew the usual factional alignments. All four candidates for governor had promised expanded state services, but none had said anything about how they were to be financed. As it turned out, the sales tax bill was the only revenue measure considered that had a prayer of being enacted. Manufacturing interests argued against the passage of anything else. The bill sailed through the House 112 to 71, with no exemptions for food, medicine, and clothing unless, like soft drinks, these essential items cost under nine cents.[9] Unquestionably, had not the Talmadge forces withdrawn their support when the state supreme court ruled for M. E. Thompson, the bill would have passed the Senate.

The antilabor bills did not come as a surprise to the AFL and the CIO. But at least there had been some assurance that they would not have administration blessing. All three major gubernatorial candidates had wooed labor during the primary. Cicero Kendrick, editor of the AFL's *Journal of Labor* and Fulton County representative, had taken particular pains to get in Herman's graces. When the issue of Eugene Talmadge's successor was presented to the legislature, he voted for Herman, apparently with the understanding that any punitive labor bills would be sidetracked and, if necessary, vetoed.

But business pressures and legislative sentiment for the antiunion bills proved stronger than anybody's campaign promises. Passed without dissent in the Senate, the bills were voted out of the House committee on the eloquent insistence of their sponsor, Herschel Lovett, a millionaire representative from Laurens. Later they were signed by Herman and, after him, by Thompson.

Though pushed by the Georgia Farm Bureau, these bills were the special pets of Georgia's biggest cotton mills. Indeed, they were written by the chief counsel for the Bibb Manufacturing Company, Baxter Jones Sr. Not surprisingly, the bills were backed by the Cotton Manufacturers Association, of which Bibb is perhaps the most prominent member.

In addition to these big items, business interests wanted some minor acts of concession. One, H.R. 229, had a curious history. Drafted and pressed by the Georgia Petroleum Retailers Association, it would authorize filling station operators to keep 2 percent of the taxes due on gross sales as compensation for gasoline lost through evaporation and spillage. The 1 percent deduction allowed in the original gas tax act benefited only gasoline distributors, said the association, whereas it was the individual operator who actually suffered the loss and had the expense of keeping books. At no time during the floor debate was it suggested that justice be done the operator by adjusting the existing rebate so that the operator would get 1 percent and the distributor none. H.R. 229 would provide a distinctly new exemption.

Having sold the bill to representatives of both factions in both houses, the association had little trouble getting it through the assembly. Governor Thompson, however, first announced that he would have to veto it. He was sympathetic toward a tax rebate for station operators, he told a press conference, but in view of the drastic budget cuts already necessary he did not think the state could afford the half a million dollars a year it would cost in lost revenue. Promptly thereafter, association members deluged the executive office with telegrams, whereupon Thompson changed his mind and signed the bill without comment. (Several months later, however, the act was voided because, according to a ruling by Attorney General Eugene Cook, it had not included a clause authorizing a special appropriation, without which no state funds were available to pay the rebate.)

Corporations sometimes had to spend a lot of time fighting "perennials." These are the bills inherently obnoxious to commercial interests that, for one reason or another, come up session after session, always with just enough threat of passing to make them worrisome. The liquor industry is said to be so vulnerable to perennials that the organization of wholesalers, the Distilled Spirits Institute, assesses each member so much a case to earmark a permanent fund for legislative action. Usually it's a prohibition bill that the industry has to buy off. This past session, though, it was a bill to establish state liquor stores, which retailers consider almost as abhorrent as prohibition.

Antiliquor bills are rarely introduced for any purpose other than shakedown. They are proposed either by some cynically and openly venal legislator or by some naive, high-principled representative who has been duped. However they are put on the calendar, the liquor industry is assured that they can be taken off for a price. Some perennials, however, are introduced in perfectly good faith. The soft drinks tax—anathema to Coca-Cola and Nehi—was pushed this year by Walter Harrison, a serious and rather courtly representative from Jenkins, in a serious effort to find a new source of revenue. Similarly, Representative Eugene Yawn, of Dodge County, had admirable intentions when he proposed a bill that would require public utilities to declare the same property value for rate fixing as they do for taxation. It seems that the Power Company, for example, regularly certifies its property for two hundred million dollars less for tax purposes, and in almost every session it occurs to some representative that this discrepancy is incredibly unfair. If rates were figured on the same property value, it can be argued, the state would gain fifteen million dollars a year in revenue. Actually, though, there are sound reasons for this discrepancy. One is that utilities spend a lot of money on the construction and maintenance of public property, such as bridges, viaducts, and roads, some of which they are thoroughly justified in certifying for rate fixing. One tax expert told us that the Power Company would probably have to go out of business if it were required to file the same value for taxable property.[10] Anyway, Yawn's bill never reached the floor.

Two bills aimed at the aviation industry were brought up for the second time in the 1947 session. They're very likely to become perennials. One called for state regulation of air commerce, which airline executives consider unnecessary in the light of existing interstate regulations. The second, which the state revenue department would like to see passed, would increase taxes on airlines routed through Georgia. Both bills were successfully squelched. Especially valuable was the influence of the late Lindley Camp, general counsel for Delta Airlines, former solicitor for Fulton County, and for a long while Eugene Talmadge's right-hand man.

A perennial is almost never debated on its merits. Good for the state or bad, it's enough that it would reduce or destroy the profits of a private industry. This patently is why efforts to raise the state income tax meet with so little success. After a few nervous moments, the corporation agents "fix" it with the House leaders. This year the leaders first used delaying tactics to keep the bill off the floor and then made sure it was safely buried when the rules committee took over the calendar during the session's last two weeks.

Of Bribes and Barter

During the 1947 session of the General Assembly stories of bribery ran around the capitol like gossip on a small-town party line. How much truth is in them is anybody's guess. Representatives who accept money won't talk, and the men who pass it out are careful never to offer money to representatives who might refuse. Bribes are almost always handled by professional politicians, many of them former members of the legislature, who know who can be had and who can't, and who are too smart to leave fingerprints.

Altogether, though, the frequency with which certain names circulated would seem to suggest that there are no more than three men in the Senate whose vote can be had for cash and no more than a dozen in the House. *Time* magazine reported as rumor that on the day and night before the assembly convened "blocks of six votes for Hummon were fetching $60,000."[11] The rumor is probably unfounded. Perhaps significantly, though, all but one of the instances of bribery we were told about took place last January during the heat and fury of the joint session that elected Herman Talmadge governor. One representative swore that he knew of two colleagues who accepted a thousand dollars apiece to vote for Herman. Another told us bitterly that the Thompson forces were offering as much as three thousand. "Although nobody approached me," said another, "men seated on each side of me were called into the corridors and given a choice of money or a road." One representative is said to have switched from Thompson to Talmadge when faced with such a choice; he didn't think it honest to accept money, but he felt he owed it to the folks back home to accept the road.

One instance suggests that more bribes are offered than taken. We were told that sometime during midsession a naive country lawyer came up to an old and respected leader of the Senate and after a few words of embarrassment thrust a hundred-dollar bill at him. "People who know," he whispered, "have advised me that the routine fee for a bill like mine is a hundred dollars—a hundred for the House and a hundred for the Senate." The Senator tried to convince him that bribery wasn't necessary, that if the bill was a good one he would see to it that it got the attention it deserved. Apparently, the neophyte lobbyist didn't believe him. When the bill came up for debate, the sudden interest of a couple of usually slow and not too bright senators showed that the lawyer had succeeded in spending his hundred dollars. Their participation drew immediate suspicion from other senators. The bill was killed on a voice vote.

It's our judgment that cash gifts to legislators are so ineffective that they can be dismissed from any serious study of what determines legislative action. Nobody but a discredited representative, one who has forfeited his opportunity for higher office, is likely to take money for his favors. It's bad politics. Once a man has accepted cash, he wears a price tag around his neck the rest of his life. Anytime thereafter the boys on the inside can whip him into line with a quiet threat to expose him. The smart politician won't be so crassly and easily bought. If he really wants to sell his support, he'll sell it for something more enduringly remunerative than cash—a judgeship perhaps, or a state building contract if he's negotiating with the governor or a contender for governor; a purchase order, a retainer, or a consulting fee if the overture comes from a corporation lobbyist.

No more than six members of the 1947 assembly have established bad character records, according to a confidential survey by a credit agency. Most assemblymen are motivated by the same things that motivate most Georgians. They're moved sometimes by principle, sometimes by prejudice, sometimes by pride, sometimes by greed, sometimes by honest ignorance. They do one thing out of loyalty to a friend, another to further a personal ambition. If a politician appears to act differently than ordinary people, it's probably because he must resolve these various and conflicting motives under pressure from various and competing sources. If he seems to be inconsistent and capricious, it is because politics is essentially a struggle for power in which pragmatic compromise is the market price of victory. Furthermore, politics has its special climate and its special code. The climate is cynical, and the code is amoral. In a reward system that usually regards it as unsportsmanlike to admit ethics into debate, it is natural for most politicians to act without reference to conscience. When they do, they find it easy to rationalize self-interest into public interest, prejudice into conviction, what is expedient into what is principle. Thus, except for a few unhappy and idealistic freshmen and even fewer God-driven older ones, most assemblymen do not recognize anything dishonest or corrupt about exchanging one's support for the promise of a political plum. To the old hands, bargaining for patronage is what the game is about. The only time that bargaining seems to be considered reprehensible is when it's done with an attitude of brazen opportunism. On the night the assembly elected Herman there is said to have been a number of fence-straddlers who were offered special benefits by both Thompson and Talmadge but who refused to commit themselves until it was clear which of the two would win. One kept a running score of the ayes and nays and delayed his vote until he was reasonably certain the count would go for Herman. He is now viewed as a bad sport.

Representatives are influenced not only by promises to share the spoils. Sometimes a man is swung in line by threats on his reputation and property. It's not uncommon for one politician to tell another apologetically: "I had to, Mac. Old What's-his-name said he'd foreclose if I didn't." But since politicians with guilty consciences often invent such threats to justify their self-inspired behavior, it's hard to tell just how prevalent or effective this practice is.

But one way or another, too many individual members of the assembly can be controlled. It simply requires one man or a group of men smart enough to control them.

The controllers must have more than the qualities of leadership. They must know the intimate histories of the majority of men in both houses. They must know which men have an antilabor bias, which are anti-Semitic, which are suckers for the "nigger-nigger" line. They must know what each representative privately and publicly wants out of life, what each man's weaknesses are, and how these weaknesses can be exploited. They must be in positions to control assignments to the strategic committees and through their parliamentary advantage exercise a free hand in the flow of legislation. In or around every legislature there are such men. During the 1947 session there were several, the most conspicuous of whom were Roy Harris, Fred Hand, and Bob Elliott.

These men, the certifiably talented leaders of the Talmadge forces, could not push through the assembly everything they wanted. The Thompson men were solid and resolute, strong enough to block any move for a constitutional amendment. Yet without the blessing of Harris, Hand, and Elliott, no bill had a prayer of passing, and—a fact of utmost importance to Georgia's corporate interests—they had virtually complete control over all measures that did not draw factional lines.

It would be going too far to say that these men are under the thumb of corporations or that the corporations are under theirs. In this kind of relationship it isn't necessary to spell out who's doing what to or for whom. It's rather a case of elective affinity, of mutual understanding and a natural dependence each on the other. The simple truth is that these three men make their living out of corporations; in outlook and instinct, they *are* Big Business.

Roy Harris isn't listed in the standard law directory, Martindale-Hubbell, and nobody other than perhaps his partners knows the size and composition of his law practice. From time to time he has handled special assignments for the Georgia Power Company. His biggest group of clients, however, is the bus and trucking industry, which he regularly represents before the Public Service Commission. In the 1945 session he pushed a bill to restrict the charter of new bus lines, a bill that Ellis Arnall vetoed on the grounds that it would set up a monopoly in the face of enterprising World War II veterans. Though he had lost his old seat as representative from Richmond, Mr. Harris ran the 1947 state legislature. Much of the time he even occupied his old office, that of Speaker of the House. Never reticent about his importance to the Talmadge program, he guided his white primary bill through the Senate in full view of the gallery. In a Senate whose top leadership was militantly pro-Thompson, his direction was needed the keep the Talmadge majority on cue. He would stand in the back of the chamber, his arms resting on the wooden railing, usually in whispered conversation with one of his faithful lieutenants. Of these lieutenants, the two most prominent were both corporation lawyers: Senator Alex Weaver of the Fifty-first District (Macon), division counsel for the Central of Georgia Railway and assistant division counsel for Southern Railway; and Senator Spence Grayson, a holdover from the First (Savannah), a lobbyist for the Union Bag and Paper Company.

Speaker of the House Fred Hand, from Pelham, is practically a corporation all by himself. He is vice president and general manager of the Hand Trading Company, president of the Big Dixie Tobacco Warehouse, secretary of the Pelham Phosphate Company, director of the Farmers Bank, a director of the Pelham Oil and Fertilizer Company, and farm administrator for the Hand family. He is kissing kin to one of Georgia's most famous cotton empires through the marriage of his sisters to Cason Callaway of Hamilton and Fuller Callaway of LaGrange. He is conservatively estimated to be worth three million dollars.

The third member of this triumvirate was Bob Elliott, of Muscogee. Sometimes called "the voice of sweet reasonableness," Elliott was Talmadge's floor leader and vice chairman of the Speaker's committee on rules. His law firm in Columbus is retained by the First National Bank, the Bibb Manufacturing Company, a string of insurance companies, Schlitz Brewers, and the Nehi Corporation. He has a personal interest in several Nehi bottling plants.

But corporations cannot afford to leave it to these three leaders, for their interests are more durable than political careers. In 1948, in 1950, and in every session to come, Big Business must face the same old "blackjack bills," the same perennial threats to their "right" to do business according to their own calls for government intervention. It will have fresh cause to implement economic aims with the authority of law. The bigger the corporation, the bigger the threat and the bigger the need.

The larger corporations cannot risk their interests to the vagaries of politics. They must be above factionalism; they must dominate all factions. If the faction they've supported the most doesn't happen to win, they must be able to switch promptly and without too much additional expense to the faction that does. To guarantee them this position, the corporations have a perfect device in the retainer fee.

Of the 259 members of the assembly, 58 are lawyers. It's a safe bet that, except for a handful of labor lawyers—and probably some of them—each is retained by one or more corporations, for corporations have found the retainer fee to be the surest and safest way to maintain a corps of supporters in all factions. Through this commonly sanctioned practice, the lawyer's private interests automatically become his client's special interests. It is not quite true that as long as lawyers make the law, Big Business can make the law. The only reason it is not true is that the corporations are sometimes at odds, that corporations aren't interested in all kinds of law, and that as long as lawyers remain human beings some of them will have integrity.

Me a Lobbyist?

Throughout the 1948 session there sat at the press table on the House floor an attractive young red-haired woman named Frances Blackmon. She sat day after day, making notes on floor debates, analyzing bills as they were introduced. During consideration of much of the legislation she was quiet and noncommittal. At other times—notably during debates on the bills to regulate voting and to provide home rule—she would seek an audience with an individual representative and talk to the point, logically and persuasively. We were impressed by Miss Blackmon because she seemed to us to be the truest representative of the people in the whole assembly. She is executive secretary and political observer for the Georgia League of Women Voters. Had there been a dozen Frances Blackmons, the history of the 1947 assembly might have been different.

Although thousands of Georgians may have had opinions about the way the legislature was doing its business, few took the trouble to let their representatives know what they were. Public response, as it might be gauged from telegrams and letters, was sporadic and limited, most of it stimulated and orchestrated by pressure groups.

From newspaper reports during the week it happened, Herman's election by the legislature seemed to have provoked spontaneous demonstrations of resentment from every hearthside in Georgia. Actually, public protest meetings took place in no more than thirty-five counties, most of them in the name of the Aroused Citizens of Georgia. Only a brief flurry of written protests descended on the desks of assemblymen during the week after Herman took office.

We were told by several representatives that the pressure to vote for Herman before the legislature met was far greater than any pressure felt during the actual session. One legislator got a deluge of postcards from people in his county several days before he left for Atlanta, all urging support for Herman. He learned later that the cards had been printed, distributed, and mailed by the editor of the county weekly, a leader of the local Talmadge faction. Although in the form of a straw poll, with space for the sender to indicate his choice for either Herman or Thompson, all the cards were premarked to show a preference for Herman.

The white primary bill brought the loudest public outcry, but, surprisingly, the mail was meager even on this highly controversial measure. Here again it was the Talmadge forces who sent the preponderance of messages. Senator Robert Knox of Thomson received a total of six hundred letters, telegrams, and postcards in his capacity as secretary of the Special Judiciary Committee. Only two hundred of these asked that the bill be rejected. It was obvious that the other four hundred had been written in answer to Herman's radio appeals, since they all were phrased according to instructions he had broadcast.

In the face of this general passivity and in the absence of any clear expression from the people who had elected him, a representative was very likely to give an attentive ear to the many spokesmen for special interests. Of these spokesmen, the most ubiquitous was Harry Lynwood Wingate, president of the Georgia Farm Bureau Federation. Right be-

hind Wingate were Charles Dudley of the Associated Indus-
tries of Georgia; T. M. Forbes of the Cotton Manufacturers
Association; and Harold Saxon of the Georgia Education
Association. And if it wasn't one of these at his elbow tug-
ging at his sleeve, the representative found Zach Arnold
of the Georgia Municipal Association; Neil Printup of the
Georgia Petroleum Industries Council; Milton Allen of the
Georgia Association of Petroleum Retailers; Francis Ham-
mack of Capital Air Lines; Hamp McWhorter of the Distilled
Spirits Institute and the bus lines; Lon Duckworth, speaking
for several insurance companies; or Tom Camp, then director of the Georgia Association of Railroads, who almost defeated Mrs. Henry Nevins for secretary of the Senate. Every
now and again, like a voice in the wilderness, would appear somebody from labor—Charlie Gillman of the CIO or
George Googe of the AFL.

Quite often these men performed a useful service to legislators by giving them facts. Quite often, too, the legislation they pushed was, if not altogether constructive, at least
not inimical to the public interest. In fact, we would say
that, since ours seems to have evolved into a government
that moves through the arbitration of competing interests
(mostly economic, as John C. Calhoun was perhaps the first
to point out), theirs is a necessary function. But in the un-
even emphasis of their special appeals and in the absence
of principled arbiters, there is a growing danger. What is
needed, and needed badly, is some agency of comparable
strength and organization that can give voice to and advance the collective interests of all the people.

"Most of us honestly try to vote what we think is best for
the state," we were assured by a representative of eight
years' experience. "But if it's a choice between voting what
we think our home folks want and what we know a special
interest group wants, I'm afraid most of us will vote for special interest. We figure the chances are the people back home
will never know, and if they do know they won't care, and if

they care enough to raise a fuss at the time they'll have forgotten all about it before next election time."

Our informant paused to reflect. "It's a funny thing," he said when he resumed. "People seem to think there's a lot of underhand play in the way a lobbyist works. That isn't necessarily true. Most lobbyists I've run into are like insurance salesmen. Their sponsors may have given them bigger expense accounts and more freedom to spend, but. . . . They're out to sell us something, and they try hard to make us feel good and not to offend us. Sometimes they get what they want just by inviting a man to dinner at the Mirador Room or the Athletic Club. They act real friendly, and to us country boys that's usually enough. We're used to doing favors for friends."

Of the bills sponsored by pressure groups, the most dramatically contested were those to do with the regulation of labor unions and to establish a sales tax. The antilabor bills were championed vigorously by the Georgia Farm Bureau and had the full, though less demonstrative, support of the Associated Industries of Georgia and the Cotton Manufacturers Association. The sales tax was advocated most visibly by the Georgia Education Association, with the quiet endorsement of Associated Industries and the declaredly personal help of the Farm Bureau's president, Mr. Wingate; it was opposed chiefly by the Retail Merchants Association.

According to Mr. Wingate, the Farm Bureau's decision to press for antilabor legislation in Georgia came in the fall of 1946 when the National Farm Labor Union (AFL) announced its aim to organize three million farm workers. Mr. Wingate's preoccupation with labor, however, dates from a much earlier time. In November 1942, speaking at the bureau's annual convention, he deplored the migration of farm workers to the factories and demanded that the prices of farm products be kept sufficiently high to attract labor and keep it. In the 1943 convention he asked for, and got, a resolution urging public officials to pass and enforce "fair labor laws which will restore peace and harmony in our nation." In 1945 he was saying that business and industry were "absolutely at the mercy of labor" and blaming labor for the wartime food shortages.

Since he took over the bureau presidency in 1941, Mr. Wingate has plugged successively for an end to farm subsidies, curbs on Farm Security, abolition of the Office of Price Administration, and the various bills that finally became the Taft-Hartley Act. If these advocacies have the suspicious smell of the National Association of Manufacturers, there's good reason. Most of the policies of the Georgia Farm Bureau are shaped by its parent body, the National Farm Bureau Federation, whose historical communion with the NAM is hardly happenstance. In the summer of 1945 Mr. Wingate appeared on lecture platforms all over the state in a series of panel discussions sponsored jointly by the Farm Bureau, the NAM, and the Associated Industries of Georgia, the NAM's affiliate. The subject was the "interdependence of farm and industry," and besides Mr. Wingate speakers included a small group of well-known industrialists and financiers. Conspicuously excluded from the advertised "discussion" were representatives of organized labor.

Almost from its inception the Farm Bureau has been criticized for representing the big farm operator to the neglect of the small dirt farmer. Wingate's sponsorship of the anti-labor bills gave his critics one more point. It is a point, however, that is not likely to be appreciated by most Georgians. Actually, these were popular bills in Georgia, especially among assemblymen. Wingate's only hurdle was the need to get them out of the Industrial Relations Committee, where Chairman Cicero Kendrick, editor of the AFL's *Journal of Labor*, had hoped to bury them. That was a hurdle easily cleared. Working assuredly in hotel rooms and capitol corridors, Wingate recruited so many legislators to his cause that when the bills were reported out of Mr. Kendrick's committee unfavorably, the House voted to override, 157 to 28, and ordered full floor debate. That done, Wingate simply busied himself encouraging members of the assembly to speak for the bills and seeing to it that they were on hand for the roll call. It didn't hurt him one bit that Representative Stafford Brooke, a labor sympathizer from Whitfield County, read him off the House floor as a lobbyist. Wingate's friends in the legislature immediately responded by calling Brooke's action typical of labor's "high-handed methods." [12]

Mr. Wingate was also helped by the one-sided sentiment conveyed in letters to legislators. Bureau members from all over the state wrote as he directed them. Some who were not quite sure what the legislation was all about wrote to ask their representatives to vote for "Wingate's bill." Businessmen in areas where there were no conceivable threats to unionization wrote similar appeals, and even in areas where unionization is a fact of life management seemed to muster impressively more support than the unions. One representative confided: "I know a lot of the telegrams signed by workers were in fact signed and sent by mill owners, but that's all right."

Only from Whitfield and Greene Counties, both CIO-organized, came more letters from union members than from management. Union members in Greene sent penny postcards; mill owners sent telegrams. The AFL made last-minute efforts to get members to write their representatives, but with feeble effect. On this occasion, the AFL seems to have been the victim of its own bad habits. Pursuing a policy more usually associated with corporations, it had relied on "negotiation" to get what it wanted; it had depended on the bargaining ability of Representative Kendrick to smother the bill in the House or to guarantee its veto, and Mr. Kendrick had failed.

Unlike Mr. Wingate, executives of the Cotton Manufacturers Association and the Associated Industries of Georgia did very little buttonholing. With both these organizations it's the practice to rely on officers of individual corporations for needed legislative muscle. Mr. Dudley of the AIG and Mr. Forbes of the CMA regard their jobs as mostly informational—acquainting the assembly with the views of their memberships and informing their memberships about pertinent legislation. Both testified in public hearings for the antilabor bills. The AIG polled its directors and, as expected, found them unanimously in favor.

The AIG also took an active interest in the sales tax bill. Its members were opposed to the first draft because it included a 2 percent tax on wholesale goods. Mr. Dudley got the draft changed to exempt wholesalers and manufacturers, so it became a true consumers' tax. The AIG staff then undertook a study of taxation in eleven southern states. The findings, which went to the sixty-one members of the House Ways and Means Committee, showed among other things that a 3 percent retail tax would provide "adequate revenue for fulfilling the pledges made the people in last year's campaign."

Organized pressure for the sales tax seemed to be generated largely by the Georgia Education Association. Somebody apparently had sold the GEA the idea that a sales tax was the only way to deliver to teachers their promised 50 percent raise. Just before the bill came up for House debate, executive secretary Harold Saxon sent circulars to sixteen thousand schoolteachers that read in part: "This is it— House Bill No. 8. . . . The chips are really down. There's a strong, active, and well financed opposition to this bill. Your Representative will hear from this opposition. Be sure to let him hear from you." Most representatives heard.

The opposition to which Mr. Saxon referred came from the Retail Merchants Association of Georgia. It was vociferous opposition, but it would hardly have been enough to block the bill's passage. General sentiment around the capitol was that, with amendments to exempt food and medicine, it would have passed the Senate about as easily as it had cleared the House, but for one thing. The supreme court decision that named M. E. Thompson acting governor came one day before the Senate vote. The Talmadge faction, which theretofore had been almost solidly for it, now turned against it, determined that the Thompson administration get no additional revenue.

To our knowledge, the most influential corporation agent in the state never set foot inside the state capitol during the entire session.

Fred Wilson, until last November assistant to the president of the Georgia Power Company, has been called by the *Atlanta Journal* "the most persistent influence for corrupt government in Georgia." [13] Power Company officials disclaim responsibility for Mr. Wilson's political activities, and it may indeed be true that his motivation is more personal than professional. [14] He may play politics only for the exquisite pleasure that comes from being a power behind the throne. Or, since Mr. Wilson is something of a millionaire in his own right (he is vice president of the Henry Grady Properties, is part owner of a radio station and a housing project in Marietta, and has other real estate holdings in Florida), it may be that his main concern is to protect his own extensive interests.

Be this as it may, for some time now Mr. Wilson has been commonly regarded as the Power Company's "fixer." He is said to have elected Ed Rivers in 1936 and 1938 and Eugene Talmadge in 1940 and 1946. The story is that in the 1942 gubernatorial campaign he backed Talmadge even though every other corporation agent in the state, with the exception of those representing the railroads, was strategically deserting him. Soured, he is supposed to have devoted the next four years to getting back at Ellis Arnall. Despite vehement denials by Roy Harris, the argument persists that in 1946 it was his support that kept Ed Rivers in the race to split the anti-Talmadge forces and elect Ole Gene.

Almost nothing has been published about Wilson. He talks politics only with his peers, and then with studied discretion.[15] To most of the press corps, as to many junior politicians, he is a mystery man who does his work in the wings and by sleight of hand. Around the capitol people will tell you that Fred Wilson always names the clerk of the House and the secretary of the Senate ("He didn't elect me," says Mrs. Henry Nevins) and that his influence with the presiding officers of both houses is so great that he often selects the chairmen of the most important committees.

A former secretary to Senator Walter F. George, Mr. Wilson became part owner of the Henry Grady Hotel in 1936 when he helped Cecil Cannon get a loan from the Reconstruction Finance Corporation. Since then the Grady, which is built on land owned by the state of Georgia, has become the politician's home away from home. On the Senate floor last winter Senator E. F. Griffith of Eatonton testified to its importance with the comment, "I don't believe the people of Georgia will ever know what's going on . . . until they put loudspeakers in the Henry Grady Hotel and a few microphones under certain beds or behind the furniture."

Mr. Wilson is in an ideal position to do petty favors and has resources enough to do some that aren't so petty. Several representatives, after being appointed to key committees, have been surprised to receive their week's hotel bills stamped "paid." Denying that Wilson is necessarily a corrupting influence, one of his longtime acquaintances explained: "Fred operates on the theory that every man has his price and the price isn't always money. He manages to control at least fifty men in every legislature—the fifty so-called key men—just by making friends with them, by doing them favors. He does this long before they get to the legislature and in a position to return the favor. He sends a graduation present to a man's son. He lends another man some money. That sort of thing. He never extracts a promise, but he always knows that if the time comes when the Power Company is under fire, he can count on these men to do what he wants."

Oddly enough, Wilson is defended as a "square guy" by some people who, it seems, would stand to be hurt most by his alleged interference in government. Pete Swim, former public relations director for the CIO's "Operation Dixie," recalls that the massive drive to organize textile workers was able to start only because of Wilson's generosity. At a time when the union's biggest problem was to house its staff, Wilson volunteered rooms at the Henry Grady and waived the five-day limit. He also has given the AFL cause to be grateful. George Googe, director for the Southeast, says, "He's proved himself a good friend to labor."

So deliberate has been Wilson's policy to avoid publicity that some people saw an ulterior motive in his acceptance last year of a Thompson appointment to the special committee on tax revision. It was an appointment that practically invited press comment, occasioning an editorial in the *Atlanta Journal* that called him "a lobbyist behind the scenes, a maneuverer for special privileges, a wire puller for dubious and sinister political deals."[16]

The code of Georgia implies a distinction between lobbyists and "legislative representatives" seldom drawn by either legislators or the public. The law defines lobbying as "any personal solicitation of a member of the General Assembly . . . *not addressed solely to the judgment,* to favor, or oppose, or to vote for or against any bill, resolution, report, or claim . . . *by any person who misrepresents the nature of his interests.*"[17] Declared to be a crime by the Georgia constitution, lobbying carries a penalty of imprisonment from one to five years. The code recognizes "legislative agents" by prescribing certain regulations for their conduct but defines their function only indirectly, by omission. Presumably, a legislative agent is one who seeks to influence an assemblyman by personal solicitation, as does the lobbyist, *but who argues solely to the legislator's judgment and who does not misrepresent himself* (emphasis ours).

In the thirty-six years that this law has been on the books, there has never been a conviction for lobbying. It is to be assumed, then, that there are no lobbyists in Georgia, only legislative agents.

Call them what you will, there are plenty of them. There's hardly a corporation lawyer of any prominence in the state who at one time or another hasn't been paid to escort a bill through the legislature or who, on other occasions, hasn't been paid to try to block a bill's passage.

The objection to legislative agents is not implicit in what they do but in the fact that they work so much in the shadows and half-light. Something needs to be done to bring them into the open.

No legislative agents active during the 1947 session were listed with the secretary of state, despite a 1911 law that requires registration of all "attorneys or agents or regularly retained counsel employed to aid or oppose, directly or indirectly, any bill, resolution, etc."[18] In recent years disregard for the law has become not an exception but the rule.

The law of diminishing returns seems to have set in on this particular measure as soon as it was written. A total of 232 persons registered for the first session after its passage, exactly half that number for the next one, then none at all for the next five years, until inexplicably thirty-seven registered in 1918. Since 1921 no more than a handful have declared themselves. The last to be recorded were four lawyers for Southeastern Pipelines during the 1941 session.

Among those listed earlier were representatives of the Coca-Cola Company, Southern Railway, the Atlantic Coast Line, the Association of Insurance Company Presidents, the American Mutual Alliance, the Southern Natural Gas Company, and the Metropolitan Life Insurance Company. Conspicuously absent are any registered agents for textile manufacturers, the Power Company, the airlines, and bus and trucking companies.

Also recognized more in the breach than in the observance are three further provisions in the 1911 law, all of them punishable as misdemeanors. The first prohibits the retention or employment of attorneys or agents for "compensation contingent in whole or in part upon the passage or defeat of any legislation." The second requires that reports of "all expenses paid, incurred, or promised" by "any person, firm, or corporation or association" in connection with legislation in which they were interested be filed with the secretary of state within two months after adjournment. And the third excludes all agents, "whether or not they have registered," from the floors of either house while the legislature is in session.

The fact is, laws restricting corporate interference in government are like Georgia's blue laws. They're on the books, but that's about all. Lobbying was first declared to be a crime in the 1877 constitution. In 1908, carried along by the national wave of antitrust sentiment, the assembly passed a law admirable for its high purpose but hardly likely to give a moment's pause to a corporation agent bent on contributing to the delinquency of a public official. This law makes it illegal "for any Georgia corporation, or corporation doing business in Georgia, or any officer or agent of such corporation to make or authorize, directly or indirectly, any contribution from *corporate funds* [emphasis ours] to campaign funds, or for political purposes in any election or primary election held in Georgia or for the purpose of influencing the vote, judgment, or action of any officer of the State of Georgia, legislative, judicial, or executive." Any violation is punishable by a fine ten times the amount of the contribution, "but in no case less than $1,000," plus a prison sentence of "from one to four years." [19]

The men who've been around in state politics don't think a strengthening of the laws would help, either. "Sure you could revise the laws so that some of them would sign the book in the secretary of state's office," they say. "But what would be the use? You'd get the names of the small fry. The big lobbyists don't hang around the capitol. They do their work from their own offices, or in the evening at the club. They don't have to go see members of the legislature. They're so big they can get on the telephone and have almost any man in the legislature trot over to see *them.*"

Georgia at the Grass Roots

After the legislature adjourned, we took off for a three-month trip throughout the state that took us into most of its 159 counties. We wanted to talk with representatives in their home settings, to catch them after they'd had a chance to relax and reflect and when they could spare the time to talk with us. We wanted to talk with other people, too—all kinds of people, common and uncommon. We hoped to find out what they thought about the session just ended; more than that, we wanted to know how well their wants and opinions had found expression in the work of the assembly. Then we wanted to get to the heart of the business, the vote itself, and see how it was being used or abused.

Popular interest in the election of the General Assembly, we found, is almost uniformly low and almost always governed by the conflict, or lack of it, between the personalities of the candidates. We found a really healthy political environment only in those counties where, under the combined stimulus of the Negro vote and an awakened white middle class, active citizens' groups have been organized.

One experienced politician told us that the counties of Georgia differ in their political complexion as much as the forty-eight states of the Union. We have found this true enough to shy from generalizations. Popular participation in elections varies in intensity and in cause from county to county. In some counties the people are complacent, satisfied, sometimes defensive of an entrenched leadership. In others the people admit to a distrust of present leadership but an inability to change it. In many—no, in almost all, and this is about as much of a generalization as we'd care to make—people exhibit keen interest in the election of city and county officials but are inclined to attach secondary importance to state and congressional campaigns.

Legislative races are quite often viewed with indifference and sometimes resolved on the basis of sentimental preference; people "feel sorry for him," or "he's a good boy, let's give him a chance." In a great many counties it's the custom for candidates to run without opposition. In those where the race is contested, the winner is elected entirely on the strength of his personal following. Issues are rarely discussed and factional lines seldom drawn. Campaigns are conducted informally, in a spirit very much like that of a fraternity election. With this kind of sentiment behind the choice of legislators, it is not surprising that two illiterates were sent to the state Senate last year.

We were particularly interested in the election of one of these two illiterates—not in the man himself, though he was by no means uninteresting, but in the psychology that had elected him.

Tourists to the Georgia lake country around Clayton enjoy Senator Tom Mitchell as they do a cartoon character. He is big and rangy and slow talking, he wears wide-brimmed Stetsons, he smiles rather vacantly, and he has an uninhibited love for hoedown music. Rabun County people also think of him as a character, but with a difference. They view him with special affection. Kind and generous, he is prone to quote the Bible often, and he can be touching in his respect for "ladies" and motherhood. He is said to have helped educate several orphans.

Until he went to Atlanta to represent the people of the Fortieth District, Uncle Tom had never held a public office higher than bailiff. He had tried often enough. Over the course of twenty years he had run unsuccessfully for about every office in the county. The people loved him and sometimes threw him token votes, but they knew he couldn't read and that his ability to write stopped with the spelling of his name, and they didn't think it fitting to elect an illiterate to a position of public trust.

But in 1946, just before the primary, a group got together and decided to back Uncle Tom for the state senate. "Why not?" they argued. "It doesn't make a tinker's damn *who* we send to Atlanta. Suppose Tom *is* illiterate. He can't do any worse than the people we've sent before, and he might do better." To the voters of Rabun County, accustomed to getting nothing out of their delegations and convinced that politics was a pork barrel anyway, such an argument made sense. It made especially good sense at the time, they thought, since Tom's only opposition came from an educated man, a schoolteacher, whom nobody liked.

So Uncle Tom went to the Senate, Stetson hat, hoedown music, and all. And sure enough, he probably did no worse than his predecessors. Although identified as a Talmadge man, he made it perfectly clear that he answered to a higher loyalty. He supported Mrs. Henry Nevins for Senate secretary against strong pressure from the Talmadge forces because "she's a mother and a widow"; and he voted for the white primary, not because it was Talmadge-sponsored, but because "my mother was a white woman."

It's said with truth that the people of Georgia vote for a personality rather than a program. This seems to be even truer of local than of statewide elections. One young representative attributes his victory to the fact that his opponent had a bad reputation with women. Representative Lawson Neel, of Thomas, said, "A lot of people voted for me simply because I was a Neel. I'm sure many of them didn't know which Neel they were voting for." A college president told us, somewhat ruefully, that he voted for a man who later turned into a savage Talmadge supporter only because "he's in my Sunday School class." Senator J. B. G. Logan, of Banks County, Representative G. H. Moore, of Lumpkin, and Representative Elliott Hagan, of Screven, all earnest anti-Talmadge men, have been returned to the legislature time and again from traditionally Talmadge counties. Their constituents either have been oblivious to the issues that would separate them or have acted more out of personal friendship than political conviction.

It is very likely, though, that the 1948 primary will see factional lines drawn for the legislative as well as the gubernatorial race. They will be drawn both by popular resentment of a representative's record and by calculated design of the leaders in the dominant factions. Try as they might, only the most rugged of individuals in the 1947 assembly could avoid aligning themselves with one of the two camps. If they voted for Herman, they are branded Talmadge men. If they voted against him, they are Thompson men. Neither Herman Talmadge nor M. E. Thompson has forgotten. Moreover, both realize the necessity for a sympathetic legislature in 1949. To have the assembly in 1949 as divided as it was last year would not only paralyze a governor's effectiveness during the two years of his term but also destroy him as a serious political contender thereafter. Therefore both Herman and Thompson are going to see to it that in all strategic counties men committed to their leadership offer for the legislature.

Similarly, the voters are going to take a more active interest in the character of legislative candidates. By and large, in 1946 the people didn't know what manner of men they were voting for. Next year they will. But any assumption that this new public enlightenment will work to the favor of the anti-Talmadge forces is the rankest kind of wishful thinking. If statistics mean anything, exactly the reverse may be true.

Fifty-nine assemblymen from counties that went for Gene in 1946 voted against Herman; only thirty-six assemblymen from anti-Talmadge counties voted for him. If it can be assumed that neither faction has gained or lost in strength since the 1946 primary and that neither will gain nor lose before 1948, then obviously the fifty-nine, who by voting against Herman voted contrary to the will of the strongest faction in their counties, will be defeated for reelection. By the same logic, only thirty-six Talmadge supporters would be defeated. Thus the Talmadge forces conceivably could win twenty-three more seats.

Nobody can know for sure, of course, what will become of the ninety-five assemblymen who voted against the dominant will of their constituents. Some of them obviously will consider discretion the better part of valor and not care to run. More experienced ones will be able to play the penitent or to explain their records satisfactorily and be reelected. Still others, particularly those from counties where the voters are about evenly divided in their loyalties, will simply face lively and unpredictable races. Whatever the total outcome, the 1948 election for the General Assembly promises to be quite unlike all previous campaigns. Voting records have been so well publicized, the factions so crystallized, and that small group of "independent voters" so alerted that the 1948 election will be something distinctly more than the usual popularity contest.

Something else, essentially far more significant, has happened in several counties that already has caused isolated changes in Georgia's political habits. That is the emergence of politically effective groups of so-called impractical politicians—citizens who finally got mad enough about the kind of government they had been getting to do something. The result has been a brand-new set of public officials in Augusta and Richmond County; a new mayor and alderman for the city of Savannah and a new delegation to the state assembly from Chatham County; a revolution in the county commission in Glynn; the defiance of the Bibb Manufacturing Company in the election of a mayor for Macon; and the defeat of an old-line machine councilman in Douglas. None of these victories is secure. The new administrations in Augusta and Savannah are making all the honest mistakes and having to cope with the disappointments and multiple pressures that inevitably accompany reform movements. It's probable that some of the new officials will turn out to be as corruptible as the men they replaced. Yet each of these reform victories has proved two things. First, the more people who vote, the less tolerance for machine control. Second, the unrestricted admission of Negroes to the polls does not necessarily give Negroes the balance of power; it may serve rather to awaken the dormant political interests of whites.[20]

In each of these five cited instances, the decisive factor in the victory was a phenomenally increased registration. In Richmond County registration went from 8,000 to nearly 30,000; in Glynn from 3,500 to 12,000; in the town of Douglas from 287 to nearly 1,700. In each area the story was the same. When the number of registrants went above the number that the machine had always been able to control (in Richmond the Cracker Party used to brag about its bloc of 6,000 votes), the machine lost out.

Significantly, each of these reform groups won with a majority greater than the total Negro vote. Indeed, in Augusta the Independent League won despite the Negro vote, which went for Roy Harris's Cracker Party. What happened in each of these communities was that the enfranchisement of the Negro was accompanied by a concerted drive by the Junior Chamber of Commerce to expand the registration list. The newly enfranchised Negro and the newly registered white, sometimes to their mutual surprise, merely found themselves in natural agreement that the old machines must go. Many white folks also asserted themselves, not under pressure from the Jaycees but, as one Negro leader described it, "out of an enlightened self-interest." If the Negro was going to vote, they reasoned, they better start voting too.

But We Don't Play Partisan Politics

The League of Women Voters is Georgia's only nonpartisan statewide organization working the year round for the promotion of the general welfare through better government. There are other groups, of course, with extensive memberships throughout the state that periodically express themselves politically. But they're of the special-interest variety. The most politically inclined among them, and by far the strongest in influence, is the Georgia Farm Bureau.

In every community where it has had time to establish itself the League of Women Voters is regarded with high respect. It has even earned the hard respect of "practical" politicians, although some of them find it difficult to reconcile the rational and restrained quality of its membership with the driving aggressiveness of its program. Perhaps what really disarms this kind of politician is the league's insistence on sticking to issues and its polite disregard for personalities.

Anyway, it can be safely said that the league holds the respect of both the disinterested citizen and the working politician. Through the work of its local chapters, the activities of the Atlanta office, and the influence of its members at large, the league probably has done more than any other single agency to raise political activity in the state above the level of barbecue, fish fries, and hush puppies. Unfortunately, the league has but thirteen locals (membership: thirty-one hundred), five college chapters with a membership of three hundred, and three hundred members at large—a total membership of about thirty-seven hundred. What further limits its effectiveness is the fact that of the thirteen locals only one is in a two-unit county. In the rural areas, where its influence is most needed, the league is virtually unheard of.

The Georgia Farm Bureau, on the other hand, has active chapters almost everywhere except in a few counties in north Georgia. It now has 52,000 family memberships, representing a total enrollment of perhaps 150,000. Mr. Wingate, its director, told us that it has sustained a 47 percent increase over the past several years and that he is confident that it will have at least 100,000 families signed up before the end of 1948.

The size of the bureau's membership, however, is deceptive and cannot be interpreted as a sign of political solidarity. Many tenant families are signed up by their landlords; they take no part in the development of the bureau policies and are in the main indifferent toward its program. Moreover, many bureau members are not farmers at all but merchants, bankers, and professional men who are persuaded to contribute to its support as a gesture of loyalty to their farmer customers. Nevertheless, the Farm Bureau is something to reckon with as a pressure group, and Mr. Wingate is proud of its effectiveness. "We don't play partisan politics," he explained. "We're very careful to distinguish between business and politics." According to his definition, it's "politics" to push one candidate over another when both endorse the bureau program; it's "business" to push a pro–Farm Bureau man in preference to an antibureau candidate. For instance, it will be the bureau's business to "get" Henderson Lanham, congressman from the Seventh District, who, alone among the Georgia delegation, voted against overriding the president's veto of the Taft-Hartley bill. It will be the bureau's business to support all the others. Mr. Wingate has so informed the county locals.

The political activities of the Farm Bureau are directed by Mr. Wingate almost entirely from its headquarters in Macon. We were told everywhere that the local chapters were little concerned with political issues and almost exclusively with improving farm conditions. They hold regular meetings, usually in the schoolhouse, and listen to lectures on such things as crop diversification, soil improvement, and techniques to produce higher yields, usually from a faculty member at a nearby A&M college. In most counties the bureau program is either directed by or in cooperation with the extension agent, who undoubtedly looks to the Farm Bureau lobby in Washington to help sustain the large federal appropriations for agriculture on which his job depends.

Perhaps because they have so much strength that they are courted by all candidates, Farm Bureau chapters rarely take partisan stands in local elections. At a word from Mr. Wingate, however, the whole membership can be activated to send telegrams or letters to state and federal representatives or to "speak to" local officeholders.

A third politically active organization is the Georgia Association of Democratic Clubs, made up of Negro leaders in more than sixty Georgia communities, with a membership of about twenty thousand. This group, headed by Mr. A. T. Walden, a prominent Negro lawyer in Atlanta, primarily seeks to acquaint the Negro population with the mechanics of registration and voting. Its work, however, does not stop with education. During the primary it had to see to it, wherever possible, that white tax assessors did not make it unreasonably difficult for Negroes to register, that registration boards did not purge Negroes without just cause, and that Negroes were admitted to the polls without discrimination and intimidation. The chapters also conducted regular meetings to instruct Negroes in how to conduct themselves at the polls so as to minimize the aggravation of racial tensions ("Don't drink the night before"; "go to bed early and get to the polls early"; "don't argue with the election managers or with white voters.")

Although the common and strong anti-Negro expression in stump speeches left few Negroes in doubt about which candidate they should support, the association did find it necessary to warn its members against the white man's double-talk and to guard against traitors in their midst. In this sense, the association has certainly been a partisan organization. But it's our conviction that the only thing required to make it nonpartisan, to destroy "the Negro bloc," is to take the race issue out of politics. With few exceptions, we found the Negro leadership sensitive, intelligent, and thoroughly responsible.

In between elections, the association has continued its orientation program among Negroes and in the larger towns maintained congenial liaison with white officials. Most recently, it has been pushing its program for the hiring of Negro patrolmen in Negro areas, with successes to date in Savannah and, more recently, in Atlanta. Thanks to its persistent advocacy, the idea is winning increasing public support in Macon, Gainesville, Brunswick, and Augusta.

Except for the League of Women Voters, the Georgia Farm Bureau, and the Georgia Association of Democratic Clubs, we found few groups at the local level engaged in political action. The labor unions exerted pressure against the antilabor bills, and the Merchants Association protested the sales tax, but neither showed any organized interest in issues that didn't affect the livelihoods of their members. Churchwomen were effective in some areas, notably in Augusta, against the white primary bill. On the county level, we found only two groups that had promotion of better government as their only purpose: the Augusta Citizens Union and the Citizens Organized for a More Progressive Douglas and Coffee County.

During the session itself we hadn't put much stock in the letters, telegrams, and postal cards received by legislators. We figured they couldn't be a very accurate index to public opinion, since almost all of them seem to have been sent at the prompting of some group with a particular ax to grind. Yet today, after soliciting opinions from people in every district in the state, we think maybe these messages were a pretty reliable guide. We think further that the turbulence of the 1947 session very well matched the ferment in the people's minds.

Briefly, this is about what we would judge to be popular reaction to the three most important bits of legislation introduced: (1) White primary. The majority of white Georgians do not want Negroes to vote and would like to see some means devised to keep them from it. What they might think if the issue could be explained to them properly, and how many might be willing to let Negroes vote, is something else again. (2) Sales tax. Georgians don't exactly cotton to a sales tax, but if it's the only way to pay school teachers, okay. (3) Antilabor bills. By and large, the people don't like labor unions. Anything the assembly can do to keep them small and weak is all right by them.

The White Primary and the "Nigger Bloc"

Anybody who wants to think realistically about the prospects for progressive government in Georgia might well start with a premise advanced by Roy Harris. "The Negro question," he told us, "is going to motivate politics for years to come."

Though it's too early to chart the course of the 1948 campaign, it's already evident that restoration of a white primary will be the issue. As much as some of us would like to think otherwise, a U.S. Supreme Court decision sustaining the South Carolina ruling is not going to quiet Herman's tirades against the "Negro bloc" or break the hold of the "nigger-nigger" line on the minds of his followers.[21] The only hope for taking race prejudice off the stump is a crippling Talmadge defeat in 1948, another defeat in 1950, and after that at least eight years of wise and dignified government.

At the moment it is impossible to weigh the relative

strengths of the pro-white primary and the anti-white primary forces. Mr. Harris claims that Talmadge's following has increased 20 percent since the state supreme court ruled him out of the governor's chair. Thompson leaders do not have such a ready figure but merely claim steadfastly that in a two-man race Thompson will win. Even if it were possible to evaluate these two statements, it would be fallacious to assume that the relative support of either candidate is determined by popular thinking on the white primary issue alone. The issue is yet to be clearly defined.

A current estimate of the situation would run something like this:

The white primary is regarded as a moral issue by only a small minority of white voters, most of them concentrated in urban areas. Because of the county unit system, these voters are virtually disfranchised and politically ineffectual. They are not happy about M. E. Thompson, but they will vote for him in a two-man race. They are almost instinctively anti-Talmadge.

The white primary issue (and Herman's unorthodox election to the governorship) has only intensified and solidified the traditional pro-Talmadge and anti-Talmadge forces. We found no evidence that any county that went for Talmadge last summer would go for Thompson in 1948 or that any county that went for Carmichael would go for Herman. In all counties where people are about evenly divided in their loyalties (McDuffie, Barrow, Greene, Bartow, Douglas, and Hall, to name a few), battle lines are forming. We have found almost everywhere that the Talmadge machine is better disciplined, more aggressive, more politically wise.

Mr. Thompson's veto of the Harris-drawn primary bill has not been accepted as proof that he is for the enfranchisement of the Negro. The people know where Herman Talmadge stands. They are not so sure about Mr. Thompson. His reluctance to face the issue squarely, his hesitancy to go on the offensive and make his position clear, has undoubtedly worked against him to date. He has said that he is for the white primary, "but not this kind of white primary." But beyond his advocacy of segregated polls and a dubious revision in the eligibility requirements, he has not suggested what his own kind of white primary would involve. As a result, many enlightened citizens have been dismayed, and the Talmadge people have only laughed at him. Moreover, his lack of a definite policy has served to further confuse the people who emotionally agree with him, those thousands of proud and prejudiced Georgians who sincerely want a white primary but reject the Roy Harris variety as being too dangerous. As far as we can tell, there has been no effort to inform these people that at the time it was drafted Roy Harris's bill was the only *legal* way to enforce a white primary and that even the Harris plan will be unlawful should the Supreme Court sustain the South Carolina decision.

The desire for a white primary varies from county to county, depending on the proportion of Negroes to the total population and the character of the county's political leadership. In north Georgia and in most urban centers, including Savannah, the white primary bill will not be an effective issue in 1948. In south and middle Georgia it will be so effective that the people will hardly listen to anything else. (This does not mean that Talmadge will carry no north Georgia counties and Thompson none in south Georgia. The Talmadge faction has an iron grip on Union, Rabun, Murray, Cherokee, and Lumpkin Counties in north Georgia. Conversely, because they are dominated by Ed Rivers, Atkinson, Berrien, Clinch, Lowndes, Ware, and Lanier counties in south Georgia probably will go for Thompson.)

It is fairly easy to summarize the Talmadge line on the white primary: Negroes vote in a bloc; in a state election the Negro vote will be the balance of power; the Negro vote will join with the CIO and city liberals to vote against rural interests. All Talmadge men are agreed on this line and recite it every chance they get. They also have some prepared an-

swers. Suggest to a Talmadge man that educational standards be added to the requirements for registration and the
answer is, "You do that and you rule out a lot of good white
folks." Ask him if he thinks it might not be dangerous to
take election laws off the statute books, as Roy Harris proposed, and he says, "You can trust the party as much as you
can trust the law."

Beyond this catechism, Talmadge men offer other reasons,
like personal improvisations on a common theme: "Niggers
don't take orders from us any more; now they listen to their
preacher." "The Negro vote will go to the highest bidder."
"Letting the nigger vote will lead to only one thing—mixing
of the blood." "The nigger doesn't want anything for himself. He just wants what the white man's got. I don't want
him in my party. Let him have his own party." "We're not
against niggers voting. They've been voting in the general
election for years. What we don't want is for them to be put
in a position in our party where they can be manipulated."
"We got to educate 'em before they're ready to vote."

It must be recognized that many Talmadge politicians are
for a white primary because they have no other choice; indeed, it may be that some of them would like to change their
stand. They started yelling against Negro enfranchisement
several years ago because it was expedient; they saw in it a
surefire appeal to prejudiced whites and a guarantee of election. Now they're out on a limb. Having lost a chance to win
the Negro vote, they can expect to stay in office only by
keeping Negroes from voting. That essentially is the present
position of the whole Talmadge camp. For its own preservation it cannot afford to let Negroes vote. Roy Harris was
quite honest when he said, "If five hundred thousand Negroes register, we might as well go fishing." Harris is confident, though, that no more Negroes will vote in 1948 than
voted in 1946. He knows that in the counties where Negroes
outnumber whites the whites aren't going to let the Negroes
vote and that the Negroes, most of them poor and illiterate

and all of them dependent on white people for jobs, aren't going to press the issue.

If the Supreme Court outlaws the South Carolina system, it will only require that Herman Talmadge change tactics. Instead of advocating that primary laws be made party rules, he may try to satisfy federal authorities with the passage of an educational qualifications law and his supporters with the tacit promise that the law won't be applied to whites. Fred Hand, Speaker of the House, says that in 1948 Herman will just ignore the Supreme Court decision in his stump speeches. Floor leader Bob Elliott says he won't ignore it but will be elected anyhow as the man "who would have given the people of Georgia a white primary if he could." Elliott goes on to say that "once in office, Herman will think up something new to keep the niggers away from the polls, and when the Supreme Court rules that unconstitutional, he'll think of something else, and when the Court rules that out, he'll think of something else again."

You can put it down that the dialogue of the 1948 campaign will differ in neither timbre nor substance from what voters heard in 1946.

A Sales Tax? Who Cares?

You can also expect to hear again much talk about a sales tax. A bill to establish such a tax is almost sure to be introduced in the next assembly, and unless events contrive to keep it in committee, it will surely pass, for the people of Georgia are about ready to accept it.

The Georgia Education Association is committed to a sales tax. Mr. Wingate of the Farm Bureau is for it. The only group actively fighting it is the Retail Merchants Association, and even some of its members are beginning to think it may be all right—that is, if the state allows them a generous rebate for collecting it. Most of the excitement among merchants stems from the fear that a sales tax would lose them customers in the border states, and most of the battle is being waged by merchants in the counties that border the sales tax states of South Carolina, North Carolina, and Alabama (the counties of Richmond, Stephens, Whitfield, Carroll, Troup, and Muscogee) and those that border the non–sales tax state of Florida (Lowndes, Brooks, Thomas, Grady, Decatur, and Seminole).

From our conversations with union leaders, we gather that labor opposes the tax in principle. "We deplore it," they told us. But we've seen no signs that labor is mobilizing its limited strength against it. In rural areas we found people generally unaware and indifferent.

What seems to have happened is that over a period of several years the people have been impressed with the necessity for additional state revenue and told that the only way the state is going to get it is through a sales tax. They are now about ready to believe it.

Anti–sales tax sentiment among legislators has been reduced through this same kind of attrition. Many representatives voted against the bill this last session, arguing that no revenue measures should be passed until a thorough examination had been made of the existing tax structure. They challenged the idea that sufficient revenue could be raised only through a sales tax, and they said they would not accept one until the need had thus been clearly established. A special commission is now making that examination. Regrettably, hardly anybody thinks it will do the job.

The commission is expected to do one of three things: (1) be so divided in opinion that it can make only weak and ineffectual recommendations; (2) submit such a burdensome, academic report that the assembly will ignore it (witness what the House did to the voluminous recommendations from a similar commission headed by revenue director Eugene Cook in 1943); or (3) recommend a sales tax. Whichever, a sales tax will likely be passed. The choice in the next session will be exactly what it was in 1947—either a sales tax or no new revenue. By that time many of the legislators who called the sales tax the most unfair and abominable form of taxation yet devised will be so beaten down that they might very easily support it.

Who Loves a Labor Union?

The average Georgian's feeling about the labor movement can be summed up in two sentences: "I'm not antilabor. I'm just antiunion."

To rural Georgians, organized labor is stereotypically John L. Lewis, the farmer's worst enemy, the agent for communism, and the destroyer of free enterprise. In their minds it is just about everything the NAM and the Georgia Farm Bureau say it is.

Understandably, the strongest antilabor sentiment is in the areas where there are no unions. With no personal knowledge of labor leadership and no experience with union methods, people here have derived their impressions almost exclusively from their local newspapers, almost all of which subscribe to services of the NAM-directed Western Newspaper Union and regularly carry its boilerplate; wire stories about strikes in key industries; visiting speakers at civic club luncheons; and a variety of special-interest periodicals, including the *Farm Bureau News*, the *Market Bulletin*, and the *Statesman*. In these areas it is a mark of respectability to be antiunion.

In communities where unionization has been accepted, however reluctantly, public opinion is still influenced by antilabor propagandists, but it is more likely to be determined by the conduct of the local unions. We found that in Savannah, after several years in bad repute, the AFL is beginning to earn public support, largely because of the restrained leadership of Representative Herbert Skinner, one of the sparkplugs in the Citizens' Progressive League. On the other hand, the seamen are regarded by many as little better than thugs, an opinion easily come by in view of the frequent dock fights and a recent assault by a union member on an elderly shipping official. In Augusta the AFL was long identified with the Cracker Party and consequently suffered from that clique's repudiation at the polls last year. The AFL further discredited itself last spring when, in a vindictive move against the Richmond delegation for supporting the antilabor bills, it joined with the Crackers to oppose the adoption of a new city charter it had previously endorsed.

In other semi-industrial towns with established trade unions—Atlanta, Macon, Rome—we found no discernible provocation for either anti- or pro-labor sentiment. Here a person's attitude toward unions is apparently governed by class and economic status; conforming to pattern, most white-collar workers identify with their bosses. It's worth noting, however, that the AFL lost the support of many normally sympathetic Atlantans last year when Representative Cicero Kendrick of the AFL voted for Herman Talmadge. Politically, labor is a factor only in the Seventh Congressional District and in the following counties: Fulton, Floyd, Bibb, Chatham, Richmond, Muscogee, Whitfield, and Greene. In a gubernatorial campaign, to quote Roy Harris, "We just forget about labor."

To combat the widespread labor phobia, especially among uninformed south Georgians, labor could do nothing better than to publicize the town of Dalton. Here the CIO has so well integrated itself into civic life, exercised such a physical change in the town itself, that it has won the manifest loyalty of white-collar clerks, merchants, and professionals. "We used to be a class-conscious people," a retired city policeman said. "We wouldn't associate with mill workers, and we wouldn't let our children play with their children. We hated to go into the homes, even on charity missions, they were that dirty. The people were ignorant, lazy, never paid their debts, and they used to fight a lot among themselves. At least that's what we all thought. Well, all that's changed now. Ever since the unions came in 1937. See that school over there? The union was behind that. They also got behind a public playground. The workers' homes are clean now, and they pay their debts, and their children are just like everybody else's children, maybe a little smarter. Some of their children have gone on to college and come back to Dalton as doctors and lawyers. We're proud of them. All in all, I guess the unions were the best thing ever happened to this town."

But Dalton is unique. Almost everywhere else we found people reflecting the biases of mill owners and telling us proudly how the unions had been licked. Management in Georgia, we have to conclude, is not opposed merely to the closed shop or to mass picketing. It is opposed to the very principle of collective bargaining.

Wherever there is an established industry or the promise of new industry, businesspeople are organized to combat "labor infiltration." After explaining that he opposed the labor movement because "it destroys the sense of personal craftsmanship and does away with the personal relationship between employer and employee," Herschel Lovett volunteered that he had guaranteed passage of the antilabor bills to the management of the Stephens Woolen Mills as an incentive to get Stephens to come to Dublin. In Dougherty County we were told that the Albany Chamber of Commerce had "offered every concession in the books" to get new industry and that the people would "fight hard at any threat of unionization." In McDuffie County a highly respected official described with obvious satisfaction the prevalent attitude in his community. Public hostility was so great, he said, that union organizers could not even find a room to rent and were forced to commute from Augusta; further, every civic club in Thomson rejected the union's request that it be allowed to state its case at luncheon meetings. In Macon, we were told that the Bibb mills would have been organized a year ago if management hadn't exploited the Negro issue so skillfully. It was in Macon, too, that we learned of the strong opposition to CIO activity by the AFL. "It was worse than those NAM posters," according to a newspaperman. "Every week the AFL paper would come out with blasts at the CIO. Ads that started off, 'All right, Macon, you asked for it; here's what will happen if you let the CIO take over.' Stuff that bad and worse. When the CIO won an election in one plant, the AFL agent stormed off in a huff and refused even to sign the tally sheet."

A typical reaction to the CIO's organizing efforts in small family-owned plants, we gather, is that of the owner of a veneer factory in south Georgia. The CIO was never able to sign up more than three workers, and all three lost their jobs. The owner didn't fire them immediately. He first had them transferred, one by one, to the hardest, most backbreaking jobs in the plant. Each man was fifty or older, and none could hold up. When a man dropped out from physical exhaustion, he was dismissed for incompetence. Having thus eliminated the union's nucleus, the owner then called his workers together for a lecture. "It's all right with me if you want to join a union," he told them. "But you should hear this, and you better believe it. If you ever try to strike on me, I'll close this plant down tighter'n a drum and never open it again. I've made enough money out of this plant, more than enough, to retire on, and a strike would make me mighty happy to retire."

Elsewhere we have found that the CIO had been unable to get inside the gates not so much because of calculated intimidation by management but because of a practiced paternalism accompanied, in some instances, by an enlightened policy of prevention—the granting of those wage increases and improved working conditions that unions could be expected to demand. Although union agents might have a different story, we were told that this was the reason for union failures at the Callaway Mills in LaGrange, the West Point

Manufacturing Company in West Point, the Mandeville
Mills in Carrollton, the LeTourneau plant in Toccoa, and the
Atco Goodyear Plant in Cartersville.

What's for Me?

Georgians are not impressed with what past administrations have done for their communities. Ralph McGill is right
when he says that the average person has never felt the impact of state government. We were told of roads that Rivers,
Talmadge, or Arnall had built, or of roads they had promised but were yet to build. But nowhere were we told that
the people had benefited so much from the administration
of a former governor that their loyalty stemmed from gratitude alone.

Of the more recent administrations, that of Ed Rivers has
made the deepest impression in voters' minds. We were told
so often that Rivers had done more for the state than any
other governor that we would almost believe it if it weren't
for the realization that much of the credit given him belongs
rather to President Roosevelt. People still point proudly to
the concrete highways (Rivers's detractors call them "death
traps") and to the many public buildings constructed during
his administration—schools, courthouses, recreation centers, community canneries. Nor have they forgotten that it
was Rivers who passed the homestead exemptions act and
set up the state patrol.

But the truth of the matter seems to be that most people in
Georgia have gotten so little from the state government that
they don't really expect much of anything from it. They
know they want two things—more paved market-to-market
roads and improved school facilities—and that's about all.
People who have made a comfortable living off the tourist
trade would like to see an expanded parks program, but
people who live in areas unsuited to park development ei-

ther couldn't care less or actively resent any proposal to spend state funds for the benefit of another part of the state. The establishment of county health clinics brought immediate approval whenever we suggested the idea, but only rarely did we find any conscious recognition of what might be done at the state level to raise health standards. We were told almost everywhere that no, there was nothing any candidate could offer as a positive program that could match in public response the Talmadge appeal to race prejudice.

Race and the Right to Vote

About 150,000 Negroes registered to vote in the 1946 Democratic primary. Legal and illegal purging in some sixty counties reduced this number to 125,000. Of these, probably 100,000 voted.

These are not accurate figures, but they are as good as can be obtained. Negro voting in the primary was something distinctly new in 1946, and no agency, public or private, was equipped to do the detailed job of collecting records on its character and extent. That even incomplete records are available is due only to the personal curiosity of some county clerks and to the self-serving fact gathering of some politicians.

County registrars are required by law to record the race of every person registered, but they are not required to break down registration figures by race in their consolidated reports to the secretary of state. If anybody had the time and money to contact every registrar in the state, and if every registrar could be persuaded to open his books, it might be possible to get an accurate count. So far as we know, nobody has tried. A month before the primary, after an informal survey of its own, the *Atlanta Journal* estimated that 116,345 Negroes were registered, a figure that can be accepted only as the minimum.[22] A. T. Walden, of the Negro Association of

Democratic Clubs, believes that before the purges started throughout the state a few weeks before the primary at least 150,000 had registered.

The inability to read or write is not enough to disqualify a voter in Georgia. In many counties, however, many Negroes were struck because they could not, to the satisfaction of the board of registrars, "understand and give a reasonable interpretation of any paragraph of the Constitution of the United States or of this state . . . read to them."[23] This kind of purging was widespread throughout south and middle Georgia and would have reduced the number of Negro registrants even more had it not been for the intervention of federal judges.

Generally, the urban counties were remarkably tolerant of Negro registration. One week before the primary, the Associated Press reported that only 100 Negroes of 24,000 registered had been purged for illiteracy in Fulton County (Atlanta) and practically none in Floyd (Rome). Sumter County (Americus), which lies smack in the black belt, was a conspicuous exception; only 92 of 650 Negroes to apply for registration were judged to be qualified.

Estimates on the number who actually voted vary widely. People who would like to believe that Eugene Talmadge failed to get a majority of white votes say 75,000; extreme Talmadgeites, who would like to explain away the fact that 97,391 more votes were cast against him than for him, say 200,000. We have settled on a figure agreed on separately by two people who ought to know. Roy Harris and A. T. Walden both say 100,000. Mr. Harris says he *knows* because he instructed his men on the county election committees to count the votes in the Negro ballot boxes first, before consolidating them with white ballots for the official tally.

All things considered, this figure is nothing less than phenomenal. Hardly half that many Negroes voted in any other southern state in 1946, even in those states where Negro participation in primaries has been long accepted.[24] The fact is that despite all the agitation about the Negro's right to vote—all the heroic struggles to obtain and secure it, and all the noisy efforts by demagogues to prevent it—the mass of southern Negroes has to be educated, aroused, and coaxed to exercise it. That 15 percent of the Negro population past their eighteenth birthday should vote in the first Georgia primary open to them can be attributed to the intelligence and diligence of the state's Negro leadership, the temper of the Talmadge campaign that provoked them to extraordinary concern, and the integrity of an unknown number of mostly anonymous election officials who insisted that Negroes be given a fair chance at the polls.

Negroes voted in a bloc against Eugene Talmadge, and for good reason. As one legislator explained it, they voted against him for the same reason anyone would have voted against him if their name was Clawhammer and he'd said nobody named Clawhammer would ever be allowed to vote again if he got elected.

In every case where there was the appearance of a bloc vote, it was because some candidate was using the race issue and his opponent was not, or because, at least in one instance, a candidate let it be known that he was *for* Negro enfranchisement. In Muscogee County Negroes voted solidly for L. N. Huff for lieutenant governor. Nowhere else in the state had Dr. Huff got anything like a bloc vote, and the suspicion was that Columbus's Negro leadership had sold out. We found, on the contrary, that Negroes had merely rallied to a positive appeal; Dr. Huff was the only man in the race to come out squarely for their right to vote.

It can be said categorically that in state elections the solidifying factor is always the Negro's right to vote. Negroes vote in blocs only when white supremacy is the issue. In local elections, the situation is a little different. Negroes do vote in blocs on county and municipal matters whenever these matters are commonly recognized as threats or promises. Indications, however, are that even in local elections the impulse toward a bloc vote is destroyed as soon as local officeholders begin to feel the impact of the Negroes' political strength. When that happens, the Negro vote becomes an object to be courted and bid for; there is no longer a rationale for bloc voting.

We are not forgetting that the lynching of the four Negroes near Monroe and the murder of another in Taylor County can be traced directly to the inflammatory nature of the 1946 campaign.[25] Nevertheless, we believe that the mechanics of the election itself went off with much less tension between the races than predicted. Slowdown tactics were used in some counties, as in Chatham, where many Negroes stood in line from five o'clock in the morning until the polls closed that night and never got the chance to vote. There obviously were instances of calculated intimidation. But practically all such instances occurred before the day of the primary or in vicinities nowhere near the polls. Almost without exception, the actual voting went off without incident.

In most counties the physical arrangements for voting were planned carefully with a view toward forestalling disturbances. Polls were segregated, usually located out of sight of one another and quite often separated by considerable distance. Negroes usually voted in the basement or in the rear of the courthouse or in another building; in Upson County the Negro poll was in the jailhouse. Almost everywhere Negroes handled themselves quietly and with great dignity. To most of them it was an occasion of special importance, perhaps a solemn one. They were voting for the first time in their lives, and they brought to the polls an appreciation of the right of free ballot that was not to be found among white voters, who tended to take that right for granted. Theirs was not an attitude that could have precipitated any outburst. In Fulton, DeKalb, and several other counties where the polls were not segregated, they took their turns with the whites, and there was no trouble.

Some interesting reflections might be made on the pattern of Negro voting. We found, for example, that in the small counties virtually all Negro votes were cast in the county seat, rarely in a rural precinct. We found, too, that more Negro women voted than men; in West Point one observer said that 90 percent of the colored vote was cast by women. In almost every community Negroes looked to their preachers for political guidance.

Reaction among white voters was mixed. We did hear considerable praise for the orderliness with which Negroes voted and quite often a defense of their right to vote. There was a general expression of regret that the Negroes were so ill prepared for their new citizenship. Among some whites it was an expression of self-reproach for having failed to provide the educational facilities that would have prepared them; among a great many more it was just another irrational condemnation of the Negro. But mostly what we heard were complaints: unqualified Negroes had voted; many of them had sold their votes; some of the ballots had been "fixed"; they had used sample ballots for pre-voting instructions, some of which had found their way into the ballot boxes.

These things did happen, but of greater interest to us were the people who told us about them. As we listened, and heard again and again the note of self-righteous indignation, it occurred to us that the real trouble between the white man and the Negro is a matter of the spirit. The problem of the Negro's entry into politics, no less than the whole problem of the Negro and the white man, would be no problem at all if the white man could only bring himself to regard the Negro as a human being. In our discussions with many white citizens—respectable people certain of their Christian motives—we detected a curious ambivalence. They either endowed the Negro with heroic character, demanding that he behave himself more honorably than the white man, or they regarded him as one of a different and lower species, from whom only the worst could be expected and therefore

to whom nothing should be given. However they thought of
Negroes, it was not as a people endowed essentially with
the same frailties and virtues of all people.

These persons knew that white voters had done the very
same things they complained of in Negro voters. Why did
they consider it so much more of an outrage when the Negro
did them? Why did they think it was all right for an illiterate white person to vote and not all right for an illiterate
Negro? "It's the bloc vote," they would say. Do they mean
that white people don't vote in blocs? What about the Talmadge bloc? "Well, there's a difference." We would ask
them for the difference, and they would say, laughing, "Oh,
you know about niggers. A nigger's like a hound dog. The
worse you treat him the more he loves you."

No use. The prevailing mind-set of such persons does not
permit honest debate. It weaves and ducks and escapes all
logical thrusts. If it did not, it would admit the one fact that
would end all this to-do about the Negro's right of ballot:
the qualified Negro has as much right to vote in any Georgia
election as the qualified white. Or, to put it more simply: any
person who qualifies to vote under the laws of Georgia is
entitled to vote.

But to face this fact, to believe it and give it the authority
of enforceable law, one must first accept the principle that in
a political democracy there are no Negroes and no whites,
only citizens.

The white majority in Georgia is not yet ready to accept
this principle.

Who is chairman of the Democratic committee in your
county?

If you don't know, you've got plenty of company.

Charged with the job of conducting the primaries, this
committee is the prime mover in the whole election process.
Whether we have fair and honest elections depends on it.

But most of us don't know how the committee is selected or what purpose it serves. As a result, in most counties the committee is self-perpetuating. Its members are either political hacks bent on furthering their own causes or men of high integrity who serve out of a sense of civic responsibility. Elections are run, whether carelessly or efficiently, purely according to the persuasions of the committee's members.

Here is how the committee is defined by Rule 25 of the Democratic Party of Georgia (the italics are ours):

There shall be a County Democratic Executive Committee for each county in the State. The members of the County Executive Committee elected in the state-wide primary held on the 17th day of July, 1946, shall hold office until the day following that on which the State Convention shall be held in 1950.

The members of the Democratic party of each County shall elect a County Democratic Executive Committee at the primary herein provided for in 1950 and every four years thereafter on said date and each shall hold office for a period of four years and until the day following that on which the State Convention is held four years after his election. Said County Committee shall consist of at least one member from each militia district and each city ward and the *County Executive Committee may provide for a larger number.* Each district and city ward shall have equal representation. Suitable blanks shall be left at the foot of the official ballot for the voters to write in the names of person or persons for whom they desire to vote as a member of the County Executive Committee from their respective district or ward. The plurality rule shall govern in determining the election of members of the County Committee. *The County Executive Committee may require that candidates for the County Committee qualify as such candidates and provide for printing their names on the official ballot. County Executive Committees may provide that the committee members be voted upon only by the voters living in their district or ward, or may require that the members of the committee be voted upon county-wide.*

Members of the County Committee elected at a primary shall

assume office as such on the day following that on which the State Convention is held after the primary. In the event any county committee fails to meet and organize, after five days written notice by any member of said committee to each member thereof, said committee shall convene and elect a Chairman, Vice-Chairman, Secretary, and such officers as it sees fit.

Each committee shall make rules as it sees fit not inconsistent with these rules and the rules of the State Democratic Executive Committee adopted under authority of these rules. The Committee can be convened at any time by five days notice thereof by any officer. All vacancies in the County Committee shall be filled by the remaining members of the committee and such appointees shall serve for the unexpired term of the vacancy which he fills.

During last year's debate on the white primary bill, proponents stressed the point that control of elections would still be in the hands of the people, even though election rules were stripped from the statute books, because the people would continue to elect the county committees. In view of the liberties granted these committees, this argument seems to have dubious validity. Party rule is elastic enough to make for easy manipulation. Furthermore, it's hardly accurate to say that the people elect their county committees. In reality, in most counties the people merely endorse nominations of the incumbent committee.

An idea of the liberties taken, most of them innocently perhaps, may be gained from a catalog of the variances among counties in the way committee members are elected. In Polk County a slate of candidates is placed on the ballot by the incumbent committee; to replace three members of the committee who had died, Chairman Roy Emmet simply asked around the community for three prominent men who would agree to serve. In Bartow it is the custom to name the committee by "street corner caucus" and by write-in votes. In Hall, where rivalry between the two factions is strong, the write-in method is used with an interesting variation. In 1946 the anti-Talmadge group had gummed tabs printed up listing its choice for membership on the committee and passed them out near the polls with instructions that they be stuck to the bottom of the ballots. (The Talmadge faction has protested that this procedure, also used in Troup County, is illegal.)

The method used in Stephens County is standard for many counties. Nominations are placed on the ballot by the incumbent committee, with a blank space to permit write-ins. Very rarely is there any concerted effort to contest the committee's nominations with write-in votes, and the committee manages to perpetuate itself through public indifference. We were told that at the time of our inquiry the chairman himself didn't know how many members were on the committee because the party rule book had been lost.

It is perhaps more common, however, for no slate of names to appear on the ballot. Rather, a blank space is provided for the voter to write in his choice. Usually what happens is that the voter scratches his head, turns to the poll manager, and asks, "What am I supposed to do here?" and the poll manager says, "Oh, write in Joe Smith. He's been on the committee so long as I can remember, guess he might as well stay on." The voter writes in "Joe Smith" and considers his civic duty done.

Interest is so low that sometimes an ambitious man can get elected simply by busying himself quietly around his precinct on election day, asking friends to write in his name. In Towns County a teacher at Young Harris campaigned for a day or so and got himself elected chairman.

During the height of the battle between Thompson and Talmadge last year, many voters discovered that the sympathies of their county committees were exactly the reverse of the dominant sympathies in their counties. Fulton and DeKalb Counties, for instance, are overwhelmingly anti-Talmadge, yet the committee in neither county would authorize a delegation to the Thompson convention in Macon, both being dominated by Talmadge men.

The Vote Shall Be by Ballot

Under Georgia law what kind of ballot is used is up to each of the 159 counties. They have their choice of three code provisions, one of which permits the use of almost any kind of ballot so long as it's printed.

Nobody knows for sure how many counties use a secret ballot. Several years ago Lyle Chubb, then research consultant to the Citizens' Fact-Finding Movement, tried to find out, but without much luck. Sixty-two counties didn't respond to his questionnaire at all, and an unknown number, he has since learned, gave him the wrong answers. Superior court clerks, it seems, sometimes don't know the difference between the official ballot and the official secret ballot.

Just to get the nomenclature straight, it might be well right here to define the three general types of ballots permitted by Georgia law:

1. *The no official ballot.* Since 1869 the law has said, "The vote shall be by ballot." It does not say what kind of ballot, and in practice the type used often depends on the preferences of the election managers. Senator J. B. G. Logan, of Banks County, told us that his county had adopted a secret ballot under this section of the code eighteen years prior to the 1941 secret ballot act.
2. *The official ballot.* In 1922 the legislature amended the election laws so as to provide for more detailed instructions for the preparation of ballots for primary and other elections. This act provides for a numbered stub and a numbered ballot. It may be adopted on the recommendation of two successive grand juries and, if adopted, eliminates use of the secret ballot, thereby permitting a check on every person voting.
3. *The official secret ballot.* Like the official ballot, this can be adopted or discontinued on recommendation of two successive grand juries. It provides for secrecy, although the

stub is numbered, by requiring that the number on the ballot be printed on a perforated tab. When the voter receives his ballot, he signs the numbered stub, receives his ballot, tears off the numbered tab, and deposits it in one box and the ballot in another. Thus there is no means whereby the ballot can be checked against the signed stub.

In our talks with people throughout the state, we found little concern for the secrecy of the ballot. It was either that the ballot they were using was secret enough to suit them or that they just didn't care if people *did* know how they voted. In some counties where the secret ballot is provided by law, it is not commonly understood that the numbered tab is to be torn off and deposited separately, so that in reality many voters simply disregard this safeguard for secrecy.

We also found that some people prefer the numbered ballot to the secret ballot, under the impression that it offers better protection against fraud. Their point seems to be that, with the numbered ballot, if a person is discovered to have voted fraudulently, his or her vote can be recovered from the ballot box and destroyed and thus have no effect on the final count. With a secret ballot this would not be possible. Election managers would know only that in the mass of unnumbered ballots there was one fraudulent ballot. Since that ballot could not be recovered, the only way to guarantee an honest count would be to call a new election.

One of the frankest objections to the secret ballot came from a veteran of thirty or more years in local politics. "Do I think we ought to have a secret ballot?" he said. "Hell no. I think you *oughta* know how some of these lyin' sonsabitches vote."

The evidence is that election irregularities of various kinds are pretty general throughout Georgia. These irregularities may result from nothing more than human carelessness, as some apologists claim. We don't think so. Most of them, it seems to us, are engineered by men who make money out of public office.

Certain politicians have tried to minimize the seriousness of the *Atlanta Journal*'s exposé of election fraud in Telfair County. "That was the general election," they argue. "The general election doesn't mean anything in Georgia. Least-wise it never did before. Things like that don't happen in our primaries. Our primaries are fair and honest."

We have found other politicians, however, as well as editors of country newspapers, who say that irregularities equally as serious occur in the primaries. Votes are sold for a dollar and a slug of stump rum; the dead and insane are voted; election returns are not counted but concocted. In a lot of the rural counties poll managers are usually, pur-posely, chosen from among the oldest adults in town, who are usually are too tired by the end of an election day to be careful about the count. Their carelessness and their vulner-ability to offers of "assistance" combine to make an election a sort of fixed routine, in which voters are privileged to drop slips of paper in boxes by political bosses who have already "counted" the ballots.

Georgia's election laws are neither uniform nor models of clarity. Subject to loose interpretation and relatively easy to circumvent, they permit fraud at many stages in the election process and irregularities at virtually every stage. Here are some of the more interesting examples we've been told about:

• Registration lists are not purged of the dead, insane, and imprisoned, nor of persons who have moved away since the last election. The result is that precinct managers innocently or knowingly allow votes to be cast in the names of persons who are unavailable, unable, or unauthorized to vote.

- Ballots are prepared in such a fashion as to make it simple to vote for one candidate and difficult to vote for another.
- Locations of voting places are not announced until the day before the election, or polls are moved at the last moment. This device effectively cuts down on the number voting.
- Watchers are not assigned to many precincts, thereby facilitating corrupt practices by poll managers.
- Poll watchers and managers are selected wholly from one faction. In Savannah in 1946 the Democratic committee attempted to select workers who were divided on the governor's race but sympathetic to local incumbents. Thus, there would have been apparent representation of all factions, when in fact poll workers would have been stacked in favor of the city machine.
- Poll managers fail to comply with the law that requires the posting of complete and correct instructions on voting procedure. In the Fifth District congressional race, instructions for marking the ballot were changed in the middle of the day, with the result that many ballots were thrown out that had been marked in accordance with earlier instructions.
- Private booths are not provided, enabling managers to watch and influence the marking of ballot.
- Managers "help" mark ballots for voters who are illiterate, blind, ignorant, or lazy. Often these people are concerned about one race only and permit managers to mark their own choices in all other races. Managers who do not actually mark ballots for such willing accessories will suggest how they should be marked.
- Some party officials take liberties with the ballots. In one county in 1946, the chairman of the Democratic Executive Committee wrote in his name on hundreds of ballots before the polls opened. When a voter questioned the legality of this act, the poll manager assured him it was all right, that the committee chairman was merely exercising a privilege of office.

- Solicitation is common by persons, even the candidates themselves, in the immediate vicinity of the polls.
- Votes are purchased by one means or another. Campaign workers are given sums of money to be used as they see fit on election day. Sometimes they give semiliterates a dollar apiece to vote as they tell them. Sometimes they are more delicate. When laborers and farmhands say they can't take the time to go to the polls because it would cost them money to leave their jobs, the candidate's man will pay them for the time lost and drive them to the polls on the assumption that they will vote "right."

It is easy to buy votes. Apparently the hard thing is to keep them bought. Several ways have been devised to ensure that the vote vender casts his ballot the way he is being paid to cast it. Perhaps the most common device is what is known as chain voting. Under this system the first man in the chain enters the polling place, receives his ballot, drops a blank piece of paper in the ballot box, walks outside, and sells his untouched ballot to a waiting purchaser. The purchaser then marks the ballot and gives it to another person, who, when he goes in to vote, deposits the marked ballot and, when he comes out, gives the unmarked ballot to the payoff man and collects his money. This procedure is repeated throughout the day.

Sometimes a simpler method is used. The buyer will have as his accomplice a poll worker, whose job it is to assist the voter in marking his ballot and to let the payoff man know if the voter reneges on his bargain. Since the voter gets paid only after he's voted, it is a pretty safe method, although in some cases a bit too obvious.

One county ring adopted a unique system several years ago. Buyers arranged with the election managers (our informant swears this is true) to require that the desired candidate be shown not by the conventional pencil mark but by removing his name with a razor blade. A voter would cut out the name of the machine candidate, drop his ballot in the box, and then present his "coupon" to a payoff man and collect his dollar.

Various techniques have been used by workers of one faction to get workers from the other camp away from the polls long enough for skulduggery. Workers will insist politely that opposition helpers go out for dinner, or fake phone calls notifying them of urgent business at the office. During one recent election a desperate worker eliminated the opposition by buying them all cokes. With hasty apologies, they got up and left, one fast after the other. The cokes had been spiked with croton oil.

Perhaps the greatest opportunity for fraud comes at the time ballots are counted. Roy Harris says he's never worried when people tell him the opposition is trying to "buy" a county away from him; he gets worried only when he's told the opposition has sewed up the election committee and plans to steal the election by falsifying returns.

A corrupt poll worker, watching his chances, can do any number of things to help his man. When the ballots are being divided into stacks by candidates, just prior to the tally, he can slip into his candidate's stack some of the ballots marked for the opposition. (If he's called on it, he's "sorry, just careless.") He can "read" the ballots incorrectly so that one candidate gets credit for a ballot marked for another. If voting machines are used, he can read the tally backward, reversing his totals in favor of the losing candidate. If he's really desperate, he might be able to eat enough ballots to throw the election; one south Georgia lawyer is now known as "Billygoat" for having done just this.

Ballots have been stolen and destroyed. During one election count a stranger ambled into headquarters, scooped up a stack of ballots, and ran. A poll worker chased him, lost him, and returned a few minutes later to find another stack gone.

But usually it's not necessary to dispose of the ballots. A simple error in arithmetic will serve the same purpose. Most of these convenient little errors (adding or dropping a digit) take place in the consolidation of returns—sometimes by the election committee itself, sometimes (in cities) by precinct captains reporting to the election committee. During the 1946 election in Richmond County, as one precaution against a dishonest count, the Independents refused to accept any reports of a consolidated vote and demanded ward-by-ward returns instead.

Alert, firm, and conscientious election managers can prevent irregularities. But all too often the managers themselves are corrupt or corruptible. In fact, in some militia districts it is a matter of common conjecture if the managers ever counted the ballots at all. The managers are men of like mind, there's nobody around to tell them otherwise, and counting ballots is too tedious and troublesome. Instead, they simply dream up some likely figures. Two weeks before one election, a legislator was told by a manager that his district would go 75 to 7 (or some such specific figure) for a given candidate. These were the exact returns for that candidate after the votes had ostensibly been counted.

Delayed returns are always suspect. Among gubernatorial candidates it's a cardinal principle that on election day everything be done until the last minute to carry out the impression of sure victory. "To let on that you're not carrying the state like a house afire," a former governor told us, "is just like handing a dozen counties to the enemy." That's why campaigns sometimes extend right through the day of the primary. Candidates aren't trying to sell themselves to the people any longer; they're trying to sell themselves to those county bosses who like to ride bandwagons, who don't care who's elected governor just so long as their counties go for the winner.

The law says that the count shall be public, but the law isn't always followed. We were told that at the main precinct in one county Carmichael received a clear majority from the first of two ballot boxes; it was counted publicly. Managers then went into a back room to count the second box; their private count showed a unanimous vote for Eugene Talmadge.

The law does not specifically authorize the presence of poll watchers, and many election officials have seen fit to bar them. At the last state primary in DeKalb County, several watchers representing Helen Douglas Mankin, candidate for Congress, were denied the right to watch the count from a point close enough to see anything. Mrs. Mankin's brother, Hamilton Douglas, was threatened with arrest if he insisted on watching the count at the DeKalb courthouse.

Conclusions

Very simply, what Georgia needs at this moment is an educated electorate and a two-party system. Until we get them, "good government" will be no more than a campaign slogan, and more often than not the slogan of a defeated candidate.

Georgia's existing political structure is not so impregnable that the people can't break it. We believe that for the people to have consistently good government they need only to decide they want it bad enough to work for it—and work hard. To make this decision, however, may first require a change in character and the rejection of an imprisoning value system more inimical to reform than any political machine.

You can explain why the people of Georgia are the way they are. You can find explanations in their history, in their fear of God, in their biracial culture, in the diversity and hard demands of their geography, in certain national discriminatory practices that have held them to a colonial-type economy. All the explanations will be true, and they will probably prove the people blameless. But the fact remains that the main obstacle to progress in Georgia is its people. The compelling reality today is that though it is essentially undemocratic, ours is nonetheless *representative* government. It is probably an accurate reflection of the needs, wants, anxieties, and prejudices of the people.

In undertaking this study the two of us had hoped that somehow we could establish that the fault lies more with the system. And yet, reviewing the things we've seen and the talk we've heard, we can only believe that the people of Georgia are bound more by their own ignorance than by any system imposed on them. It may not have been like this always. But today it can be said with conviction that the chief reason we have a one-party system and a county unit system is that most of our people want them, and the chief reason we are ruled by a coalition of political hacks and corporate wealth is that the people don't know enough to care. Our politics is what it is because our people are what they are— and they are either impotent, indifferent, or destructive because of their individual economic circumstance, their allegiance to custom, their spiritual impoverishment, and their ignorance of what works and doesn't work for justice in our tragically flawed society.

Money, we repeat, *does* run the politics of Georgia. But this does not refute the fact that ignorance is the root evil. The powerful men of wealth who back a candidate for private gain, who block legislation for the general welfare to gratify immediate self-interest, are ignorant. They are no less ignorant than the woman who walked two miles into town and sold four dozen eggs in order to make two dollars to "help Gene's son along," or the hundreds, perhaps thousands, like her who give their mites to a man who can prop up their failing sense of dignity. If the rich and privileged were not so ignorant, they would prefer to invest their money in honest government rather than pay it to shakedown administrations; they would know that government by the few can only lead to government by the fewer; and they would put their surplus profits in a program for human advancement, knowing that only through the advancement of all the people can they themselves continue to profit.

All this considered, it seems to us that before we can plan any campaign to rid ourselves of a perpetuating condition of political injustice, we must answer these basic questions:

Is it possible to educate our people to the responsibilities and sacrifices of democratic government?

Assuming that we can educate only those people without property interest who now derive little benefit from government, would the resistance of men with money now controlling the forces of government be so great as to keep the enlightened majority politically sterile?

Is there enough money to be had from people opposed to the present political setup to launch and sustain such a campaign?

If these three questions can be answered yes, then the general pattern of a long-range program becomes clear. But equally clear, we believe, is that any potentially successful program will require two complementary statewide organizations—one for orientation and one for political action; one to awaken Georgians to what "good government" can be, the other to show how good government can be achieved.

An education agency is needed that can effectively reach people of all ages and economic groups. Its purpose should be threefold: (1) to acquaint people with the facts of Georgia politics and government; (2) to stimulate thought and discussion on the needs of the state as they can be met through government; and (3) to sell actively a nonpartisan program of advancement, the program to be decided on by a policy board composed of known and respected leaders in the fields of politics, human relations, public health, education, agriculture, industry and commerce, and so on. Its program should be directed toward a mass audience, and it should employ the full resources of all communication media—radio, newspapers, and public forums.

At the same time, a second party is needed to build a shorter route to reform. Two things argue for this: (1) under the county unit system of the currently constituted Democratic Party, the state's progressive forces are virtually disfranchised; (2) the current leadership of all too many county election committees is venal, careless, or indifferent to democratic values. Since the county unit system perpetuates itself through assemblymen dependent on it for election, the only way to bypass it is to force the decisive vote into the general election, where the winner is determined by popular vote. Similarly, rather than try to replace the present Democratic Party's election managers, it would be easier to elect new managers for a second primary and to ensure an honest count of general election returns by the presence of trained poll watchers. To do both things requires organization, and that organization logically should be a second, distinct political party.

If these recommendations seem too demanding, then it is only because these are demanding times. The situation is such that nothing less can offer a prospect of constructive government and guarantee its permanency. We can no longer afford to default to the cynical men of wealth and to the politicians of vaulting ambition, whose pursuit of profit and power degrade the idea of democracy and would deny us the right and the means to make it real.

PART 2

The Interviews

William T. Dean, president pro tem of the state Senate, Thirty-fourth District (Conyers, Rockdale County), interviewed in the office of the Senate president, March 31

As Senate presiding officer, Bill Dean probably proved to be the most valuable man in the Thompson camp. Talmadge men outnumbered Thompson men, but the Talmadge program was stalled and sometimes blocked by Mr. Dean's skillful use of parliamentary rule and by his adroit appointments of Thompson sympathizers to key committees. He has the manners of a gentleman, and in the handling of his Senate duties he was consistently fair, direct, and unequivocal in his decisions from the chair. In private conversation he is just as polite, and just as fair and firm in his opinions, but for one accustomed to speaking from a podium his voice is surprisingly low.

Mr. Dean was unrestrained in his observations on the behavior of his colleagues. At one point we asked if he could confirm the story about the representative from Cherokee County, a medical doctor from Canton. The story was that, after first publicly voicing support for Thompson, this man had switched to Herman at the last minute. The reason, according to rumor, is that Congressman John Wood had told him that unless he voted for Herman, the C&S Bank would foreclose on his clinic. Dean said he'd heard this story, was inclined to believe it, but couldn't confirm it. He said that the doctor has "a bad conscience. He acts mean when he's drunk, and he drinks a lot. In fact, he is the only man I know who drank on the Senate floor this past session—or even in the cloakroom."

Even more of a troublemaker, he volunteered, was Senator Wideman, who was always challenging him on parliamentary procedure. Dean described Wideman as a "frustrated schoolteacher who's just naturally perverse." He expressed disappointment in Spence Grayson, one of the most ardent Talmadge spokesmen. He said that in the previous session Grayson had been thoroughly polite and cooperative, that he actively "hated the Talmadges, both father and son." This year Grayson never missed an opportunity to rise from his seat and defend the Talmadge program. "He was one of the most stubborn men I've ever tried to deal with, and I cannot understand what came over him."

Dean was more tolerant of Senator Alex Weaver, a normally "right-thinking man. I think he's just crawled so far out on a limb he can't get back."

He voiced strong dislike for Roy Harris. "Roy's got the power bug," he said. "He's always the bridesmaid, never the bride." He said that perhaps more than anything else Harris wants to be reinstated by the folks in Richmond County who turned him out last spring. "He wants to control Richmond County as much as he wants to control Georgia." Harris has always intended to run for governor, according to Dean. He was bitterly disappointed when Ellis Arnall backed out on what Harris had thought was a tacit promise to support him in 1946. "I wouldn't be a bit surprised if he didn't run in 1948 instead of Herman."

Most legislators do not think Harris is crooked, Dean said. "I'm not sure that he gets paid in a black satchel, either." But Dean knows of at least one occasion when Harris went back on his word, and he doesn't intend to let Harris forget it— even though it may be the only time Harris ever defaulted on a promise to another politician. Before the white primary bill came over to the Senate, Harris and Herman came to Dean and asked him to limit debate to thirty minutes. Dean thought it was a reasonable request but agreed to it only on the condition that the Talmadge forces accept five amendments. Harris and Herman pledged their support for the amendments and, when Dean asked them to put in writing, signed a memorandum to that effect. So debate was limited to thirty minutes, and in time the bill passed the Senate, with its five amendments. By the time it got to the floor of the house, however, Harris had changed his mind. He reneged on his promise, and when the bill finally passed, it lacked the amendment that the Thompson forces had hoped would protect the ballot from fraud. Dean showed us the signed memorandum. "I'm gonna hold on to this. It ought to come in handy some day."

Dean said that bribery is not as prevalent it's said to be and relatively unimportant as a factor in the course of legislation. He has been approached only once with a bribe. A young man from one of the small farm counties offered him one hundred dollars for his support of a local bill. Dean refused the offer, but he knows that "some of the boys" did not. He said that once a man takes money, he sacrifices all his influence, for thereafter his price is known to everybody.

Dean does not consider Ted Forbes, executive vice president of the Cotton Manufacturers Association, a lobbyist, apparently because Forbes doesn't go in for arm-twisting. He denied that Farm Bureau dues were ever paid by the National Association of Manufacturers. He said that he had paid dues for four of his tenants, but "only to meet my quota," and he did not bill these tenants for their dues. Dean, who is head of a Farm Bureau local in Rockdale County, said that the bureau's main purpose is to keep the best lobbyist in the country, Ed O'Neal, in Washington and in the employ of farmers.

Dean has absolutely no respect for Fred Hand, Speaker of the House. "Emotionally, he's a child." He knows that Hand has ambitions for the governorship but doubts that he could ever be elected.

Dean is hopeful that Herman's reputation as an alcoholic might catch up with him before the 1948 primary. He told us that Herman had taken the cure at White Cross in Atlanta and hinted that Thompson had photostats of the hospital

records. He also said that some of the old Talmadge leaders
are becoming disaffected. "Herman's making too many mistakes." Among them, he cited Herman's acceptance of an invitation to speak on the same platform with Gerald L. K.
Smith,[1] an invitation that Harris later rejected for him. He
said too that Herman practically had thrown recognition by
the National Democratic Party to Thompson by telling the
press, "I don't give a damn what Washington thinks, I'm
running the Democratic Party in Georgia."

Dean would like to think that someday we could have
clean elections. "That would be Utopia."

Lon Sullivan, director of the Georgia Citizens Council and former director of the Department of Public Safety, interviewed at lunch at the Piedmont Hotel in Atlanta, May 13

"Lord knows I've said the corporations run Georgia," said
Mr. Sullivan. "But to be more nearly accurate, *some* of the
corporations run Georgia." He paused. "No, to be accurate
you'd have to say that some individuals in some corporations run Georgia."

"Undoubtedly the most mysterious and most effective
corporation meddler is Fred Wilson of the Power Company.
You can't put your finger on him, but anybody who's had
anything to do with Georgia politics during the last ten
years will tell you it's true. The other Big Boys are Sam Hew-
lett of Atlanta, Fred Scott of Thomasville, W. S. Mann of
McRae, John Whitley of LaGrange, and Bull Blalock of Atlanta. Whitley and Scott are road contractors, you know, and
Blalock deals in road machinery. Dick Arrington, president
of Greyhound, used to be active in state politics. He may not
be so active now. Oh yes, one other man is Buck Murphy,
lawyer for the C&S Bank.

"Ed Rivers is essentially an honest man. His main fault is
that he can't say no to his friends. I don't believe Rivers was
at all corrupt during his first administration. Actually he
was something of an idealist. I do think, though, that Ed allowed himself—knowingly—to be used by the Power Company last summer to draw votes from Carmichael.[2] I'm disappointed in Ed, of course, but I can't help remembering
how fair and decent he was with me when I started up the
state patrol. He told me that the only way the patrol could
function was for it to enforce the law indiscriminately. And
he let me run it that way. We arrested plenty of important
people, including Ed's own son, and Ed protected us every
time. He'd get these threatening calls—from some local big
shot, say—telling him that if he didn't get the patrol to re-
lease this friend, he'd see to it that Rivers lost his county next
time. Ed would talk to him a while, explain to him how necessary it was that the patrol treat everybody alike, and somehow manage to pacify him. Of course, the guy would be unhappy for a while, but then Ed would come along and do
him some favor and everything would be rosy again.

"I'm afraid at the moment Arnall is out of the Georgia
picture. He just didn't play ball with the corporations. I
remember Ellis told me once, 'The difference between me
and Rivers is that I know how to dance around these
boys'—meaning the corporation agents. I don't think we
can read Arnall off, though. He stands a good chance for a
comeback in 1950. It's absurd to count out any politician in
Georgia. Four years ago I'd have said Gene Talmadge was
through.

"I think Walter Harrison may be the only man in the
General Assembly who can be considered a possible candidate for governor. Walter's got a lot of integrity. Only thing
wrong with him is his impulsiveness. You just can't put
reins on him, and he's likely to go off half-cocked. I've been
told that Bob Elliott plans to run. The Lord forbid."

Eugene Cook, attorney general, former
commissioner of revenue, interviewed in his
office in the state capitol, May 14

Mr. Cook is of the opinion that lobbying is a matter for the
legislature. "The laws are on the books. It's up to the legislature to enforce them." He is not too hopeful that anything
might be done to require lobbyists to declare themselves or
to reduce their influence. "You might reduce the registration
fee. It's much too high, $250. But I don't think more than one-
tenth of 1 percent of the lobbyists were ever registered, even
when the fee was practically nothing."

Mr. Cook does not quite refute the popular idea that the
Power Company has a commanding voice in the decisions
of state government, but he does minimize the company's
efforts to control its property evaluation. "Twice while I
was revenue commissioner I raised the evaluation on the
company's property. The company accepted both increases
without any protest at all." During his two years as commissioner, he did not find any evidence that the company was
declaring nontaxable certain property from which it derived
a profit. The Yawn bill, which would have required the company to declare the same property value for rate making as
it did for tax purposes, is a pure shakedown bill, Cook said.
Although the discrepancy in evaluation does exist, it exists
for a sound reason. "A lot of property used every day by the
public—viaducts, bridges, roads—was built by the Power
Company at its own expense, without any government sub-
sidy at all. It has every right not to declare it for taxation."

The commissioner of revenue is doing a superb job collecting income taxes, according to Cook. "It's not very likely
that many people get away with anything. Some people
think it's funny they don't read any reports that the state is
suing people for nonpayment when they read often that the
federal government is suing them. Well, that's just because
it's not necessary for us to sue them too. After the IRS has

collected, we're right behind them." Similarly, the state revenue department sees to it that the income figures filed with
the state coincide with those filed with the federal government. "One of the first things I did as revenue commissioner
was to arrange for photostatic copies of federal income tax
returns to be made available to our state collectors. We recovered something in the neighborhood of three million dollars during the first year we started that policy. Photostatic
copies have been available to the state ever since. Most of
the cases are settled out of court with a penalty of 25 to 50
percent over the amount originally due."

Although he spoke proudly of his term as commissioner,
Mr. Cook intimated that irregularities under his predecessors, and perhaps subsequent ones, have been fairly common. He told us this story: in 1942 a Savannah corporation
was discovered to be $125,000 in default on corporation
taxes. In the midst of the Arnall-Talmadge campaign that
summer, Cook found in the desk of one of his department
heads a memorandum addressed to the corporation offering
to settle the state's claim for $25,000. Cook implied that this
memorandum had been prepared at the direction of Eugene Talmadge, then governor. As soon as he discovered it,
Cook sent one of his agents to Savannah. Within twenty-
four hours the agent was back with a check for $125,000.

The most immediate reforms needed are administrative,
according to Cook. He says that the very awkwardness of
routine in the department costs the state untold revenue
each year. Records are apparently poorly kept. "It's not unusual to find critical records destroyed just before a new administration takes over."

During his term as commissioner he submitted forty-
three different proposals for reforming the tax structure.
The assembly adopted only one: a provision for an additional exemption. "You're smack up against ignorance when
you recommend any changes in taxation practices. The
assembly—and probably the people generally—automati-

cally fear and oppose any suggestion of new taxation. They think *any* change is going to raise taxes. They're just against change, no matter what. Before we can do anything we've got to educate our legislators."

At this moment Cook is leading the state's fight against twenty-nine railroads—twenty-two through the federal suit to end discrimination in freight rates and seven in Georgia on charges of violations of tax laws. He quoted Ellis Arnall as saying that the national railroad lobby, the American Association of Railroads, is now in a position to have Congress pass the Reed bill. "We're up against the strongest lobby in the country."

Ralph McGill, editor, *Atlanta Constitution*, interviewed in his office, May 20

We had tried to arrange to see Mr. McGill in the evening at his home, where we could talk with him without being interrupted every few minutes by the telephone. He had first agreed, but when we called to check with him this morning, he said he wasn't "sure about tonight," would we come instead to his office this afternoon. Mr. McGill's private life has been fodder for gossip in Atlanta for some time (his wife is rumored to have a drinking problem), and it occurred to us that he may have been moved to change his mind for fear of some domestic unpleasantness. Our presumption may have been right; during one of the several interruptions this afternoon he accepted an invitation from Hamilton Douglas to attend a graduation ceremony tonight.

As it turned out, the interview was the most unsatisfactory we've had with anybody to date. Mr. McGill was nervous and distraught. He kept taking off his glasses and putting them on again, rocking in his swivel chair, sighing heavily, and running his fingers through his hair. He looked terribly tired. It would be only a slight exaggeration to say that he seemed on the verge of tears. We were embarrassed to see him like this. For many years he had been somebody special to both of us, and to see him as he was this afternoon was like watching the face of a champion who'd taken one too many punches. We left feeling more than a little sorry that we'd come.

We asked him how extensive he thought corruption was in Georgia politics. He replied with a loud sigh, which we took to be in both sorrow and disgust. He went on to say some things, perhaps out of frustration, that he couldn't have meant, beginning with a line we remembered from one of his columns: "It's all right to steal an election if you steal it for the right man." He then went on to tell us something of what he'd seen and heard during the Ellis Arnall campaign of 1942. "I used to watch Roy Harris get on the phone and call a dozen men in a dozen undecided counties. When the returns came in, those counties went for Arnall." He said as a statement of fact that there were forty counties in Georgia, all of them two-unit counties, each controlled by a courthouse ring, that could be bought up until the day of election. Moreover, he said, there were forty more that could be described as "venal"—counties that couldn't be bought for cash but could be had by a crafty bargaining agent like Harris who knew with whom to bargain. It was difficult for us to understand exactly what he meant by a "venal" county. "I don't think Chatham was a venal county," he said, as if in explanation. "It gave the people good government."

McGill is already convinced that Herman will carry the 1948 primary. "He's stronger right now than his father was last summer. He's pulled in at least twenty-four more powerful men, some of those who were hard workers for Carmichael last year. That man Lokey in Thomson, for instance." He recognized the severity of Herman's alcoholism, however. "Herman got drunk within two hours after the court decision and stayed drunk for four days."

Nor does McGill think last year's victories in Augusta and

Savannah will last. "Johnny Bouhan will go back in Savannah and the Crackers in Augusta," he said decidedly.

Asked if he thought there was some sort of conspiracy at work to deny Georgia decent government, he shook his head. "What we've got is a conspiracy of mores. And that's the long battle we've got to fight. Look at what's happening in Greenville today. A lawyer gets up and says he's glad that Negro was lynched and then attacks the FBI for its Yankee interference. What can you do with a man like that? What can you do with a shoe salesman who'll get down on his knees to fit a pair of shoes on a Negro but will refuse to sit next to him on the street car? There's a conspiracy of mores working all over the South, and I don't think a damn thing can be done until we change those mores."

We asked Mr. McGill what he thought about a grand-scale mass education program for Georgia, one that would use pamphlets, the radio, public forums, slogans and songs, public service ads, and the like to help change those mores. "I don't know. Maybe if you could do pamphlets on Georgia like the CIO did on politics. Maybe *then* you could get to the people. And that's what we've got to do, get to the people."

We had been in his office for more than an hour. He had been distracted by telephone calls, messengers with galley proof, and at one point by the arrival of one of the *Constitution*'s star cartoonists, Milton Caniff, who kept him out of the office for about a half hour. Now the telephone rang again. "Okay," we heard McGill say. "He's going to sue?" He took off his glasses and put them on his desk, leaned back in his chair, and ran his fingers through his hair. "What can I do about it? . . . All right, Ray. All right." He started to hang up but pulled the mouthpiece back in time to say, "Thanks, Ray."

Mr. McGill then sat, looking beyond us at some horizon of his own. After a long while he brought us back in focus. "You boys come back again, will you?" He got up and rushed us to the door.

Note: Next morning we read that the Reverend Frank Norris had filed suit for libel against Ralph McGill and the *Atlanta Constitution*.

Malcolm Bryan, vice chairman of the board, Trust Company of Georgia, interviewed in his office, Atlanta, May 22

Until recently Mr. Bryan was a vice president of the Federal Reserve Bank of Georgia.[3] A professional economist and a onetime professor, he was apparently brought to the Trust Company not only for his knowledge but also for the prestige of his presence. Some of the banking reforms he has recommended have been resisted by the older, more "practical" heads on the board, and we have been told that his position is insecure. We've also been told that he has been distressed to learn that the vice chairman doesn't have as much authority as he had been led to believe. This distress may be the reason for the caution and the hesitancy he showed before us this morning. But perhaps it's just his nature to appear resigned and philosophical. His friends, who recall the circumstances of his conversion to Catholicism, call him "a merchant of despair."

"I don't deny that there has been some sort of coalition between corporation officials and politicians," he said. "But I don't think there's been any closely knit, bargaining relationship. I don't think corporation officials always act politically for their corporations. Bob Strickland and T. K. Glenn [former chairman of the Trust Company] both were for Gene Talmadge, and the Trust Company was often called a Talmadge bank. But as far as I know they were for Gene Talmadge purely because they were personally devoted to the man. In the six months I've been here I've seen no evidence at all of Trust Company interference in politics or government. As a matter of fact, through this recent business the

Trust Company not only didn't support Herman Talmadge but, by neglecting to cooperate with him, caused him a lot of embarrassment."

Mr. Bryan was one of the leaders in the Weltner Movement in 1936 that sought to elect Judge Blanton Fortson as a "people's governor." That movement failed, he said, because of the ineptness of the well-intentioned men who directed it. "We didn't get started soon enough, and we were politically naive. Why, Judge Fortson wouldn't even accept a lot of campaign contributions" for fear that the contributors might be trying to compromise him. The Fortson campaign was run for fifteen thousand dollars, which was about a hundred thousand less than either of the other two candidates spent. "And yet, it was amazing how much we got done with only fifteen thousand." Mr. Bryan is dubious that any similar movement could ever win in Georgia, political conditions being what they are. "The problem is how to defeat the machine politicians without stooping to machine tactics. I don't know if it's possible." He seemed to say that he and his generation had tried to do their bit for good government and that it would be up to our generation to try again—an attitude that Mr. Weltner had also expressed when we interviewed him last week.

"It's not too hard to list the things wrong in Georgia," he said. "The hard thing is to decide where and when and how you should start to right them. Some people have a mechanical gadget, like the county unit system. They say get rid of the county unit system and all our problems will disappear. Well, I don't think there is a single remedy, and I'm afraid I'm one of those people who doesn't know what the remedies are. I don't think we're ever going to get decent government as long as we cling to a one-party system. I further think that any new movement has got to start at the grass roots. But don't ask me what direction that movement should take."

We told Mr. Bryan of our conversation with Mr. McGill and of McGill's comment on the venality of Georgia counties. "If Ralph says that, I guess it's true, although it doesn't sound quite right to me that as many as forty counties can be bought. I don't think it's a matter of buying counties anyway. Take Pickens County, for instance. I know from personal experience that six men control that county. But they don't do it for personal profit. They do it to satisfy their vanity. It's a thing of pride with them. They just like to be in a position where people will ask them how to vote, where politicians will seek them out, and where they can have the privilege of calling on the governor and being assured of an audience."

He then talked for some time about Mr. McGill. "I'm afraid Ralph may be heading for a crack-up," he said with genuine sadness. "I think he needs to get away from politics for a while. What he needs is to go to the beach and lie in the sun for six months and think of nothing more important than what he's going to have for his next meal."

"What do you think is wrong with Mr. McGill?" I asked him.

"Ralph's worked himself into a box," he answered. "Lots of people think Ralph's being told what to write and that he's rebelling. That's not true. Nobody, not even Clark Howell, is putting any pressure on McGill. He's the victim of his own mistakes and of his own emotional makeup. Ralph put his heart in the campaign last summer, and it almost killed him when Gene won. But Ralph hates to be on the losing team. He hates it so much that on the night of July 17 he was about two hours premature congratulating Talmadge. You remember that, don't you? He went on the radio with Talmadge several hours before the returns were all in and praised him for being such a good fighter and said he hoped he'd have a good term in office. Well, that was his first mistake, and Ralph knew it. After that, he proceeded to make another. He kept writing those front-page pieces, under his own name, saying flatly that Gene Talmadge was in the best health he'd been in years. Everybody around Gene knew he was dying, and everybody kept telling Ralph that. All the same, Ralph kept writing about how Gene was just suffering from something he ate. Well, when Gene died, Ralph realized he'd made his second mistake.

"You can't correct a mistake. If you try, you only make another. You have to forget about it and start all over again. And what Ralph should have done was to sit down with himself and examine where he'd been wrong and start writing and acting as if he'd never made the first mistake. But no, he went right along and made a third. After Gene's death he spent a whole week and Lord knows how many columns eulogizing the man. It went even beyond the point of showing honor to a great man—assuming that Talmadge was a great man. It got downright sickening and more than a little embarrassing. Well, all Ralph's friends chided him about that, and Ralph's not one to be chided. It became a personal thing with him then, and the only thing he knew was to defend himself. Then, after Herman had forced himself into office, McGill made still another mistake. He got hold of some quack lawyer who told him Herman's position was sound, and Ralph sat down and wrote a column about it. Now he's writing in such a way as to give not only comfort but some degree of honor to Herman. All of his friends are concerned about him. The *Constitution* staff is worried. All during the squabble between the two governors, his friends would get calls from one of the people at the *Constitution*, asking them to see Ralph and please speak to him about what he was doing. About once a week I'd get a call from Jack Tarver. It'd usually come right after Ralph had done an editorial or a column for the next day's paper. 'For goodness' sake,' Tarver would say, 'have lunch with Ralph today and give him hell. I've just read his tomorrow's piece.' So I'd have lunch with him, I guess about once a week, but he wouldn't listen. Whatever I said made him all the more nervous and all the more defensive. What Ralph needs is a good long rest."

Roy Emmet, editor, *Cedartown Standard*; member, State Board of Regents, interviewed in his office in Cedartown, May 28

Polk County shows great interest in the election of representatives to the General Assembly, but elections are always decided on personalities, never on issues. Mr. Emmet is pleased with this year's delegation but says one member of a former delegation was a chiropractor, a near illiterate, whose only interest was in getting through a bill recognizing chiropractics as a legitimate form of medicine.

To his knowledge there has been no outside interference in recent elections. Many years ago, though, the Georgia Power Company tried to elect a man to the city council. Emmet says he sees no harm in outside interference; "it's all in the game of politics."

The League of Women Voters has been organized only during the last six weeks, he said. It now has a membership of about two hundred. It was organized largely through the efforts of Mrs. Emmet. The Farm Bureau is inactive in the district; likewise the Cotton Manufacturers Association.

Although Senator W. D. Trippe had been defeated once before because he favors a sales tax, during this past legislative session popular sentiment was for it. Emmet attributes this change in public attitude largely to his own editorials in the *Standard*. He's long advocated a sales tax, believing that the "tax burden should be shared." People in the Cedartown mill community, he said, get five-room homes for as little as twenty-four dollars a month, water and lights either free or for a ridiculously low rate, and police and fire protection free, and yet they contribute nothing to the cost of running the city or county. These people, whom he calls decent, God-fearing Anglo-Saxon Americans not long off the farm, show no interest at all in civic improvement, and he believes that the only way to get them to pay their share is through a sales tax.

The county showed hardly any interest at all in the white primary bill; that was "just another fight in Atlanta." In his opinion the county unit system is undemocratic and a disgrace, but he doesn't believe we can do away with it. He favors readjustment of the vote, however, so that the larger counties may have a more nearly equitable influence in the running of the state.

Dick Duke and a man named DeVitt are the two Talmadge leaders in the area. Duke was a longtime partisan of Governor Eugene Talmadge. He runs a chain of service stations throughout north Georgia and Tennessee. Emmet believes that Duke's only interest in Talmadge is the prestige that he gets by supporting him. To Emmet's knowledge Duke has never benefited financially by working for Talmadge, but he has always enjoyed Talmadge's favor and likes to be regarded in the community as the man who can "fix it" with Gene whenever a local boy gets in trouble with the law. Emmet himself is considered the leader of the anti-Talmadge forces. No one man, no few men, in the county can decide an election, but Emmet thinks he may be the most influential.

The county Democratic committee, of which Emmet is chairman, is elected by popular ballot. Candidates are nominated by the committee and are offered on the ballot without opposition. To replace three members who died last year, Emmet simply asked around the community, found three respected residents who agreed to serve, and put them on the ticket. In the last election Emmet himself supervised the polls and is sure there were no irregularities. (He believes that in most other counties the committees could stand to be investigated.)

In Cedartown about 276 Negroes voted at a segregated

poll handled by a strong but principled Talmadge man appointed by Emmet. In each of the other precincts, where polls were not segregated, no more than 3 or 4 Negroes voted.

Emmet says emphatically that there are no men in Polk County who depend on state business for a living. Somewhat significantly, all the major roads were improved and paved during Talmadge administrations that the majority of the county's voters had opposed, thanks entirely to pressure on the highway department by a very "clean" and competent county commission. Until 1930 there was only one paved road in the county; "today you have to go out of your way to find one that isn't."

Sentiment in the county is swinging against the CIO, which Emmet fears for its "mob rule" and irresponsible leadership. The textile people lost their chance two years ago to lick the CIO, he said. At the time, he tried unsuccessfully to convince management to go after the CIO with an "information campaign" and explain to workers what unionization would cost them. "The CIO wouldn't have had a chance." He said if necessary he would have condoned calling the CIO organizers "communists and nigger lovers. Mind you, though, I believe in organized labor."

Emmet doesn't believe farmers are concerned with issues at all. "They're interested in politics only because it offers them a good show." He believes that most farmers want good schools and that they'd feel very bitter if any governor tried to cut down on the seven-month school term or tried to reduce teachers' salaries.

The county has seen no recent Klan activity. Emmet told us he'd cleaned out the loft in his newspaper plant several weeks ago and come across a cabinet and a chest full of old Klan regalia and records, including minutes. The cabinet and chest disappeared, however, before he had a chance to study the records, which he believes were of a Klavern active from about 1914 through the mid-twenties. He saw a lot of "interesting names" on the rolls during the few minutes he had the opportunity to scan them. He believes that a carpenter who was doing repairs in the loft secretly removed the stuff.

Mr. Emmet was generous with his opinions, and our interview often drifted into interesting tributaries. He volunteered that one constructive move might be to organize a very quiet, statewide political action committee. "The committee should be nameless, members should represent only themselves, and its purpose would be to coordinate the efforts of progressive-minded people in every county." He considers Ed Rivers a damaging influence on M. E. Thompson. He felt the *Atlanta Journal* injured its reputation by its "vindictive" reporting of the Talmadge campaign but thinks the Telfair exposures "great journalism." He said Ralph McGill "sold out" after July 17; "he was exposed to too many facts to justify his wrong-headed stories on Gene Talmadge's health and political developments after his death." He expressed embarrassment over the *Journal's* picking up several of his byline stories and running them on its editorial page. "I write for a small-town newspaper, not the *Atlanta Journal*." He said he was working through the Board of Regents to improve the Agricultural Extension Service; he believes the job of commissioner of agriculture could be abolished and never be missed. He was one on a committee of three regents who investigated and recommended Raymond Paty for chancellor and considers him "a tremendous asset." He said he was unimpressed with the several visits Herman had paid him and doubts that Herman can command the loyalties Gene did.

Ben Cooper, editor, *Rome News Tribune*, interviewed in his office, May 28

"None of this year's delegation will be returned because of their stand against the white primary bill," according to Mr. Cooper. "People here want a white primary bill and expect to get one after the next election." A lot of "respectable" citizens were members of the old Ku Klux Klan and "won't stand for Negroes voting."

The county Democratic committee is self-perpetuating, and, as in Polk County, nominees go on the ballot without opposition. Nevertheless, Cooper says he's going to see to it personally that at the next election Grover Byars, the committee's chairman and an ardent Rivers man, is opposed.

Opposition is growing against Henderson Lanham, whom Cooper regards as "definitely pro-labor," but the dissatisfaction may not be enough to turn him out. Any congressman is in a tough spot, he says. "People expect him to stick on the job in Washington and at the same time keep up his contacts and patronage at home." Lanham does a weekly column from Washington and has a regular transcribed radio show. "I admit, he's doing a pretty good job keeping in touch."

Cooper thinks there are "plenty of people in this state capable of being governor, some of them right here in Floyd County." He went on to suggest Barry Wright, a corporation lawyer. "It's about time we had a governor. Haven't had one since Joe Brown."

Cooper impressed us as shifty, opinionated, not wholly reliable, something of a wishful thinker, very much an opportunist. He resents the Atlanta newspapers. "If you believed what they wrote about Herman, you'd have thought we were having an invasion." He says Thompson had no business calling a "rump convention." To his mind, Thompson and Rivers are "the real bolters," implying that, just because Herman, Roy Harris, and Jim Peters "did something he didn't like," Thompson had no right to go against the "legal" acts of the Democratic Party convention. He sees no danger in repealing primary laws. "We had better and cleaner primaries before the Neill Primary Act." Harry Wingate, he insists, wouldn't have a prayer being elected governor because "his only interest is the farmer." Wingate is going to "wear himself out, just like Ellis Arnall." As for Arnall, Cooper says he will never be elected to office again in Georgia. "He's made himself a national figure, and in order to be a national figure a man has to sell out the South."

J. Roy McGinty, editor, *Calhoun Times*; former state senator, interviewed in his home in Calhoun, May 30

Local interest in the 1946 legislative race was higher than usual, McGinty says, because he had campaigned editorially against reelection of the incumbent representative. It seems that during the special session Roy Harris, taking the floor to argue against the constitutional amendment that would have permitted Ellis Arnall to succeed himself, quoted this representative as saying that Roy McGinty had threatened him with "political destruction" if he opposed the amendment. Accosted by McGinty, the legislator denied that he had told Harris such a thing and promised to repudiate Harris on the floor and then vote for the amendment. He failed to keep his promise. "He didn't repudiate Harris, and he voted against the amendment." Back home, McGinty exposed this representative through the *Times* and so thoroughly discredited him among the people of Gordon County that "the man couldn't be elected dogcatcher."

A man of conscience, Mr. McGinty is said to be largely responsible for the recent change in Gordon County's political mix. The county used to be about sixty-forty for Talmadge; now it is seventy-thirty anti-Talmadge. The county supports a pro-Talmadge weekly, the *Gordon County News*, but Mr. McGinty's *Times* is the more respected and more influential.

Mr. McGinty said he knew of no recent intrusions by outside economic interests in local elections. But he does recall a city election some years back when the Georgia Power

Company played a curious role in the reelection of a mayor. "This mayor, a renegade doctor, favored selling our municipal power plant to the Power Company. He was defeated and has since left the county for good."

Mr. McGinty has editorialized often against the idea of a sales tax and feels that most of his readers are similarly opposed. Told of Roy Emmet's attitude, Mr. McGinty looked pained. "It's absurd to say that tenants and non–property owners don't pay taxes. Everything we buy is loaded with taxes."

About the white primary: "People say they want a white primary, but not this one. Thompson says it too. It's ridiculous. Harris offered the only kind of white primary possible. Although most of the people around here probably would prefer a white primary, they're not strongly anti-Negro, and I think they're too smart to be sucked in by the Talmadge line. As a matter of fact, I think our people probably will be even more opposed to Herman next year than they were to Gene last year."

His attitude toward the county unit system is that of most serious-minded small-town leaders. "The system could stand some adjusting," he said. "But I've never taken any public stand against the system because I think without it we might see the rise of big city machines that could dictate to every county in the state, and I'd hate that. The Supreme Court suit was valuable, though. They started people to thinking. At least more people know what the system is all about now." He doesn't think the system is the root evil in Georgia. "What we need—maybe the only thing we need—is an honest vote and an honest count. I think the most important objective in the state should be a mandatory secret ballot. You let the people vote as they want and guarantee an honest count of their votes, and you'll elect people who'll correct these injustices. After that business in Telfair in the general election, I'm convinced that Carmichael won the primary—yes, even under the county unit vote. It's significant that in the legislature the greatest opposition to election reforms always comes from the south Georgia delegations. Historically, our primaries have probably been subject to more abuses than our general elections."

Judge "Red" Townsend of Dade County is undoubtedly as shrewd a politician as there is in the district, Mr. McGinty said. He spoke grudgingly, admitting his dislike for Townsend and his methods. In Calhoun, the most influential politician is Otto Langford, former clerk of the superior court and now cashier of the local bank.

Gordon County uses the official secret ballot. Reflecting on his earlier comment, Mr. McGinty said he would like to see mandatory use of voting machines. "Maybe *that's* the only way we can guarantee honest elections."

To date, Gordon County has felt the impact of unionization only through the organization of one small chenille plant, where the CIO recently won a contract. Shortly thereafter mill owners called on McGinty and asked him to suppress news of the CIO victory. McGinty repeated with some pride what he told them. "I told them first that it was about time they faced up to the fact that the unions were coming and must be accepted. Then I gave them a little lecture on freedom of the press. I told 'em newspaper editors didn't like to be told what not to print and I'd appreciate it if they remembered that hereafter."

In Mr. McGinty's view the Klan is of no consequence in Gordon County. "I'm a Klansman myself. You know that? Back in 1917 or '18 a friend of mine was a Klan organizer. It was sort of fashionable to join the Klan back then. It was considered an honorable sort of social fraternity, a way to perpetuate the memory of the men who 'saved the South' or something."

He's reserving judgment on Henderson Lanham. "Last summer I was inclined to think that maybe Lanham was riding liberalism hard just for political expediency. But he's done a good job so far, and I don't see much opposition to him."

We told him that we'd heard many of his friends suggest that he run for governor against the Talmadge machine. He looked pleased but said nothing. Asked if he knew of any prospective candidates, he shook his head.

What do the people here want of state government? "Good roads, and I guess that's about all. We haven't played politics in this county, and we haven't put any organized pressure on the state. So—we've gotten hardly anything. This county probably is in worse need of paved roads than any county in the state."

Ralph McGill, he told us, has lost considerable stature all over the district. "I went to see an old sick farmer the other day. Hadn't seen him in nine, ten months. You know what the first thing he asked me? He rose up in bed on his elbow and asked, as I was coming into the room, even before he said hello, 'What the hell's come over Ralph McGill?'"

McGinty is unimpressed with Herman Talmadge. He doubts that he can hold his father's following "unless he can get the old gravy train running." He considers Roy Harris the most dangerous man in the state. "I don't think he'd sell out to just anybody, but he'll certainly listen to Georgia Power."

He hates factionalism, "of whatever stripe. I'd like to see a new political movement get started, but I don't want to have anything to do with the old crowd of practical politicians." Pointing out that some of the anti-Talmadge leaders are every bit as unscrupulous as the Talmadge leaders, he referred to Murray County. "My son, Roy Jr., is editor there. He's for Talmadge. That surprise you? Well, he is. The boss up there is corrupt, and Roy just won't have anything to do with him. And yet this boss is always the man the anti-Talmadge candidate deals through. Roy's a Talmadge man purely for reason of local politics. He figures he just cannot afford to endorse anything the boss does and still keep his integrity."

Note: Gordon County struck us as being one of the few counties in the state where the intelligence and wealth of the community are being mobilized behind a program of planned improvement. At the Rotary luncheon today, to which Mr. McGinty invited us, local people expressed genuine concern over the possibility that the federal government might drop its hot-lunch program. Not content to express mere concern, some in the audience offered to help continue the program at their own expense.

At the luncheon we listened to a presentation by schoolboys from Sonoraville, all members of the Future Farmers of America. From their report we gather that the work of the vocational teacher and the cooperation of the Calhoun townspeople had actually changed the landscape of their small community. New buildings had gone up and old ones had been renovated; eroded land had been converted to pasture; unprofitable food crops had given way to livestock and sheep farming. During the discussion period, the businessmen talked of the need for paved roads and for consolidating more rural schools. Answering one old-timer's complaint that people were too immoral, Jack Lance, the county school superintendent, said, "A man hasn't got much time for religion if he has to make a living in a gully," and was applauded.

W. A. Britton, state representative,
Whitfield County, interviewed in
his home in Dalton, May 30

A retired city policeman, Mr. Britton is in his sixties and has lived in Whitfield County all his life ("There's no better place in the world").

Interest is usually high here in local elections, although the races are rarely more than popularity contests. It may, however, be a bit different in 1948, when Mr. Britton expects the Talmadge people to draw factional lines in the election for state representative. He says they will be defeated, for the county is predominantly anti-Talmadge. Judge Stafford

Brooke, who served with Britton in the legislature, is leader of the Thompson forces. ("Thompson will make as good a governor as anybody, if we just back him up.") Gordon Kettles, Dalton's mayor, was campaign manager for Eugene Talmadge in 1946 and is now trying to build a following for Herman.

During the 1947 assembly Mr. Britton received about two hundred telegrams from merchants opposing the sales tax. He got messages from acquaintances in the labor unions asking him to speak up against the antilabor bills, as well as a few similar notes from nonunion members. Sometime before the session opened, he got a letter from the Christian Americans in Fort Worth enclosing copies of two bills that later proved almost identical with the antilabor bills that were passed, with a request that he introduce them in the House. He threw the letter away. H. L. Wingate was the most conspicuous lobbyist in the 1947 assembly. "He's a nuisance and a danger," Mr. Britton said. "It's people like Wingate who'll drive us to communism." He says he heard a lot of talk about bribery during the session and is fairly convinced that some of it went on. He himself was not approached.

The white primary will undoubtedly be an issue in 1948, "but it won't have much appeal around here. My people aren't interested. I think the nigger line is wearing thin, anyway. After all, colored people voted last summer, and nothing horrible happened. I think most people are going to realize it's just a scare."

Mr. Britton paused. His eyes signaled that he was about to confide something that he might later wish he hadn't. "I guess you know, I voted for the white primary bill. Last summer the Talmadge people came to me and said that if I didn't agree to support the bill, they'd put up a man against me. I told them that I would and ran without opposition, so when it came up in the House I had to keep my promise. It was a bad bill, though, and I'll never vote for it again."

About two hundred Negroes voted in segregated polls in the Dalton precinct in 1946. Mr. Britton said that they voted unanimously for Carmichael. "They wouldn't have, though, if race hadn't been made an issue." No Negroes voted in the rural precincts.

The Whitfield people are sold on labor, according to Mr. Britton. "The unions have done a lot for the county. The union people made a lot of money during the war, and they're beginning to send their children off to college. Some of 'em have already come back, too, as doctors and lawyers. We're mighty proud of them.

"I don't understand the Farm Bureau," he went on. "If Wingate gets his way and does manage to destroy the unions, the farmers will be eating only what they can grow. They'll have destroyed their biggest market. I don't understand why the people in south Georgia feel the way they do about labor, either. They've had no experience with unions, the way we have. I think it must be a conspiracy, with people like Wingate being paid to run around stirring up trouble against the unions. Seems to me the best thing could happen would be for unions to go in strong in south Georgia. Once the people saw what the unions were really like, maybe they'd realize that union people are just like everybody else."

Mr. Britton does not believe the Klan has any significant membership in the county. "When I was on the police force there were a couple of cross burnings, but I think they were done by pranksters, schoolboys maybe, playing Halloween."

Britton has a clear idea of what he'd like to see in Georgia. "I want better schools and after that better roads. Why, right here in Whitfield County there are some roads that are so bad in winter that RFD carriers and school buses can't get through. Then I'd like to see a real parks program. I think one of the most important things we've got to do is to get the people of north Georgia and the people of south Georgia to know one another better. Maybe if we get those coastal islands developed for the public, and if we made more parks around our mountains, then maybe the people in south Georgia would come up here more often, and we'd go down there more often. I also want to see something more of a health program. We ought to have a clinic in every county in the state—at least one clinic for every two counties."

Paul and Warren Akin, lawyers (father and son), Bartow County, interviewed in their law office in Cartersville, May 30

Voters in Bartow County are anything but passive. Although they rarely organize behind issues, more than five hundred people met in the courthouse to protest continuance of the General Assembly session while the Supreme Court was deliberating on the "who's governor?" issue. Interest is higher in local than in state elections, perhaps because voters don't expect very much from state government ("Roads first, schools second. That's about all. Negroes are happy about homestead exemptions.") The Akins personally oppose the sales tax but describe the general opinion as "indifferent." Majority opinion favors a white primary bill. Deploring it, Mr. Paul said, "You cannot oppose the law of progress and of God."

Paul Akin is one of three men who handle party affairs in the county, the others being Judge McIlreath and Bob Knight. The Democratic committee is elected by "street corner caucus" and write-in votes. The committee does not perpetuate itself. Bartow uses the official secret ballot, and to the Akins' knowledge there have been no irregularities. Carmichael carried the county in 1946 without the help of the four or so hundred Negroes who voted.

According to the Akins, Georgia Power runs the county. Its law representatives, Neill and Ault, are close to the city

manager and usually get anything out of municipal government the Power Company wants. Most recently, this has
meant the discontinuance of natural gas service. The Akins
call Fred Wilson a crook and cite the fact that he was indicted for bribery, though the indictment was nol-prossed.
"It's a shame and a disgrace for the Power Company to
have a man with his record as their public relations man,"
Paul said.

Paul Akin has been active in politics for half a century. "You can't get elected in Georgia without money," he
told us, "and you can't get money except from the wrong
people." He said that Herman Talmadge will be a threat as
long as he's alive. "If his alcoholism gets too bad, the crowd
that would benefit from his being governor will prop him
up and, if necessary, keep him under guard."

Dick Kenyon, state representative, Hall County, and Bill Gunter, his law partner, interviewed in their office in Gainesville, June 3

We ran through our usual questions. The answers can be
summarized like this:

Popular interest in local elections. Last summer five men ran
for the legislature, generating much interest. Votes were
cast mostly on the basis of personal following, although
Kenyon was identified as anti-Talmadge and Howard
Overby, though not clearly aligning himself, was suspected of being a Talmadge man. Kenyon led the ticket by
close to fifteen hundred votes. Although issues were not a
factor in 1946, Kenyon believes that issues will be decisive
in the next election, with Overby representing Talmadge.
Outside interference. None.
Civic or special-interest groups. No League of Women Voters. Farm Bureau growing. Cotton Manufacturers Asso-

ciation politically inactive. Public sentiment favored anti-labor bills and sales tax; pressure pro and con on white primary bill, but Kenyon feels that no place in Georgia were people more aroused over the challenge to "our form of government" by Herman's takeover. Mass meetings, informal gatherings, prayer meetings.

Pressures on legislature. Kenyon says strongest pressure came from schoolteachers favoring passage of sales tax. One teacher got Kenyon out of his sickbed (bad flu) to urge him to vote for it. When questioned, she admitted that she hadn't read the bill, that she was calling because the Georgia Education Association (GEA) had told her to; the sales tax, according to the GEA, was "the only means for getting enough revenue to pay schoolteachers."

Kenyon first favored the sales tax, thinking it the only revenue measure possible of passage. As the session wore on, however, he began to wonder if this was necessarily true; he became increasingly aware of the gross deficiencies and peculiar exemptions in the way the income tax was structured. He tried to get George Ramsey of Toccoa to introduce a bill to raise the income tax rate; had it passed, it would have almost doubled revenue to the state.

County unit system. Kenyon and Gunter both believe that the system is undemocratic, that some adjustment should be made.

Political leadership and election procedures. Talmadge leaders in the district are Ed Dunlap, chairman of the Jefferson Day Dinner, and a "boy" named Frank Stow, who was named chairman of the rump executive committee thrown together to support Herman. Kenyon is recognized as leader of the anti-Talmadge majority. The legitimate county Democratic executive committee is selected by popular vote. No slates presented, simply blank spaces on ballot for write-ins. During the last election the anti-Talmadge forces had stickers printed up with their choices for committee members and passed them out at the polls. Hall uses the official secret ballot. Both sides kept vigilance during the counting of ballots at the last primary; both satisfied of an honest count. About 770 Negroes voted, almost all of them in Gainesville proper. Ballot boxes were segregated. No incidents.

Labor bias. Public feeling ran against CIO's effort to organize Chicopee Mills. No unions in county now.

Klan resurgence. No signs.

Congressional race. Gunter says John Wood is losing support, could have been defeated last time if he had a strong opponent. Believes such an opponent will offer next campaign. Some talk that Phil Landrum, Thompson's executive secretary, may be the man. Both are sold on Landrum; "he's in politics out of a sincere desire to improve Georgia."

Potential gubernatorial candidates. Kenyon has growing faith in Thompson's integrity and independence but not in his judgment. Says that Thompson has made several serious errors, all contrary to advice from his closest associates. Admires Thompson for having vetoed the white primary bill despite advice from Rivers to sign it. He's sympathetic to Walter Harrison, thinks he could make a good governor.

Program for Georgia. Kenyon says "the people have gotten just about the kind of government they deserve." He says voters have no crystallized ideas about what they want and expect from government other than "roads, schools, and an honest administration."

Miscellaneous. Both Kenyon and Gunter say highway department must be removed from politics. They say people were generally satisfied with Ellis Arnall's kind of administration until Talmadge got them inflamed over the race question. They do not believe that any constructive, positive program can be offered in the next campaign to match the effectiveness of Talmadge's racism, because Talmadge will embrace all proposals for extended services made by his opposition. They believe Talmadge's opponent should say simply that the Negro is a citizen, has been declared so by the United States Supreme Court; that we must recognize him as a citizen and devote our energies toward making him a better citizen.

Gunter, formerly of Commerce (Jackson County), says he knows for a fact that the Farm Bureau uses the quota method (i.e., landlords pay dues for tenants). Both feel that Wingate is a threat. Kenyon was disturbed by the inconsistency between Wingate's argument against a closed shop for unions and his advocacy of an agriculture bill, which he himself had drafted, that in effect would have created a closed union of farmers by forcing them to contribute and participate in certain practices without their consent. Gunter feels that Wingate's record as a big-farm man would make him "awfully vulnerable on the stump."

Kenyon distrusts Bob Elliott, adding that some of the strongest Talmadge men also distrust him. He remembers what an old-timer told him on his first day in the assembly: "Bob Elliott always starts off in a blaze of glory, but by the end of the session he's got nobody listening to him."

Kenyon thinks there could be an effective working coalition among fifteen to twenty young men in the assembly, and he likes the idea of setting some long-range as well as short-range objectives.

He says as far as he can tell the Agricultural Extension Service has had little impact in the county, although he acknowledges that the county agent is a "superior" person who had done a great deal of good by encouraging diversified farming, primarily by promoting increases in livestock and poultry. He thinks maybe Tom Linder's job could be abolished without harm and admits that he frequently can't understand what Linder is trying to say in his *Market Bulletin*.[4]

Kenyon says he feels sure there was bribery in the legislature, but he can't prove it. Rhodes Jordan of Gwinett, he says, was clearly in fear after the Talmadge crowd had worked him over with offers of bribes. "Jordan voted against Herman in the face of threats of bodily harm." He also says that Roy Harris tried to buy Henry Eve by offering him a corporation account; he was to handle a ten-thousand-dollar collection, most of which he could expect to retain. To earn his fee would require only that he write one letter on his office stationery. Eve turned Harris down.

J. G. B. Logan, state senator from Banks County; hometown, Homer, interviewed in Cornelia, June 4

Senator Logan was chairman of the Senate Special Judiciary Committee. It was his adroit maneuvering that delayed passage of the white primary bill. He looks like a character out of Dickens: short and stout, white hair cropped close to his scalp, and pince-nez glasses. He must be easily sixty-five.

He had not meant to run last summer, he confided. But when Talmadge men put up a young veteran plugging for the white primary, he announced forthwith. The Talmadge candidate was financed by friends in the county and also by substantial contributions from the Talmadge headquarters in Atlanta. Logan believes that the only reason he is always reelected in his Talmadge-minded county is the personal respect that people in Banks have for him.

Except for what was obviously inspired by Herman's radio speeches, he felt no public pressure during this past session of the assembly and was free to vote pretty much as his conscience and intelligence led him. The Farm Bureau has a large and active membership in Banks, but, curiously, he heard very little from it during the session. He is personally and strongly opposed to the sales tax; he thinks it "ridiculous to take money from a poor man and then give it back to him through state welfare services." The home folks, however, don't seem to care one way or the other. He feels sure that the white primary bill will be an issue in the next campaign. He is nevertheless hopeful that the U.S. Supreme Court will rule on the South Carolina system (after which Roy Harris's bill was patterned) soon enough to change the nature of the debate. He is sure that the court will declare the South Carolina primary unconstitutional. He is "a mite" fearful how the Talmadge people will react.

Logan sees no candidates in the 1948 gubernatorial race other than Herman ("If not Herman, a Talmadge man equally bad") and Thompson. He doesn't know Wingate "well enough to judge him." He thinks there's a chance that Herman may not run, that older and cooler heads in the Talmadge faction—like Jim Peters and Charlie Redwine—won't let him.

Logan thinks the county unit system is undemocratic. He brands as "hogwash" the notion that without it city machines would control the state. No more than ten Negroes voted in the last election. The county adopted the secret ballot eighteen years before it became law.

He says the county has benefited very little from state services. It has only one paved road, a gift from Eugene Talmadge that the Talmadge people "have never let us forget."

George Ramsey, state representative from Stephens County, interviewed in his law office, Toccoa, June 4

Ramsey ran unopposed for the legislature. His election was assured because of the strength of his personal following and the influence of his senior law partner, Clyde McClure. He is on friendly terms with the Talmadge faction, who may or may not put up somebody against him should he run again. He's not sure that he will try again, since "I don't have a political practice. No domestic relations, no criminal practice, strictly corporation law."

Ramsey grew up in Atlanta and is a graduate of Atlanta's Boys High School. He defends the county unit system nevertheless. "The people here like it and want it."

Stephens County has been sharply divided in recent years, but the factional alignments do not necessarily correspond to the pro-Talmadge, anti-Talmadge factions of state politics. Stephens uses the secret ballot. About one hundred Negroes voted in the 1946 primary, almost all of them from Toccoa and all at one segregated poll at the courthouse. Ramsey said that from his office window on election day he could see ten-dollar bills being passed out to farmers and millhands. (He commented that he himself would rather risk defeat than buy votes.) Nobody pays much attention to the election of the county Democratic executive committee. Names are on the ballot, and people simply endorse them unless "they choose to write in somebody else." The committee is "pretty much self-perpetuating, and not even the chairman knows how many members there are. The party rule book has been lost for some time."

About the only thing the state has ever done for the county is to give us "Hollywood Drive," a handsome paved road built under one of the Talmadge administrations. It connects Toccoa with Hollywood, Georgia, and has "very little traffic."

During this past assembly session Ramsey says that the most pressure on him was for the antilabor bills. He knows that a lot of the telegrams were sent by mill owners in the names of their workers, but "that's all right." He speaks with approval and pride of the effectiveness of management's "public relations program, which has made popular sentiment strongly antilabor." The AFL and the CIO have both been unable to organize workers at LeTourneau and at the other factories in town, including a thread mill that's owned by J. P. Coats. "Unions have no place in Toccoa," he says.

"I can see some justification for a union at a place like Fulton Bag where people live in company-owned mill villages. But here workers own their own homes, they're well paid, they're an integral part of the community, and they already have everything a union could give them."

Ramsey opposed the white primary bill not on "religious, moral, or ethical grounds" but because it would hurt him personally. (How it would hurt him personally he didn't make clear.) He considered the bill dangerous and said as much in a speech to the local Kiwanis Club. He's proud that after his speech "a great many who'd favored the bill changed their minds."

Of the prospective candidates for governor, he thinks Charlie Gowen and Harry Wingate are perhaps the best qualified. He likes Gowen, though "he's cold, never warms up to you." Wingate, whom he calls "a thoroughly honest man," could be elected tomorrow, and "I'd be for him."

Ramsey is for a sales tax because "the people are only concerned about government when government affects them personally, and the best way to get 'em concerned is to tax 'em." He doesn't favor broadening the electorate. "I don't believe in Roosevelt's kind of democracy. I think we ought to go back to real democracy and let only freeholders vote."

Lillian Smith, author; Paula Snelling, teacher; and Frank Smith, Rabun County ordinary and Miss Lillian's brother, interviewed in the library at Miss Smith's camp for girls at Laurel Falls near Clayton, June 4

There is something about the people of Rabun County that must be understood before the political situation here makes sense. They are poor people and proud people, and they nurse an abiding grudge against the rich from Atlanta who have made private playgrounds of the Georgia Power lakes.

Sometimes their resentment manifests itself in aggressive exhibitionism. The tourists call them "hillbillies"; all right, by God, they'll show 'em just how much licker a hillbilly can drink, just how ignorantly a hillbilly can talk, and just how smart a hillbilly can be driving a bargain. Conditioned to live by the code of the clan, they take for a leader only a man who has identified himself as one of their kind. What the leader says, what he does, and what he says do are rarely questioned.

No wonder, then, that Rabun County has regularly gone for Talmadge. Ole Gene could act like a hillbilly, too. He would tell them that the city folks were scheming hypocrites, that it was only country folks like themselves who could be trusted to run the state of Georgia. They believed him, for it was what they wanted to believe and had been telling themselves, and they loved him for saying it where the city folks would hear it. Besides, one of their own leaders was an intimate friend of Ole Gene's. If Fred Derrick, a Rabun County boy with an education, wanted Ole Gene for governor, that was enough—they'd vote for Ole Gene.

The psychology of these people also explains why they elected an illiterate, Tom Mitchell, to represent them in the state Senate. "Atlanta thinks we're hillbillies," they seemed to say. "All right, let's send them a real hillbilly." It explains, too, why the county administration is one of the best and most efficient in Georgia. The county, you see, is run by one of their kind, too—Frank Smith, the ordinary, no less honored and respected than Fred Derrick. They trust Frank Smith; "he can run the county just about any way he wants to." What this means, of course, is that the people of Rabun have an exclusively provincial interest in politics and government. Their reliance on "Fred and Frank" has, in effect, been a forfeit of their right to self-government.

Miss Lillian described all this as a preface to her discussion of the 1946 legislative race. "What the people did here last summer was a slap in the face of democracy," she said. "The people have grown to think of the state assembly as a pork barrel. They don't think anybody goes to the legislature except for what he might get out of it for himself. For years we've sent the wealthiest and most respectable people in the county to Atlanta. As far as we can tell, they have done absolutely nothing for the county. Well, last spring a group of veterans decided that, in view of the selfish behavior of our previous representatives, this time we might as well elect Tom Mitchell. Old Tom has been running for something for the past twenty years, and they thought it was his turn now to be elected. They knew he couldn't read and he couldn't write, but they didn't believe he could possibly do any worse than the 'respectable' people we'd sent before. Most of the people in the county agreed with the veterans. They'd been betrayed too many times to think it made any difference who got elected. Maybe if there'd been a better man running against Old Tom, he would have been defeated. But as it was, Tom's only opponent was a rather unfortunate man named John Arondale. John's a fine person with fine instincts, but he's a schoolteacher and somehow manages to make everybody dislike him."

No outside interests interfered in the primary or, as far as the Smiths and Miss Snelling know, in any prior election. "The Power Company is pretty important in Rabun County," Frank Smith commented. "But its chief concern with government seems to be to keep its low property evaluation. Certainly it's never openly endorsed a candidate for local office. Mostly it depends on its Atlanta people to get what it wants. The Power Company owns thirty thousand acres in the county. It pays two-thirds of the county taxes. It ought to pay more, but then I've never been able to get a really accurate figure on the value of its property. That's handled by the state, you know, and the state assessors seem inclined to play ball with the company."

The county has no organizations for political action. Almost entirely through the efforts of Misses Smith and Snelling, a small group of church women got sufficiently aroused to go to Atlanta and testify against the white primary at the

Senate hearing. Miss Lillian thinks their action was supported by most of the people in Clayton, if not in the county,
despite a strong bias toward Herman Talmadge. "We have
only 106 Negroes in the county," she explained. "By and
large, I think people here have an amazing degree of tolerance for the Negro. That's why a man like Talmadge [she
was referring to Eugene] is so dangerous. He came up here
for a campaign talk and whipped up race feeling where it
had hardly existed before. I know, because my friends in the
Negro community—they live just down the hill here—told
me. Talmadge fired the imaginations of all our poor whites.
He told them about mixing the blood and how uppity the
black people were getting. That caused the poor whites to
search out the Negroes in hopes of some excitement. White
boys started sitting in the Negro balcony at the theater. They
would sit there and insult the Negro boys and girls, tease
them, do all manner of annoying things, hoping something
would happen. It got so bad that older Negroes ordered
their children not to go to movies until the primary was
over. They kept them home nights and told them that under
no circumstances were they to lose their tempers if a white
boy teased them. The Negroes behaved themselves beauti-
fully." The primary went off without incident. Only a few
Negroes voted. The first one did what Fred Derrick told him
to do and voted for Eugene Talmadge.

Derrick, a prosperous Ford dealer, heads the Talmadge
faction in Rabun. His brother Claude, who runs a service
station next to the Ford agency, is second in command and
handles the polls at election time. (Derrick is said to have
used his Ford distributorship to the splendid advantage of
Talmadge's state headquarters; he guaranteed delivery of
1946 Fords to influential leaders in other counties on the
condition that they support Talmadge.) The Talmadge machine has also relied on a family of bootleggers named
Ramey, who are close kin to Cecil Cannon, Fred Wilson's
partner in ownership of the Henry Grady Hotel. Frank
Smith is assumed to be leader of the poorly organized anti-

Talmadge faction, though he disclaims any strong participation in partisan politics. Interestingly, Fred and Claude
Derrick are his brothers-in-law.

The county Democratic executive committee is self-
perpetuating. For the last two years the committee has
nominated whomever it liked, placed the names on the ballot, and elected its members without opposition. Apparently
Rabun uses the official numbered ballot. Anyway, Miss
Smith knows it isn't secret. "Some years ago when Paula and
I wanted to protest against Roosevelt, we voted Socialist.
Two hours after the polls closed everybody in town knew
we had voted Socialist."

The county has no organized labor and has had no experience with union people. Yet the popular sentiment is
vigorously antilabor. "That's not so unusual," Frank Smith
commented. "I think you'll always find the strongest antilabor feeling in the nonindustrial areas. Farmers simply
can't pay sixty cents an hour for labor, and they see in the
organizing efforts of the unions serious competition for farm
labor."

Little of the antilabor sentiment has been cultivated by
the Farm Bureau, in Mr. Smith's opinion. The bureau is
only now beginning to organize in northeast Georgia. Frank
Smith has met Mr. Wingate and considers him a shrewd
man of great energy. "I don't like him," he said. "I don't
trust him."

None of the group could think of a potentially good candidate for governor. "I know a lot of men who would make
competent governors," Frank said. "But they'd never have a
prayer of getting elected. In fact, the ridiculously large number of counties makes it almost impossible for a competent
man to be a decent governor, anyway. The demands of 159
counties—meeting delegations from all these counties, day
after day—he doesn't have any time left to tend to the state's
business. He's kept too busy satisfying the county leaders
so he can count on their support when he comes up for reelection."

The Smiths were equally depressed about the prospect for selling a constructive program to the people. "You ask me what I expect of my state government," Miss Lillian said, "and I can tell you. But I'm afraid most of the people around here can't. They have gotten so little from their government, they have been so disillusioned with people in high places, that they no longer look to the state government for anything more than a bit of excitement. They want good roads and better schools, I suppose, but that's about the sum of it."

Miss Lillian then proceeded to enumerate the things she thought she had a right to expect from the state. "I'd put education at the top of the list. And by that I mean education without discrimination. Next I'd put adequate hospitals, and that includes adequate mental hospitals, maybe *especially* adequate mental hospitals. I expect honest and intelligent administration of tax money. I expect a humane penal system, one motivated by a policy of corrective justice. I think good roads are important, though I think maybe their importance has been overemphasized. I also want a good, efficient, incorruptible state highway patrol."

Frank Smith sighed. "Of course, the bedrock of all our problems is our people. It's a fact we have to accept, the government cannot be far ahead of the culture. What we really need is a revolution in our educational process. People must be brought to understand from the ground up what democracy and self-government require of the individual."

Fred Derrick, chairman, Rabun County Democratic Executive Committee, interviewed in Clayton, June 5

Derrick confirmed the Smiths' analysis of the negative character of public interest in the election of legislators. (Tom Mitchell is a good man; "horse sense but no education.") The only issues that Rabun voters seem to care about are the white primary and the sales tax. They're against the sales tax and for the white primary bill. "Eugene Talmadge would never have signed the sales tax bill," he said emphatically. "Gene told me that if the state ever came to seriously consider a sales tax, he'd favor a manufacturer's tax instead." As for the white primary bill, Derrick is all for it. "You can trust the party as much as you can trust the law." He said Gene wouldn't have pushed the Roy Harris kind of bill, but admitted he could think of no alternative. "You can't have any legal white primary unless you take all primary laws off the statute books." He paused and added, as if uncertain of its significance, that only six Negroes had voted in the 1946 primary. "The polls were nonsegregated."

He went on: "This nigger vote business has been pressed on us too fast. After all, the nigger's only 150 years out of the jungle." He paused again. "Niggers vote in a bloc, and that's bad. If you enforce your qualifications rule, you'll rule out a lot of white men, too. Can't do it without ruling out a lot of white men." Another long pause, then: "God made us white for a purpose and the nigger black for a purpose. I don't think He intended niggers to marry white folks. What we got to do for the nigger is educate him."

The county has got a couple of roads and the promise of one from the South Carolina line to Hiawassee as a result of good work on the part of his brother-in-law, ordinary Frank Smith. He said that he himself had got the county a couple of paved roads because of his friendship with Gene.

"Gene Talmadge never broke a promise to his friends. I took a lot of trips with him, including his last one by air, to Mexico. He looked in perfectly good health then. He had tremendous energy, drove himself right up to the last, killed himself campaigning. I was devoted to him."

Derrick recalled a banquet in Atlanta after the primary when M. E. Thompson "made an ass of himself" bragging about the number of counties he'd carried. He said Thompson told him he could have taken Rabun "if I'd wanted to."

Later with Gene in the hotel room, Derrick said, "Gene, I thought you were elected governor in that primary. But anybody who didn't know better would have thought M. E. was elected, way he was carrying on tonight." Gene said, "Oh, let the boy have a good time. I ain't worried."

Except for Herman, whom he thinks in some ways smarter than his father, Derrick sees no plausible candidate for governor. He says Herman's strength is growing, especially in south Georgia, where some counties report a 20 percent growth in Talmadge strength since the Supreme Court decision.

Derrick doesn't believe Roy Harris will be "in the picture much longer."

G. H. Moore, state representative from Lumpkin County, livestock dealer, real estate agent, interviewed in Dahlonega, June 5

Lumpkin is a Talmadge county, and Moore, a strong anti-Talmadge man, owes his election to his personal friends, many of whom he says are Talmadge partisans. He says he entered the race for the legislature "out of civic responsibility," knowing that if he didn't run, "there'd be one more man down there for Talmadge." He is a longtime supporter of Ed Rivers, whom he considers honest but too inclined to give in to his friends. "Every man has his price," he says, "and the pressure just got too much for Ed."

During this last assembly Moore "felt very little pressure" from people on anything. He heard very little from his constituents about the sales tax, although his niece told him, apparently judging from town gossip, that the county was split fifty-fifty on the issue. At Thompson's urging, he voted for it. He was opposed to the white primary bill and feels confident that he voted in accord with majority opinion in the county. Of the hundred-odd Negroes in the county, between thirty-five and forty voted in the 1946 primary.

Moore thinks the county unit system unfair. He would not, however, take a public stand against it unless there was an obvious move, as he thinks there was by the Talmadge forces this last time, to use it for personal political advantage. The system should be adjusted, he believes, possibly by rearranging proportionment in the lower house.

Moore's brother John is one of the three Lumpkin county commissioners and is generally understood to be anti-Talmadge. The former Talmadge leader, a man named Jones, has been succeeded by his son, a veteran who opposed Moore in the race for the legislature, and a filling station operator named Sheldon. Moore says the courthouse, including the sheriff, "is stacked with Talmadge men."

Lumpkin uses the numbered ballot. Moore says he knows of no errors in the counting of ballots, but there is often some "skulduggery" by poll managers who fill out ballots for illiterates. "The rule is that whenever a man can't fill out his own ballot, two men must watch the man who's making it out for him." He says the rule is rarely followed. The Democratic executive committee is selected by ballot, but nominees are always put up by the committee itself.

Lumpkin has benefited from state services "lots more than other counties." Rivers gave the county a lot of good roads, but so have other governors. He also credits Rivers with free schoolbooks, homestead exemptions, public buildings, and social security. "Our county gets back four dollars for every one we give the state treasury."

Typically, Lumpkin people are strongly antilabor, although there is no union activity in the county. Some of this attitude may be attributable to the Farm Bureau, which is well organized locally, but to Moore's knowledge Harry Wingate has never even visited here.

There's been no revival of the Klan in the county. Moore recalls that in the early twenties a Klavern was organized by

"a bunch of men who needed working over themselves."
The Klan made one visit to a Negro home and was met by a
Negro with a shotgun. Scared, the Klansmen fled and dis-
solved the Klavern.

Volunteering the common view but in a tone that suggested he wished otherwise, Moore said that "people want
roads and good schools, and very little else." He seems to
favor "broad planning" and speaks as if he sees planning as
an alternative to "petty politics," which he thinks ruinous.
Road letting, he believes, is the source of most graft; R. M.
Lyles, in Gainesville, "has grown rich by getting state road
contracts."

Moore doesn't know of any "potential governors," though
he thinks Walter Harrison "might be a good bet." He feels
optimistic about Thompson. "I think we've got the Talmadge people licked for good." The Aroused Citizens, he
believes, had a determining influence on the Supreme Court
decision against Herman and have shown convincingly that
"decent-minded Georgians won't tolerate any more Talmadgeism." In his opinion Eugene Talmadge never did anything progressive for the state. "He duped the people into
believing that he was serving the little man, when actually
he served the Big Boys." Talmadge's three-dollar tag and his
low ad valorem taxes "saved the little man pennies and the
big man thousands."

Henry Grady Vandivere, solicitor, Cherokee Circuit; hometown, Canton, interviewed in his office in the Cherokee County Courthouse, June 5

Politics in Cherokee County, according to Vandivere, is characterized mainly by blind loyalty to the Talmadges. The ordinary, sheriff, tax collector, and two of the three county
commissioners are all Talmadge stalwarts. The fact that the
county Democratic committee has an anti-Talmadge chair-

man is an aberration; "he wouldn't have been named chairman if the court hadn't made Thompson governor." Personalities, not issues, rule campaigns and elections here. Representative Manous is very popular, as is Dr. Grady Coker, whom Vandivere calls "an admired and respected surgeon." There has been little feeling about the white primary; it was enough that Talmadge wanted and promoted it. Nor has there been much talk about the prospect of a sales tax. Organized pressure groups are nonexistent. A family named Jones, which owns the two textile mills, has great influence, but how the Joneses are inclined politically Vandivere says he doesn't know. "Their main concern seems to be to keep the unions out."

Cherokee uses the numbered ballot. Although he knows ballots to have been doctored in prior elections, Vandivere says the 1946 primary was conspicuously clean. Of the 700 Negroes in the county, about 110 voted, all at the same segregated poll in the basement of the courthouse.

Personally, Vandivere thinks the county unit system needs adjusting and that proportionment in the lower house should be changed to allow for more representation for Fulton and other big counties. He doubts, though, that many people in rural Cherokee County would agree. "A progressive program for Georgia has got to start with the farmers," he says. He advocates abolishing the office of commissioner of agriculture and turning its functions over to the College of Agriculture administered by the Board of Regents. "That would take it out of politics." He says that no more than one out of eight of the inspectors in the Agriculture Department, all political appointees, are qualified and feels that juniors and seniors in a well-run college of agriculture would be more competent. Under his plan, competitive scholarships would be offered one girl and one boy in each county. The winners would go to college for twelve months during each of their first two years, but during their junior and senior years they would work six months and go to school six months. During the work periods of their senior college cur-riculum they would take over the jobs of county agents.

He thinks the departments of wildlife and game also could be done away with and possibly reconstituted under a single department of conservation. College students could serve as game wardens. He'd like to see punishment for game-law violations revised. "As it is, game wardens make criminals of first offenders, and the state collects only five dollars for each fine." It would be far better to warn the first offender and "tell him to get a license within five days at seven dollars, exactly double the current license fee. If he didn't comply, he should then be fined fifty dollars or more." Vandivere feels that his plan would triple present revenue from game violations and be better for the violator, who would not be stamped a criminal.

Vandivere is a great admirer of Ed Rivers, whom he thinks honest and capable but unable ever to be elected again. He thinks Herman "a brilliant boy" who might be a fairly good governor if he could get over some of his prejudices and stay out of bad company. "If Herman hadn't tried his coup last winter, nobody could beat him in 1948."

Ira Butt, editor, *North Georgia News*, interviewed in his newspaper office in Blairsville, June 7

Mr. Butt is a slight, wizened man who looks older than he probably is. He seems to have an amazing amount of vi-tality. He produces one of the few remaining hand-set week-lies in the state, piecing his paper together out of type from mixed fonts and printing it on an old-style flatbed press. He has a frank, salty tongue and an engagingly friendly man-ner. He probably is the nearest thing to a "wool-hat boy" we've talked with—earthy, almost pugnaciously proud of his county, and a defiant Talmadge apostle.

Legislative races in Union County are always pretty "hot," he told us, and yes, campaigns are always fought out on the basis of personalities. "It ain't likely that anybody against Talmadge could get elected."

The sales tax? Mr. Butt's "agin' it," and "so are all the other decent people in the county. It's a rich man's tax, and we ain't got many rich folk hereabouts."

The county unit system is the only protection Georgia farmers have against the cities, Mr. Butt believes. "'Course I know you boys come from a big county, and I can understand how you feel about it. All the same, if we didn't have the county unit system, the niggers in DeKalb and Fulton could outvote all the white people in north Georgia. That's the only way M. E. Thompson can beat Herman—with the nigger vote. I wouldn't be surprised if Thompson doesn't go into the general election, 'stead of running in the primary, just so he can count all his nigger friends."

Mr. Butt considers himself leader of the Talmadge forces. "Some dope fiend" named Wellborn heads up the anti-Talmadge crowd. "No one man can rule this county, but old Doc Wellborn would like to try." Butt seems to recall that the chairman of the county Democratic committee was elected last summer in a mass meeting, which if true would mean that Union County had violated party rules. Butt went on to say that Dr. Wellborn, who was named chairman, appointed all the committee members.

"What kind of ballot do you use here?" we asked him.

"The Australian ballot."

"The secret ballot?"

"Sure, the secret ballot."

"Is it numbered?"

"Yeah, it's numbered."

"The stub numbered too?"

"Sure, the stub's numbered."

Jamie smiled and shook his head. "That way, you can check on how a man has voted. Don't you think that's wrong? Don't you think it'd be better if you had a ballot that wouldn't permit you to find out how a man voted?"

Mr. Butt leaned over. He smiled broadly, and his eyes

brightened. "Why, hell no," he said, laughing. "I think you oughta know how some of these lyin' sons of bitches vote."

Mr. Butt laughed long and loud, and we had to wait for him to catch his breath. Finally, I asked him if there'd been any signs of irregularities in the primary last summer.

"No, don't think so," he said. "But that Carmichael crowd—they'd have pulled some fast ones if we'd let 'em. They tried to fix it so our watchers wouldn't be around when the votes were counted. Kept suggesting we go to supper. 'We ate early,' I told 'em. Had to watch 'em like a hawk."

No Negroes voted, Mr. Butt said. "Ain't got no niggers in Union County."

Asked what Union had gotten out of state government, Mr. Butt pondered for a long while. "Not much, I don't guess," he said. "Nothin' at all." He reflected for a moment, and then his eyes brightened again. "But you take this man Thompson. Here," and he thrust a copy of last week's *News* at us. "Read that."

We looked and read. Almost all the front page was taken up with a reproduction of the lead article in last week's *Statesman* about the number of pro-Thompson representatives Thompson had appointed to state jobs. A smaller article of Butt's own composition was an attack on Thompson for spending state money on electrically powered lawn mowers. The mowers were to be used at Vogel Park, "where there ain't enough grass to keep a lazy field hand busy more than an hour a week."

Mrs. Henry Nevins, secretary, state Senate, interviewed in her office in the Senate chambers, June 9

Mrs. Nevins's husband was secretary of the Senate until his death several years ago, but it was more than sympathy that elected her to take his place. A charming woman in her mid-

forties, she knows her job, likes it, and has the necessary political skills to keep it.

Mrs. Nevins does not believe bribery figured importantly
in the controversial session just past. "No more than three
or four senators at most sold out," she said. "I'm inclined to
believe that a great many more in the House did, though."

What makes a man vote for Talmadge? "Conviction, often as not," said Mrs. Nevins. "Take old man Darby. He's
a banker. An old southern gentleman—really. He doesn't
think Negroes should vote, and with him that's enough.
There are others, of course, who vote with Talmadge because they think they stand to get the most out of his administration, and there are others who vote out of a sense of
loyalty—they're beholden to the Talmadge crowd for past
favors. Leonard Wood, for instance. A couple of years ago
Wood passed a string of bad checks. Lindley Camp saved
him from the chain gang, so last session Wood voted the
way Camp told him."

Mrs. Nevins doesn't think senators vote a Big Business line
so much from Big Business pressure as from the fact that they
are Big Businessmen themselves. "You'd be surprised at the
number of wealthy men in the Senate. Darby owns three
banks, Tarbutton owns a railroad, Kiker has made millions
out of a sawmill, and Porter Carswell—he's Tarbutton's
brother-in-law—is tied into the Candlers. The Candlers, you
know—Asa, that is—always backed Talmadge."

The two most effective lobbyists in the state, Mrs. Nevins
thinks, are Tom Camp, former secretary to Congressman
Robert Ramspeck and now executive director of the Georgia
Association of Railroads, and Fred Wilson, assistant to the
president of the Georgia Power Company. It was Camp who
opposed Mrs. Nevins for Senate secretary. Some of her disaffection for the Talmadge group may be traced to the fact
that Camp was favored and pushed by Roy Harris, Jim Peters, and Herman himself. She also suspects that Fred Wilson was for Camp. "He certainly wasn't for me," she said.
"The thing is, Mr. Wilson works so quietly that you just

never know. It's always been said around the capitol that
Fred Wilson could name the clerk of the House and the secretary of the Senate, but I'm pretty sure he didn't name me."
H. L. Wingate is influential, she admitted, only because he
gets behind "sure things." He's "too clumsy" to be seriously
considered for governor.

Mrs. Nevins has little or no respect for Herman Talmadge
and repeated with obvious pleasure a rumor discrediting
him. On the night of Gene's death, she said—"or it may have
been the day after"—M. E. Thompson saw Herman and
asked him to support his claim to the governorship. Herman
agreed—"told M. E. he thought there was no doubt, the
man elected lieutenant governor should take over." During
the next day and night, however, Harris and Peters got to
Herman and gave him a going-over, "plying him with liquor. Then, when Herman was out cold, they announced to
the newspapers that Herman had decided to ask the legislature to elect him governor."

How did she feel about the white primary? "I'd rather see
Negroes vote than a lot of white people I know."

Tom Herndon, lawyer and former director, Carroll County Service Council, interviewed in Carrollton, June 11

"Talmadgeism" is now an issue in Carroll County, and
Herndon believes that this is the issue that will decide the
next election to the assembly. Representative Willis Smith is
now clearly identified as a Talmadge man, Herndon says,
and "he'll be forced to run as a Talmadge man next time."
By some mysterious means, Smith got Carroll County Negroes to vote for him in a bloc in 1946. "They're wise to him
now, as are lots of his white supporters, and he won't be
elected again." Furthermore, Smith defeated W. A. Alexander, a former legislator, by only fifty votes, largely owing to

the endorsement of an unscrupulous newspaper publisher named Tuttle who then owned the *Carroll County Times* and *Free Press*. (Herndon described Tuttle as a "floater" who came to Carrollton and created such a stink by his libelous reporting that the best people were happy to buy him out, at a profit to Tuttle of seventy-five hundred dollars.)

The Farm Bureau is active, but Herndon doesn't believe it took any prominent interest in the last legislative session. Perhaps on Wingate's cue, its members wrote letters urging passage of the antilabor bills, but he isn't sure. The president of the local Farm Bureau chapter is a man named Craven, a well-to-do farmer, now county ordinary and very active politically. Craven has a tie-in with the county agent, whom Herndon considers incompetent and who spends most of his time "buttering up the bank president and the county commissioners." He spends so little time on his job, Herndon says, that he now can afford to open up his own business, a small factory making infant wear.

Relatively few people in the county care about legislative issues. Merchants were against the sales tax, because "Carrollton is near the Alabama state line and merchants feel they might suffer a loss in Alabama trade." Most protests against the white primary bill, as against Herman, came from West Georgia College.

Herndon's father chairs the county Democratic committee, the members of which are elected by write-in votes, three members from each of the fifteen precincts. The county uses the numbered ballot with signed stubs, an anachronism that Herndon is campaigning to have replaced with a genuinely secret ballot. Blind people vote, and there's rarely any formal provision for filling out their ballots. "Sometimes committee members mark ballots for the blind, sometimes just anybody who happens to be around the poll. Fortunately, the strong personal rivalry among candidates is enough to guarantee an honest count." About two hundred Negroes voted last summer in the Carrollton precinct, at

segregated polls, "of course." There were no reported incidents of intimidation. Negroes voted only in Carrollton,
Villa Rica, and Bremen; none in rural precincts. "Some areas
in the county where anti-Negro feeling is the strongest have
no Negroes."

Carroll County benefited a great deal from the Rivers administration, some from the Arnall administration, none at
all from Talmadge administrations. Carroll County has always gone anti-Talmadge, the Carrollton precinct having
voted four to one against him every time he's run. The local
mill owners have always been anti-Talmadge ("They're just
not the Talmadge kind"). Herndon believes that over the
past ten years there's been a growing tolerance for union activity in the county, although the majority opinion is still
antilabor. The textile union is represented at the Mandeville Mills but not strongly enough to force a contract. "Most
mill workers are also farmers for at least three months out of
the year and have never identified with labor." Another factor, Herndon thinks, is that wages in the Carrollton mills are
higher; the minimum, for sweepers, is eighty cents an hour,
and the average is better than ninety cents. "Workers simply
don't feel the need of a union." Town sentiment there is
largely antilabor because of the resentment toward John L.
Lewis and because of NAM propaganda in the weekly
newspaper. Scripto came to Carrollton with the declared
purpose of escaping union "harassment" in Atlanta.

Herndon believes that Carroll County people have an
awareness of what government can do and a belief in progress largely because of the influence of West Georgia College
and of the Carroll County Service Council. People look to
the county for roads, rarely injecting the highway issue into
state campaigns. They expect the state to contribute to the
upkeep of the schools, and "they want everything Rivers
gave them." He commented that the Service Council has
encouraged crop diversification and that great strides have
been made in the dairy and poultry industries.

M. E. Groover, state representative, Troup County, interviewed in LaGrange at his funeral home, June 12

Interest in the election of state legislators is above average in this county. Usually as many as six men offer for the three positions. H. T. Caldwell, whom Groover considers "a splendid man," faced unexpected opposition from a veterans' group after the AP quoted him saying he felt veterans deserved no special privileges. Veterans didn't have enough time to campaign before the primary but managed to muster about two hundred write-in votes against him in the general election. They vow now they'll defeat him in 1948. The veterans are led by a young man named Robert Hammond, who operates a group of service stations in the county and makes his headquarters at the Woco-Pep station in La-Grange. Hammond was one of two veterans elected to the LaGrange city council.

Groover felt most pressure to support the antilabor bills, most of it from Callaway Mills executives. Public opinion is so strongly antilabor, he says, that if the CIO tried to organize the mills, the Callaways would simply close down. He heard very little one way or another about the sales tax bill, though he tends to believe that people recognize the need for additional revenue and would probably support a sales tax as the best possible source. He doesn't expect much to come of the newly appointed tax commission; he doesn't believe "a bunch of economizing experts of mediocre ability should be allowed to dictate tax policy." He is convinced that most people in the county are opposed to the white primary bill and maybe even more opposed to Herman Talmadge. "They resented Tom Morgan's vote for Herman on the last ballot, and they'll probably beat him if he runs again." Groover thinks Morgan is too ambitious (he tried too soon to be Speaker pro tem) and too much of "a bandwagon rider."

"The Callaways have right smart influence," Groover said. Although he's never known the Callaways to endorse a candidate publicly, he believes them to be sympathetic to the Talmadge crowd—"at least to Gene"—if only because in 1935 Gene sent the militia to LaGrange to settle a labor dispute. He's positive the Callaway family has never tried to tell their workers how to vote.

O. W. Coffee, editor, *Chattahoochee Valley Times* and *West Point News*, interviewed in his office at West Point, June 12

A Talmadge faithful, Mr. Coffee is disappointed that more public interest isn't shown in elections to the General Assembly. Nevertheless, Troup County is "pretty well pleased" with its delegation. "Tom Morgan is a good personal friend, but I don't go along with some of his politics."

The county has been spared contentious political action groups. The Farm Bureau is inactive, although H. L. Wingate has spoken here several times and has become a favorite among West Point businessmen. Coffee says that merchants were generally opposed to the sales tax bill, not so much because they feared the loss of Alabama trade, as they said, but because they considered the business of tax collecting a nuisance. He thinks maybe a sales tax is justified, but he would prefer a manufacturer's tax if one could be worked out and administered without an army of collectors and auditors. The people favor some form of white primary, he thinks, and were disappointed in Thompson's position. He believes the white primary will be the big issue in the next campaign and that Herman will win on the strength of it. As for the county unit system: "I know it's wrong, but since it favors me and my kind of people, I want to keep it."

The Callaways (Cason and Fuller) exert a very quiet but

strong political influence, Coffee told us. "They determine who's sheriff and who's chairman of the county commissioners." Farmers in the county are led by a West Point family named Zachry ("fifty thousand acres, many tenants, and a very profitable business in grain and farm implements"). "I can't think of anybody else in West Point much interested in farmers."

Troup uses the numbered ballot. Coffee thinks it may be a good thing for "leaders" to know how people vote, else they "couldn't keep track of how people are lining up." Exactly 103 Negroes voted in the West Point precinct. "I know." He says that 100 Negroes voted in a bloc for Carmichael at a segregated poll; 3 voted for Talmadge. Most of them, "90 percent," were women, and all of them were disciplined to vote for Carmichael—so much so "they didn't recognize any other name on the ballot. I'd ask a Negro who she was going to vote for. 'Carmichael,' she'd say. 'Who're you going to vote for for attorney general?' 'Carmichael.'" Negroes outnumber whites in West Point, he maintains, and "could actually control elections if they wanted to." Further, "as long as Negroes vote in a bloc throughout the state, they can control Georgia." He doesn't believe in letting Negroes vote and doesn't believe in enforcing an illiteracy rule, since that would rule out "too many fine white people."

Coffee seems to believe that the best editor is the editor who holds stubbornly to strong opinions. He thinks Wingate might be elected governor and would make a good one. He calls Ellis Arnall "a four-flusher." The court decision, he insists, made a martyr out of Herman, and popular reaction will be in his favor. "Georgia people will never submit to Negro voting."

As if suddenly moved to explain himself, he told us he'd been imbued as a child with the "leadership principle." His father had told him not to be too disturbed about the failure of democracy because "the leaders will always see that things are handled right." He worries, though, that nowadays "leadership doesn't seem to be any better than the people. Sometimes it seems to be worse."

Tom Morgan, state representative, Troup County, interviewed in his home in West Point, June 12

Tom Morgan has had it in the back of his head for fifteen years that someday he would be governor of Georgia. The idea first occurred to him at Emory University, where he majored in political science, and it kept recurring to him for ten years after his graduation. He was a professional executive for the Boy Scouts during most of the ten years, a job that demanded no little political acumen and one in which he did very well. Today, an elected representative to the state assembly, he has settled into a regimen that he calculates will qualify him for the governorship within the next ten years. He has an office in his home that is crammed with books, two file cabinets, and a typewriter. The books are almost exclusively political in theme, with a heavy emphasis on the history and structure of Georgia politics, and he studies them with admirable self-discipline. In one of the two cabinets he keeps an up-to-date file of press clippings, all on the general subject of Georgia and carefully indexed. The other one contains more press clippings, correspondence, and an abundance of typewritten notes, arranged alphabetically in folders bearing the names of prominent and not-so-prominent political personalities. "I figure that if I'm serious about a political career, I may as well be businesslike about it."

Morgan didn't decide definitely to enter politics until he returned to West Point in 1945 after a couple of years in the navy. When he did, he first thought he'd have a try at Congress, running against Tom Camp. His friends talked him out of that, arguing that the key people in the county were already committed to Camp. If he ran for a state office, though, he could have their support for the asking. Besides, they told him, Georgia needed smart young people like him at home, not in Washington. He thought about it a while and then made his choice. His books showed him that the best training ground for governor was the state assembly, so he figured the first step would be to get elected representative. He made a conscientious canvass of all the influential people in Troup County, including the Callaways, and after enlisting their support began actively campaigning. There were six men in the race. He led the ticket by a thousand votes.

Next, Morgan was advised to cultivate the acquaintance of political leaders in all the other counties. He thought the best way to do that would be to run for Speaker pro tem. Taking his cue from Ellis Arnall, who had done the same thing many years before, he took an extensive trip through Georgia, stopping off at every county seat and introducing himself to every representative as well as to the most important county officials. Although George Smith beat him for Speaker pro tem, Morgan feels that his objective was served. He met everybody of any political consequence in the state.

Morgan has much to say in defense of Ed Rivers, and one would gather that, for the moment, he is quite willing to be regarded as a Rivers satellite. In fact, he is indebted to Rivers for his job. He is district director for the Woodmen of the World, a fraternal insurance society, which seems to be an ideal springboard for ambitious young Georgia politicians, having launched not only Rivers himself but his onetime handyman, Roy Harris. Morgan travels eight counties for the Woodmen and says he hopes to earn enough money in the next several years to subsidize his political career for several years thereafter.

Morgan was not too happy about the turn of political events in 1947. In this first year of his career, he had hoped to avoid any definite alignments and somehow manage to build up friendships and support from all factions. When the legislature split over the Herman-Thompson issue, however, he had to declare himself, and he declared for Thompson. Once committed, he proved to be one of the hardest working of the Thompson followers, appearing to the gallery to have almost as much to do with Thompson floor strategy as Charlie Gowen or Adie Durden. His impression on other politicians, however, was not as favorable. For a first-termer, he seemed a mite too busy advancing himself.

In conversation this afternoon, Morgan spoke of the Talmadge faction as if it were guilty of nothing more than a breach of good manners. His restrained criticism, however, may be only evidence of his own good Boy Scout manners. In reality his attitude toward Talmadge may be much stronger. "It didn't seem right," he said, describing the political atmosphere at Gene Talmadge's funeral, which he attended with Ed Rivers. "Even while the casket was being lowered, Jim Peters and Charlie Redwine were sifting through the crowd, lining up representatives. Miss Mitt too. [Miss Mitt is Mrs. Eugene Talmadge.] She must have known what Jim Peters had in mind. If she didn't, she was certainly doing her unconscious best to establish Herman as the logical heir. All during the afternoon she kept saying over and over, 'Well, Herman can carry on. We've got Herman.'" Morgan spoke reservedly, too, of Herman's deceitfulness. "Several days after the burial, M. E. and Rivers had a conference with Herman and got his pledge to back M. E. for governor. The very next day, though, Herman announced his own candidacy."

Morgan was a classmate and a fraternity brother of Bob Elliott's at Emory, but today he has little use for him. "Bob's a has-been in Columbus," he said. "He ran third out of three

last summer, and he won't stand a chance next time. The
people are that sore with him for the way he sold out to Talmadge." Morgan recalled that, sometime before the assembly met, he had a discussion with Elliott in Columbus about
the pending white primary bill, to which Elliott expressed
his objection. "'Negroes are going to vote in Georgia,'"
Morgan says Elliott told him. "'Maybe not for a while yet,
but they're going to vote. All of them will be voting within
ten years, and there's nothing we can do to stop them. We
may as well face it and prepare for it. As for me, I'm for
letting them vote.'" Morgan says he got the surprise of
his life, on the first day of the session, when Elliott took the
floor to speak for Herman as the only man who could guarantee white supremacy in Georgia by keeping Negroes from
the polls.

"I should have known about Bob," Morgan said. "Back
during my senior year, when I was president of Lambda Chi
Alpha, we pledged a Cuban boy while Bob was off on one
of his debate trips. Golly, when Bob got back, he almost
broke up the chapter. 'You might as well have pledged a nigger,' he said. He made such a stink about it, he made me call
a special chapter meeting. But you know what? Nobody
showed up for the meeting outside of Bob and me. All the
other brothers stayed away. They said they liked Pedro, they
had pledged him and wanted to keep him, and they'd be
damned if they were going to attend a meeting and give Bob
Elliott a chance to talk them out of it. They were sort of
scared of Bob, I guess. Even then he could talk you into believing black was white. Well, anyway, after that Bob didn't
show up around the chapter house any more. We went
ahead and initiated Pedro and he turned out fine."

Commenting on the local attitude toward Negroes, Morgan seemed pleased. "Negroes make up about 47 percent of
the population, but we've got excellent schools—really jam-
up schools for both white and colored—and the result is a

pretty high degree of tolerance. I don't believe people in this county can ever be sold a white primary. Not Roy Harris's kind of primary, anyway." One out of every eight registered voters in Troup last summer was a Negro, but the policy of the election managers was not to segregate the counting of ballots, so nobody seems to know how many actually voted. Morgan, however, knows that he ran third in the Negro vote; he had a friend on the committee examine Negro ballots before they were consolidated. "I wasn't surprised," Morgan said. "Most of the Negroes voted in LaGrange, and naturally they knew Groover and Caldwell [the other two representatives] better than they knew me. I think I can get the Negro vote next time. Since July I've had a chance to prove myself the Negro's friend."

The Callaways don't run Troup, according to Morgan. They only have the most influence. Fuller Callaway is definitely a power, he says, and so is the president of the Callaway Mills, a man named Edge. "Any ambitious politician will cultivate the Callaways," he explains, "but it's foolish to think they can control an election. If the family could ever pull votes from its mill workers, it was before 1935. That was the year the Callaways got Gene Talmadge to use the state militia to break up a strike. Gene herded the workers into bullpens, and one of the troopers killed a pregnant woman. The workers have never really forgiven the Callaways, and naturally they're dead set against Talmadge, *any* Talmadge. It's largely because of what happened in 1935 that the county is now two to one anti-Talmadge."

The Troup County Democratic Executive Committee is selected by write-in votes, with nominees commonly proposed by poll watchers. In the LaGrange precinct, according to Morgan, the practice is for the committee to print and pass out at the polls stickers carrying the committee's choices. "People don't have to write in a lot of names that way," he said, perhaps facetiously. "It saves a lot of time."

The county uses the numbered ballot, but Morgan hopes to get the next grand jury to recommend adoption of a secret ballot.

J. B. Hardy, editor, *Thomaston Times*, interviewed in his office in Thomaston, June 13

Although there wasn't much interest last year in the election of representatives to the assembly, Hardy believes candidates will be clearly identified next time as Talmadge or anti-Talmadge and will attract more voter concern. He thinks people are tiring of the "nigger-nigger" cry and the white primary issue may be less important in the 1948 campaign. Upson has "quite a few Negroes," however, and nobody can predict what may happen if racial tension continues to be stretched.

People are probably divided on the sales tax, but Hardy has heard little about it one way or another. Upson has no organized political action groups "unless you count the Farm Bureau." He considers the county unit system undemocratic, but "people want it and would resist any attempt to do away with it."

Upson uses the numbered ballot. Hardy can remember the time when "machinations" were common at the polls, including the passing out of half dollars to illiterates. In recent years, however, he's seen no evidence of irregularities. In 1946 no more than a thousand Negroes voted in the Thomaston precinct and none at all in outlying precincts. The polls were segregated in Thomaston, the Negro poll being located in the county jail.

Hardy says Upson people have no clear idea of what to expect from government, though they're all sold on the need for all-weather roads and good schools. Highway 36 from

Woodland is next on the list to be paved, and he hopes the county can get it from the Thompson administration.

A self-defined optimist, Hardy believes there's been considerable progress in the last six or so years and regrets that Ellis Arnall couldn't have succeeded himself so that people could get used to dignified, good government. He says race relations have noticeably improved in Upson; we have nothing to fear from the Negro "who knows his place."

John J. Flynt, state representative, Spalding County, interviewed in his law office in Griffin, June 13

Flynt says that he felt the most pressure from his constituents for passage of the antilabor bills, somewhat less for the sales tax and white primary bills, about both of which opinion in the county seemed to be mixed. Merchants in Griffin opposed the sales tax, so Flynt voted against it. He was in "so much hot water" for having voted for Herman and the white primary that he figured he "better do *something* to please the home folks."

Spalding County is about fifty-fifty on the white primary issue, according to Flynt. He hesitates to predict how the county will vote when it comes up again in the next campaign, as he's sure it will. He himself favors letting the Negro vote but seems to deplore the fact that the Negro's right to vote in primaries has become a matter of public controversy. "Ellis Arnall forced the issue by sponsoring the Primus King case, and all Talmadge did was to exploit the people's resentment."

Flynt then went off on a track that he'd obviously been down before. "I don't feel like worrying about these things because in no time at all we're going to be involved in the damndest ideological warfare you ever saw, maybe war itself. The niggers are going to be a factor in that ideological war. They'll support the communists, just as every downtrodden race has always supported the communists. The niggers voted in a bloc for a very simple reason. If a candidate went on the stump and said, 'All people named Clawhammer won't be allowed to vote if I'm elected,' all people named Clawhammer would be damned sure to vote against him. That's what Talmadge did to the niggers, and that's why they voted in a bloc for Carmichael."

What Flynt meant by this we couldn't decipher, and our efforts to probe his real convictions were futile. We asked him, "If, as you say, Negroes are downtrodden and therefore will inevitably support the communists in this coming ideological war, what do you propose to do—keep them downtrodden?" "No," he said. "Educate 'em."

Between a thousand and twelve hundred Negroes voted without incident in the 1946 primary—"in segregated polls, of course."

Spalding uses the numbered ballot, he thinks. Nobody cares much who's on the county Democratic committee. Its members are selected by write-in votes, and the membership changes hardly at all from election to election. Flynt says the county unit system is "here to stay," although it wouldn't hurt to do "a little reapportionment."

Cason Callaway would make "a wonderful governor," and Flynt thinks he could be elected. His immense wealth wouldn't hurt him because he's proved himself to be a man of real enterprise. "Nothing succeeds like success." Flynt also thinks Fred Hand or H. L. Wingate would make good governors, but he doesn't believe Wingate could be elected. Curiously, Flynt doesn't think Wingate could count on "solid support from farmers."

We asked Flynt what he thought about the role of corporations in Georgia. "We don't have political machines here like Hague's or Curley's or Crump's," we pointed out, "but don't the corporations perform the same function—if only because it's their money that finances campaigns and determines who'll win?"

To this Flynt answered, "Absolutely," but declined to say more.

He said there wasn't much, if any, cash bribery in the legislature. "Offers of state jobs, highways, that kind of thing, are much more important than cash bribes." Flynt took a beating from the local press and many of his constituents after he voted for Herman and again after a report that he'd told a citizens' group that he and some friends had been offered bribes amounting to almost a hundred thousand dollars. "I was misquoted."

As evidence of the quality of the Georgia legislature, Flynt told us that last summer the Georgia Association of Beverage Bottlers, concerned about the prospect of a soft-drinks tax, commissioned Retail Credit to do character reports on all members of the assembly. The report found only six of "low character." Most of the others were rated "superior."

Flynt has been put on the defensive by his vote for Herman. His friends have told him he's going to have to work hard to justify himself. Throughout our interview he kept saying that "politics is rotten" or the equivalent and that "it doesn't make much difference who you vote for anyway." He also kept repeating that in his opinion politics in Georgia "are no worse than anywhere else in the country."

Blanton Fortson, judge; 1936 candidate for governor; president, Southern Mutual Life Insurance Company, interviewed in his office in Athens, June 22

Judge Fortson immediately impresses you as a man of good will, good humor, and good sense. He's sixty-five, bald, clear eyed, and candid. He looks as if he exercises regularly.

The walls of his office are decorated with framed pictures of his graduating classes. Within arm's reach of his desk is a shelf of law books and a standing ashtray filled with pipes.

Interest in the election of representatives to the General Assembly varies from time to time, Judge Fortson told us, depending on the appeal of the candidates. Until this last election (he thinks the law may have been changed in 1947), a candidate for the legislature had to name his opponent— that is, contest the seat of an incumbent, so that people could choose between candidates rather than simply vote for the two top men. Sometimes as many as five men run for the two positions, and when this has happened, the turnout has been reasonably good.

Fortson considers Representative Jake Joel an unstable man with a mixed reputation as a lawyer. He says that Joel got the largest Negro vote. But he knows that Joel has made a lot of money swindling Negroes, and he wouldn't be surprised to learn that Joel had paid off a couple of Negro leaders to swing the Negro vote his way. All told, about two hundred Negroes voted "as a bloc" in the 1946 primary. Fortson deplores the Negro bloc vote but recognizes it as inevitable. He said he'd advised M. E. Thompson to veto the white primary bill.

Clarke County uses the numbered ballot, which Fortson thinks may be a good thing, since "a numbered ballot tends to discourage stuffing the ballot box." Nobody pays much attention to the composition of the county Democratic committee, which is elected by write-in. There was a rumor last summer that the Talmadge faction, simply because of public inertia, had succeeded in getting a majority on the committee, but, so far as Fortson can tell, they have exercised no sinister influence. Clarke County votes consistently anti-Talmadge.

Fortson considers the county unit system the crux of Georgia's political instability. Because of it, he says, a candidate can spend the same amount of money to win over leaders in ten counties that it would otherwise take him to win support from only one leader in a county, say, the size of Fulton. He is confident that the big money men—the corporations—have relied on the system to control the state vote and that they represent the system's chief defenders. The only way around the county unit system, he believes, is to set up an effective second party and force the decisive vote into the general election.

Fortson is convinced that the Power Company has an excessive influence in Georgia politics but can't prove it. He's sure, though, that the company keeps a lot of lawyers on retainer who perform no discernible service to Georgia Power and who are being paid for political favors or tasks. He recalls a bill during the Rivers administration that authorized issuance of county revenue certificates for a number of public works projects but conspicuously omitted the construction of hydroelectric plants.

Fortson believes there may be as many as fifty counties in the state that can be swung or controlled by one man. In the latter group he mentioned Columbia County (Glenn Phillips), Laurens (Herschel Lovett), and Treutlen (Jim Gillis). Until recently, Rabun County elections were also subject to one man's call, he said. There is an operative state machine, too—"a loose alliance between Big Business and the politicians"—that serves to perpetuate the county machines.

Judge Fortson admitted Ellis Arnall to the bar. He considers Arnall one of the most brilliant men in America and a politician who can handle patronage in such a way as not to interfere with a constructive program. Effective politics must rest on patronage, he added. Any new party, which he would like to see started, must offer young political workers the promise of good jobs and good rewards—"patronage honestly administered."

B. O. Williams, head of the Department of Sociology, University of Georgia, interviewed in his office on the campus, June 22

Williams bears a striking resemblance in appearance and manner to the character actor Porter Hall—slight, receding chin, pale blue eyes, a posture of modesty that approaches timidity. He is a native of South Carolina, where he was relief director for the Works Progress Administration (WPA) in the early days of the New Deal, one of the first officials in the Agricultural Adjustment Administration (AAA), and for ten years director of 4-H Clubs, both Negro and white. He speaks almost lovingly of Ben Robertson, author of *Red Hills and Cotton*. He speaks, too, of having spent all his life trying to advance the interests of the Negro and thinks himself a man compelled by a strong sense of justice. Still, he says he has avoided the Negro issue publicly, for fear that to be outspoken might cause the state government to take reprisal action against him and his teaching. He said that after the Cocking affair Talmadge sent a man to his office to examine his textbooks.[5] Williams says he was afraid for a while that he might be fired, but he has since learned that Gene knew about his "sane attitude" on race and did not consider him an agitator.

Williams was of interest to us primarily as his conversation afforded an insight into one kind of professorial mind—a mind full of academic tenets and a great deal of information but slow to make up. He puts a lot of stock in America's system of checks and balances and feels that we move forward only through a process of action and reaction. He said that until recently he had never put pressure of any kind on his representatives in Congress but felt compelled to do so yesterday when Truman's veto of the Taft-Hartley bill was returned to the Senate for action. He wrote Senator Maybank, saying very carefully, so he could not be thought to be taking a stand, that he felt the people were now displeased with labor and wanted labor's power curbed.

He also holds as one of the verities that leadership loses its following when it steps out too far beyond popular mores. He feels that the "AAACP" [*sic*] has done this in the last ten years and has consequently hurt the Negro's cause. For the same reason, he says, Ellis Arnall has lost his Georgia following.

The more he talked, the more ambivalent he appeared to be. He said he resents reports on the South in northern newspapers. "The South has made much progress in the last twenty years. It can settle its own problems if left alone to solve them." He believes *Strange Fruit* a "sensational book" with an unjustifiable theme and one that in the long run will damage the South. So too the novels of Erskine Caldwell. The Greenville trials, he maintained, represented a marked improvement in the South's judicial system and did not deserve the sensational treatment they got in the New York press.[6] "They had a lynching last year in New York. Only up there they called it murder."

Williams regards the "Triple-A CP" the most "racistic" organization in the country; he doesn't believe in any organization dedicated solely to the advancement of a single race, however oppressed. He says, however, that the Negro is going to vote, that it's merely a matter of time and methods. "Everything's a problem of method, a matter of means and ends."

Then, as if he might have exposed a liberal nerve: "Before you can improve race relations, you've got to stop niggers from raping white women. . . . Prejudice won't be wiped out if you wait three hundred years. . . . The white primary is, in a sense, simply an organization to protect white people."

Mell Williams, head, CIO local, Textile Workers Union of America (TWUA), interviewed at his home in Greensboro, June 22

Williams was attending a revival meeting at the West End Baptist Church when we called. We drove around to the church—a small, narrow, white frame building with a steeple—and parked until the service was over, caught Williams on the church steps, and drove him and his family back to his home in the mill village. Williams lives in a three-room wood house. He is married and has two children. The front room, where we talked, serves as a combination living room and bedroom. A double bed fills most of one side of the room. Against the opposite wall is a maple bureau. The only other pieces of furniture are two upholstered chairs, a magazine rack (containing old issues of *Liberty* and *Reader's Digest*), and a small radio, which sits on a round oak table. On the walls are two framed religious mottoes. In the corner of one of them is stuck a blue ribbon and an identification card certifying Williams as a delegate to the state CIO convention.

Williams looks to be in his thirties. He has a cast in one eye and has lost three lower front teeth. He talks easily, very much in the idiom. He referred to the Negro workers in the neighboring planing mills as "a right smart bunch of hands." Perhaps significantly, half the time he called them "niggers," half the time "Negroes."

The CIO, he told us, organized the local textile mill in 1941 against considerable management resistance. The mill now employs more than three hundred workers. The latest contract calls for an eighty-cent minimum wage, which Williams considers a victory. During recent negotiations management sought to set up a separate minimum for the eleven Negroes in the plant, all union members. The labor representatives balked, said there'd be one minimum for both whites and Negroes or no contract. Management conceded. "I'm no nigger lover," Williams said, "but you can't keep the nigger down without keeping us down, too. We've learned that." The union is still trying to organize Negro workers in the nearby sawmills and planing mills but so far has had no luck. "Every time organizers get active, management either closes a mill down for a day and says it won't reopen, or threatens to close all the mills down for good." It was pressure from sawmill owners that caused textile management to try to establish a lower minimum for Negroes.

The labor vote is well organized, Williams said, and for this reason no one man or one group of men has sufficient influence to control an election. When the antilabor bills were introduced, union members solicited and got the promises of both Representative Lewis and Senator Brown to fight against them. He said Lewis voted "down the line for us" but Brown "didn't go along." The Farm Bureau has a chapter in Greene, but Williams has no idea how active it may have been promoting the antilabor legislation. He knows that Lewis got a letter from one local bureau member that referred to the bills not by name but as "Wingate's bills."

Greene County people showed little concern about the sales tax, which Williams himself opposes. As for the white primary, opinion seems to divide along factional lines. Since Greene went for Carmichael, Williams is hopeful that the white primary won't have too strong an appeal in the next election. About two hundred Negroes voted in the 1946 primary. "A lot less would have voted if Talmadge hadn't fired 'em up."

Miles Walker Lewis, state representative, Greene County, interviewed in the Greene County Courthouse, Greensboro, June 23

Except for the three hundred union members, Greene County people take little interest in elections to the assembly. Last July, Lewis polled 2,330 votes to about 600 for his opponent. Lewis attributes his remarkable showing to the fact that his opponent has a bad reputation with women.

Greene elected a state senator, Lawrence Brown, who ran without opposition. Later he was exposed as a check forger, a passer of rubber checks, and "a consorter with lewd women." The voters are generally disaffected with Brown now, not because of his bad record in the Senate but because of his low moral character, and they will undoubtedly vote against him should he run for reelection. Brown first ran as a Rivers man, then switched to Carmichael, and on the night of the election in the legislature switched from Thompson to Talmadge.

Shortly before he went to Atlanta to take his seat, Lewis received a batch of penny postal cards asking his support of Herman for governor. The cards were made out in the form of a poll and had spaces for the sender to show a preference, Thompson or Herman. All were marked for Herman. Lewis learned that the cards had been printed and distributed by Carey Williams, editor of the *Greensboro Herald-Journal* and leader of the county's Talmadge faction. Obviously, Williams had given them to Talmadge sympathizers only. Lewis received messages from merchants, mill owners, and Farm Bureau members urging him to vote for the anti-labor bills. The CIO pressed him to oppose them, which he did. (The Greensboro local is the largest textile union in the state. Lewis says the Mary Lela Mill is controlled by New York capital, although many local people own stock in it.) "Greensboro has about accepted the fact that the CIO is here to stay. I think the union leadership here is thoroughly responsible and pretty intelligent."

Lewis's constituents said very little, pro or con, about the sales tax bill. He voted against it, convinced that Herschel Lovett, chairman of the Ways and Means Committee, had stifled other measures that would have raised as much revenue on a much fairer basis.

By his vote against the white primary, Lewis has antagonized the Talmadge faction. "The Talmadge people want a white primary, and they don't care how they get it." Before he went to the assembly, Lewis had told three or four people that he would support a white primary bill, but he changed his mind when he saw the actual bill. He then wrote these people personal notes explaining that he could not support the Harris bill because it would permit boss rule. Unfortunately, he also said he opposed it because it would abolish the county unit system, a statement that caused him considerable embarrassment when several weeks later he voted against extending the county unit system into the general election.

"The county unit system? Of course it's unfair—terribly unjust. I'd like to see it changed. But if I were to say that out loud, I'd be done for."

Lewis is a young man, barely over thirty, and was helped to the legislature by his record as a veteran. It helped too that his brother Lloyd, the strongest anti-Talmadge man in the district, is the county ordinary. He is unhappy about the fractious state political situation, not only because he thinks it damaging to the general welfare but also because it has seriously and unexpectedly handicapped his legal career. He spoke at length about the difficulties he was facing in Greensboro because of his identity as an anti-Talmadge man. "I have to be mighty careful now of jurors. If as many as six Talmadge people serve on a jury, I'm sunk, no matter what the merits of my case. It's a hell of a note, but I have to strike juries on political grounds now, and that's something they didn't teach me in law school."

Lewis saw no instances of cash bribery in the legislature. On the night Herman was elected, however, a legislator sat down next to him and began to talk around the subject. "There's a lot of money changing hands tonight," the man told Lewis, "a lot of it." He kept talking like this until Lewis said, "I guess a man could get a lot of money if he were a stupid enough sonofabitch to take it." The legislator rose abruptly and walked away.

Just before he announced for the legislature, Lewis complained to friends about the high entry fee. Later one of these friends suggested he get in touch with Hamp McWhorter, lobbyist for the bus lines. McWhorter, his friend assured him, would be happy to pay the entry fee for him. At the time Lewis thought his friend was kidding but now believes he was serious. "McWhorter and other lobbyists undoubtedly do pay entry fees for young politicians."

John Bell Towill and Henry Eve, state representatives, Richmond County, interviewed in Towill's home in Augusta, June 24

Organized opposition to Augusta's Cracker Party began in the fall of 1945 when boss John Kennedy arrested a boy named Bridges Evans for shouting derogatory remarks about the Crackers from a grandstand during a local ball game. Inspired by Berry Fleming and a few others, a loose-knit movement got under way that immediately got Evans out of jail and forced an apology from Kennedy. From that incident started the Independent Citizens League, whose vigorous campaigning elected three men to the state assembly and three men out of five to the Board of County Commissioners.

When first approached by this group of public spirits, Eve and Towill had no hope of winning; they merely wished to provide people in the county with some names to vote for in protest against the Crackers. Once committed, however, they took the campaign seriously and directed a concerted barrage against Cracker inefficiency and Cracker dictatorship, discussing personalities freely and, as Towill said, even resorting to a little Talmadgeism (no Negro- or labor-baiting, though). Eve says that one of the big factors in their victory was an extraordinary increase in the number of registered voters, thanks to the Jaycees. The Crackers heretofore had always held about six thousand votes, which in a registration of eight thousand guaranteed their election. In advancing the primary to April, though, the Crackers had erred; they could not close out registration, and under the impetus of the Jaycees' program, the registration list skyrocketed to thirty thousand before election day.

One Cracker tactic was to put some loose money with the city gamblers and have them make absurd bets, such as offering ten to one that no Independent candidate would be elected. The tactic backfired, however, when a lot of Augusta people began accepting the bets. Roy Harris didn't start Negro-baiting until about ten days before the primary, when he then went all out with the idea for a white primary. Before the campaign was over, Harris was distributing handbills that read in part: "If you want your children to go to school with niggers, vote Independent; if you want to sit side by side with a nigger on a street car, vote Independent," and so on. The Crackers were defeated by a record turnout. But neither Towill nor Eve considers them beaten for good. As Eve says, people simply like to be able to call a politician and get what they want immediately. "Under the Independents' kind of democracy, they can't do that any more."

Nether Towill nor Eve has any knowledge of outside interference in local elections. But Inman Curry, local attorney-lobbyist for the Georgia Power Company, has been a leader in the Cracker Party, and because of him the Power Company has been suspected of having contributed to the perpetuation of the Cracker regime.

The League of Women Voters has an active chapter in Augusta. There's also an Augusta Citizens Union that concerns itself with municipal affairs. The Augusta Merchants Association was active during this past legislative session, especially against the sales tax. The Methodist churchwomen were outspoken in opposition to the white primary.

Towill says the most pressure on him came from advocates of the white primary. Oddly enough, he received only one or two letters from union members urging him to vote against the antilabor bills, while businesspeople put strong pressure on him to vote for them. The Augusta Merchants Association is now leading the statewide fight against the sales tax. Its leaders claim that Augusta business draws on neighboring South Carolina for as much as 50 percent of its retail trade, and this would be lost to them were the state to adopt a sales tax. The Richmond delegation voted against the sales tax—not because of pressure from the merchants, who the delegation thought acted "too high-handedly," but because in their honest judgment "no sales tax should be passed until after a thorough study had been made of Georgia's existing tax laws and we could be assured that such a tax was needed." Both Eve and Towill feel that Richmond County would go along with a sales tax if the necessity for it were established, despite the attitude of the merchants.

Eve says that Richmond County has had a long record of tolerance for the Negro and that the anti-Negro sentiment that surfaced last year was almost entirely of Roy Harris's making. He doesn't believe that Richmond can ever be sold on Talmadge's white primary bill. About four thousand Negroes voted in the last primary. They did not vote in a bloc, and, suspiciously, the Negro vote went for the Crackers. Eve says there was evidence of Cracker chicanery.

Like most urban areas in Georgia, the county feels chronically cheated by the state government. It is second only to Fulton County in the amount it pays the state in taxes and has never felt it gets anything close to a fair share of services in return. No governor in memory, Towill says, has ever done anything commendable in the county. Thompson has just approved a new bridge for Augusta, a bridge promised by every governor since 1930. He says things would be different, of course, if the county unit system could be done away with, but he sees no hope of that.

Up until now labor leadership (AFL) has been identified with the Cracker Party, perhaps not by conviction but simply because for so many years any organization in Augusta had to support the Crackers as the price of survival. Except when labor is directly concerned, however, Eve and Towill have seen no evidence of a bloc vote. Both were troubled by labor's participation in the recent battle to get the new city charter accepted. This charter, modeled after one prepared by a team of consultants known as the Read Commission, had been approved by the Central Labor Union (CLU) when originally proposed. But when the Richmond delegation, with misgivings, voted for Wingate's antilabor bills, the CLU immediately sided with the Crackers in trying to defeat passage of the new charter. Both Eve and Towill consider this a sign of shortsightedness among local union leaders, since similar charters in other cities have had enthusiastic backing from labor.

Roy Harris is, of course, recognized as the most effective Talmadge leader in the county and probably in the state as well. Inman Curry, the Power Company's lobbyist, and the city boss, John Kennedy, who once held the title of commissioner of public safety, together with some AFL leaders, head the repudiated Crackers, whose influence in the city and county governments is still very strong. Berry Fleming, the author, is one of the spark plugs behind the Independent League. Besides Eve and Towill, other Independent leaders include Bill Morris, chairman of the pro-Thompson Democratic executive committee and the third man in Richmond's delegation to the assembly; Otis Benton, the group's treasurer; and James Hull, one of Towill's law partners. Hull, incidentally, is retained by the Power Company, which presumably gives the company a say in both camps, considering that it also employs Inman Curry.

The county Democratic committee is elected from a panel

of nominees put on the primary ballot by incumbent members, augmented by write-ins. Talmadge men used to dominate the committee, according to Eve, and may still hold a majority, although the Independents were able last year to put a few of their men on the committee and name its chairman.

Eve says that the Crackers tried to steal the 1946 primary by reporting a consolidated vote to the executive committee instead of reporting a ward-by-ward count. Independents forced a ward-by-ward count, however. They were reasonably satisfied of an honest count except in Ward Four, the Negro ward, where Harris's men were known to have destroyed ballots marked for the Independents. Richmond County uses the numbered ballot.

Although the Klan is either dormant or dead, a racist organization called the Aroused White Citizens has bobbed up mysteriously during the past year. It is led by a man named Howard Newcomb Morse, a young Huey Long acolyte from Louisiana who apparently was attracted to Augusta by the Crackers. Also during the last several months a scurrilous sheet called the *Augusta Courier* has made its appearance. Eve and Towill believe that it's being sponsored by Roy Harris, although its editorship is secret. The *Courier* preaches the Talmadge and Cracker lines and refers to the Independents as the "Zebra Party." It is circulated by hand at no cost, and Eve is thinking about arresting one of the carriers for failure to have a handbill license, with the hope of forcing its editorship into the open.

Eve and Towill think Bill Morris will probably run for governor. They acknowledge his lack of color but believe he has the ability to get his ideas and personality across in the small counties if he can just talk with enough people. They think he'd make a good governor, too. They don't know H. L. Wingate too well but don't think much of him from what they've observed. Fred Hand, according to Towill, is not dishonest; he's "just congenitally reactionary."

Berry Fleming, novelist (*Colonel Effingham's Raid*),
leader of the Independent League, interviewed
at his home in Augusta, June 24

We saw Fleming almost by accident, shortly before mid-
night. Towill was driving us back to the Richmond Hotel
when we saw lights on at the Fleming home—a colonial-
style mansion set back from the road—and on impulse
drove us up to the front door. Fleming seemed glad to see
us. He said he'd been up reading and would be pleased to
talk. Mrs. Fleming was sewing when we came in. She spoke
very pleasantly to each of us, chatted briefly about the Georgia Academy meeting at Pine Mountain, and then excused
herself and went upstairs.

Fleming is a balding, middle-aged man with a physique
that suggests he's led a very healthy, privileged life. He
speaks fluently, though without too much substance, and
some of his ideas were, as Towill said later, a little "half-
baked." He said emphatically that the Georgia Power Company runs Georgia and the "burden is on the Power Company to prove that it doesn't." To a novelist, he said, a lot of
little things add up, and what he's seen and been told about
the Power Company convinces him that the company uses
its organization for political purposes. He cited two instances. Once, in the early days of the war when he was
serving on the local committee of Protect America by Arm-
ing the Allies, he got fed up with successive resolutions con-
demning Hitler and suggested that the committee pay more
attention to conditions in Richmond County. The man who
threw a wet blanket on his suggestion was the Power Company's lawyer, Inman Curry. (Towill quietly pointed out that
a committee to aid the Allies was hardly the logical group to
take up the ax against the Cracker Party.) And again, when
he was interested in getting justice for Bridges Evans, the
boy arrested for derogatory talk against Boss Kennedy, it

was Jim Hull, Towill's law partner and another representative of the Power Company, who told him to go slow, that this was no time to start battling the powers-that-be. (To which Towill replied that Hull had defended Evans; that he had gotten Evans out of jail; that he had obtained a public apology from Kennedy; and that his talk with Fleming had been merely to point out that he, Hull, had done everything that he could as Evans's lawyer and that nothing would be gained by pushing the case further.) Fleming said, "Of course I don't *know* about the Georgia Power Company. I can't tell you what makes a rotten egg. But I know a rotten egg smells, and I know one when I smell one." He went on to say that he felt the Power Company was determined to use the Savannah River valley for its own profit and that its political involvement throughout the valley was calculated to prevent the federal government from making it a public project for flood control and navigation.

Robert Knox, senator, Twenty-ninth District, interviewed in his office in Thomson, June 24

Knox is a prominent lumber man in McDuffie County and owns considerable real estate. He practices law and also has an insurance agency, the Philadelphia Fire Protection Association.

He was elected to the Senate last summer as a Carmichael man, as was his colleague Leonard Lokey, who has since swung to Herman. Knox remains anti-Talmadge. He was secretary of the Senate Special Judiciary Committee that considered the white primary bill, and most of the communications that came to the Senate were addressed to him. He says he received about six hundred letters or postal cards, about two-thirds of which were pro and had obviously been prompted by Herman's radio appeals. He feels that Herman will exploit the white primary issue in 1948. "If he's opposed only by Thompson, he'll be licked. But if there's a third man in the race, Herman probably will be elected."

Knox says elections in McDuffie are usually determined through a contest between followers of two men: Arnold Ansley, leader of the Talmadge faction, and Sheriff Lynn Morris, a strong anti-Talmadge man. He considers it fortunate that, since Ansley and Morris can't agree to support Thompson, they also can't agree to support Herman. In his view, there are about two hundred such men in Georgia who can determine the outcome of any state election. "The candidate's problem is to know who the right men are and to get them on his side."

Before the last primary the board of registrars purged the voters list of all but 120 Negroes. Of these, only about 60 went to the polls. The board was bipartisan, according to Knox, but a lot of anti-Talmadge members were strong advocates of the white primary, and "they did their best to keep down the Negro vote."

Ellis Arnall probably has done more for McDuffie County than any other governor, Knox says. People are soured on him, though, for having "sold out for national prominence." Knox considers Arnall a dead duck politically.

Public opinion in the county is predominantly antilabor. The CIO tried to organize some of the local mills but failed. "People here refused to rent to the organizer, and he was obliged to commute from Augusta." When labor representatives asked to speak at Thomson civic clubs, the clubs said no.

Knox knew Herman Talmadge as a student at Georgia and liked him. He considers Herman a vast improvement over his father. Herman's mistake, he says, was in listening to Jim Peters and Roy Harris. "If he hadn't tried to take over the governorship the way he did, he'd be unbeatable." Knox went on to say that he had counseled Herman to speak out for Thompson's position. "I told him that if he didn't, I'd fight him. And I did."

William Morris, editor, *Augusta Chronicle*; state representative, Richmond County; chairman of the state Democratic executive committee, interviewed in his office in Augusta, June 25

Morris is a short, plump man with a round face, cleft chin, and short black hair—a physical type that lends itself to political caricature. He has a pleasant, friendly manner, but somehow he fails to give off any impressive amount of warmth. He has been plugged by fellow Augustans as a possible candidate for governor someday. Indeed, he admitted to us that he'd once had his eye on the governorship. He wouldn't have it now on a silver platter, he says, having seen enough of politics to make him wary. Yet the way he said it implied that he had not entirely abandoned the idea and invited efforts to persuade him. Our conclusion, after talking with him about twenty minutes, was that though he may have considerable ability, he lacks the necessary color for a successful politician and may lack the depth and breadth necessary for a really competent governor. Beside a man like John Bell Towill, say, he looks lightweight.

Morris talked glowingly about the Thompson convention in Macon. The way the audience handled itself, the dignified response, and the general atmosphere of the convention proved that there were people in Georgia who could take politics seriously and who felt a genuine concern for the Democratic Party. From this comment, he switched to an analysis of the part Ed Rivers plays in the Thompson administration. He minimized Rivers's influence, saying emphatically that nobody was telling Thompson how to run his office and that Rivers was merely "a good and valuable friend." In answer to our question as to the wisdom of Thompson's appointment of Fred Wilson to the tax committee, he said he felt Thompson was thoroughly justified, that the House resolution called specifically for the appointment of a representative from a public utility, and that Wilson was the logical choice. He said he knew nothing about Wilson except that he was "fixer" for the Power Company.

Morris then deplored the excessive presence in the capitol of certain powerful corporation lobbyists, naming specifically the bus lines, the railroads, the telephone company, the Power Company, and the liquor interests. On the other hand, if voters would send better people to the assembly— men with more intelligence and enough strength of character to resist the pressures—"special interests" would give "to the general welfare." He feels that the county unit system is contributing to this poor representation and expressed a strong desire to get rid of it.

About the 1948 race, he said substantially what Bob Knox told us yesterday: in a three-man race, Herman would probably win. Knox said he knows of nobody in the state who might be persuaded to be that third man, though he recognized only too well "the ability of the Talmadge crowd to dig one up."

C. E. Irvin, business manager, Paine College, interviewed in Augusta, June 25

Mr. Irvin is a man in his late forties. He has lived in Augusta for more than twenty-five years and feels good about the fact that in this time he has earned and maintained the respect of Augusta's white elite without sacrificing his position as a leader of the Negro community. He talks not so much with authority but with a becoming self-confidence. He knows that many whites would prefer that he keep his place and stick full-time to his job at Paine, a college for Negroes. To "go along," however, is not his nature. He has been active in the (all Negro) Augusta Citizens League, serving as its president during the fight to unseat the Cracker Party. The league has several thousand members and could easily rally two or three thousand Negroes on short notice. Mr. Irvin volunteered that Richmond County has "a healthy attitude" toward the Negro and that much progress has been made in the past few years. He went on to tell us the following:

Until a few outraged whites organized the Independent League, the Crackers were the only party in town. Some Negroes voted Cracker because the party rewarded them with jobs and money; Irvin said he could name eight or ten who have prospered "right handsomely " from Cracker control. But most of the others who bothered to vote did so because they had no other choice. The Negro vote for state legislators, he said, would have been split had it not been for the ten-day race-baiting campaign carried on by Roy Harris just before the primary. Harris forced the Negroes, about 90 percent of them, to vote Independent. (Note inconsistency here with report from John Bell Towill that the Crackers carried the Negro wards.) Naturally, Negroes were fiercely opposed to the white primary bill, but Irvin was gratified that many white people opposed it too.

Great pains were taken to instruct the Negroes in voting procedure. This, Irvin said, is perfectly natural when any group has been denied the ballot and is voting for the first time. At several mass meetings Negroes were given the following instructions: "Go home early; eat supper; stay home with your families; take a bath; go to bed early; don't drink, but if you must drink, let someone hand you a drink after you get in bed; get up early; go to the polls; don't put off voting until later in the day; don't let rain or procrastination keep you away; don't get in arguments; just vote." At 6:30 A.M. there were as many as four hundred Negroes waiting when the polls opened.

About four thousand Negroes voted. About 90 percent of them voted for Independent candidates, with one major exception. Although a Cracker, Judge Franklin of the superior court had been a fair judge. His opponent, an unfamiliar man from Waynesboro, made an overt bid for the Negro vote. Both were invited to speak to the Negroes. The new man spoke and made a good impression; Franklin only showed up when he realized he might lose. The Negroes checked both records carefully and decided that Franklin was the best man and cast their votes for him. Franklin was defeated. Irvin feels that this defeat may have been worth the price because it spiked the charge that Negroes would vote in a bloc for one faction. "It showed that we're capable of sizing up each candidate on his merits."

Not long ago "a bad Negro" killed a white man in Augusta. The Negro was arrested, tried, and sentenced to death. Irvin got busy and personally raised more than a thousand dollars for a defense fund. The defense succeeded in getting the sentence reduced to life imprisonment. "Solicitor Hines called me and said he'd heard about me raising all that money. 'In the future,' he said to me, 'don't waste money like that. Come to my office, it's open twenty-four hours a day.' And I said, 'Mr. Hines, we've never had such an invitation, and we're glad to know that you'll receive us; the reason we raised the money is not that we fear you personally, but that we fear the office of solicitor. It will be a good thing for us to talk over these things, but we felt it was up to you to suggest when we might talk. You live way up in the hills, and we live down here in the flats.' And Hines said, 'Come in any time. I can save you a lot of time and expense.'"

Irvin paused. "It takes a lot of starch to be a Negro political leader," he said when he resumed. Candidates had insisted that he take money to cover expenses, but he told them that the Negroes were willing to pay their way. He is absolutely convinced that the Negro vote cannot be controlled, because he has seen too many attempts to control it. The main failing of white people is that they can't see this.

Irvin said that Mr. Guy Merry, head of the Chamber of Commerce, is an eminently fair man, perhaps the best white man in Augusta. But even Merry is at times a victim of fear and rumor. For instance, Merry called him up once and said, "What is this about the NAACP telling you people not to vote Independent?" Irvin replied that it was "hokum," a false rumor designed to frighten white friends like Merry.

Irvin stressed that "our racial pattern is unique." A lot of Negroes who haven't lived with it a long time cannot function effectively in it, he said. He told the story of a Negro ward worker from Chicago who came to town thinking all Negroes and southern whites were stupid. "She soon learned that there were many of us who could run circles around her."

Dr. J. M. Kittrell, optometrist, Dublin; chairman, Laurens County Board of Registrars, interviewed in his office, June 26

Everything else we'd seen in Dublin was remindful of the day forty years earlier when agents for the Central of Georgia Railway had been told to get out of town and take their progress elsewhere. But not this building. It was made of concrete block and in design like thousands of others that have sprung up all over the country since the war—flat roofed, low and wide, and almost militantly modern. The letters in the sign above the door stretched out against the outline of a monstrous eye: "Dr. J. M. Kittrell, Optometrist."

The waiting room was empty except for one patient, a man, and we had a good chance to look around. It was clean and cool and simply furnished. The walls had been freshly Kemtoned in green; on one of them hung the room's only picture, a lithograph of a doctor and a sick child. The chairs and sofa were of twisted, sprung steel, with plastic cushions. Popular magazines overflowed a magazine rack, and a set of six books stood on top of a small filing cabinet. I had to twist my head to read the title. It was *The March of Democracy* by James Truslow Adams.

We walked over to the patient. "The doctor in?"

The man nodded and gestured with his head toward a corridor. "Down there," he said, blinking. "He's coming now."

We turned at the sound of the doctor's footsteps. He acknowledged my nod with a tentative smile, went to his patient, bent over, and started adjusting a pair of rimless glasses. When he was done, he straightened up and, without a word, managed to indicate that everything was all right now and the man could go. No longer blinking, the patient rose, tested the bridge to his glasses with a forefinger, and smiled.

"Whatta I owe you, Doc?"

Dr. Kittrell waved him away and turned to us.

"We're making a junket through the state," Jamie told him after we'd introduced ourselves and sat down. "Listening to people talk. We're trying to find out who runs Georgia."

The doctor spoke for the first time. "The politicians," he said with conviction.

I nodded. "Other people, too."

"Sure," he said. "All the people who want to help themselves to whatever they can get. The politicians and the people who want to help themselves. They run Georgia."

He looked tired and sad. He was a slight man with a perceptible stoop—gray haired, with dark eyes that looked out through, and sometimes over, silver-rimmed glasses. He had purplish lips, his complexion was spoiled, and his face was in folds, as if there were too much skin for his skull to accommodate. Any flaws in his physical appearance, however, were canceled by a generous smile and a candor that put us instantly at ease.

"We were told that you had a little trouble here last summer," I said. "With your registration list."

"It made me sick," he said. "Really sick. I didn't know how sick till it was all over. When it was, I decided I had to get away for a spell. I went to Chicago. But it was in Chicago it hit me. I got so sick, so sick at my stomach, I couldn't enjoy my vacation. I stayed that sick for six weeks."

"They tried to purge the Negroes?"

"Mostly that was it." He studied us for a moment and apparently was satisfied with what he saw. He relaxed, took off his glasses, and rubbed his eyes.

"I've been in this county fifty years," he began. "I've served as chairman of the board of registrars for the past ten. I used to tell the judge I didn't want the job any longer. I'm pretty busy, and the job takes up a lot of time just before an election. I told the judge I'd like to give it up. Several times I told him. But every time the judge'd insist I stay on. 'You're a fine, honest registrar,' he'd say. 'We'd have a hard time finding somebody to take your place.' So I stayed on. I sort of believe in citizenship. My father was a Universalist. He didn't go to church, but he believed in citizenship."

He paused for a moment and replaced his glasses. "First time I knew they were up to anything was one day the judge called. It was right after the courts had decided the colored should be 'lowed to vote. 'J.M.,' said the judge, 'you gonna need any help striking the list?' I told him no, I thought I could handle it all right, just like I always handled it. He didn't press me, either, that time. But about a week later I met him on the courthouse steps, and he brought it up again. I told him what I'd told him before. 'I may need a stenographer,' I said, 'but when I do, I'll ask for one.'

"Well, the judge thought for a moment and then said, 'Hear you don't like Mr. Lovett.'

"'No,' I said. 'I don't like Mr. Lovett. I'm not going to vote for him.'

"'He's a big man,' said the judge, as if I didn't know. 'Biggest man in the county. You can't fight a man like Lovett.'

"'Yeah,' I said. 'Maybe too big.'

"'But you aren't gonna vote for that little nit, are you?'

"'Yes,' I said. 'I'm gonna vote for that little nit. I don't have anybody better to vote for. Tell you what, though. I might change my mind and vote for Lovett if you get him to do one thing.'

" 'What's that?' asked the judge.

" 'You get Herschel Lovett on the courthouse steps someday, and you ask him about that road contract. You ask him why in 1937 he submitted the lowest bid on a contract to pave nine miles of the old Macon road, and then why he withdrew his bid in favor of another contractor who'd cost the state twenty-three thousand dollars more, and then why he accepted ten thousand dollars from that contractor. You get him to answer all that in public here someday before the election and I might, I just might, reconsider.'

"Well, the judge didn't have anything more to say after that, so I didn't hear anything more from him. But next thing I knew there's this article in the paper. The paper's owned by Lovett, you know. This article said the judge had appointed a special board of assistant registrars. Didn't consult me or anything. Just appointed a board of what he called assistant registrars, out of the blue, just like that.

"Now, the official board of registrars has only three members, the chairman and two others. But this special board—it had four people. See?

"Soon's I read that story, I called a meeting of both boards, and when we were all together, I explained that I didn't quite understand the situation. So far as I know, no other county in Georgia has ever had two boards of registrars, and I didn't know exactly how to proceed. The chairman of the new board, though, had a suggestion. He wanted me and him to retire and serve simply as advisers, leaving the striking up to the other five. I said no, I wouldn't agree to that, for to follow his suggestion would mean that his three men could outvote my two. I said instead that my board would agree to let his board do the purging if mine had the right of review.

"There was an awful lot of wrangling, and we didn't seem

to be getting anywhere until one of the board members said he wouldn't serve at all until we made up our minds who was chairman. That meant getting the judge to decide. The judge refused to come to our meeting, so we had to go in a body to his office. Then, maybe because he was embarrassed, remembering all those nice things he used to say about me, he decided I was to be chairman.

"Next meeting, one of the special board members insisted we immediately strike all the Negroes off the registration list. I said no, our job was to follow the law, and the law didn't allow discrimination in the purge. We could strike only the names of people who'd died since the last election, or those who'd moved away, or those who'd been convicted of felonies. We couldn't purge anybody simply because his skin was black.

"Then somebody moved to purge all those in the county who'd been convicted on misdemeanor charges since the last election, the idea being that the Negroes in the county had the worse record for misdemeanors. I protested, pointing out that the law said only felons should be struck. They overrode me, though, and passed a resolution to wipe off the lists all those with misdemeanors. But a couple of meetings later they discovered that the white folks had almost as bad a record for misdemeanors as the colored, and the idea began to pall on them. They stuck to it, though, till I tricked 'em.

"I paid a visit to the local bootlegger. 'Don't tell anybody,' I said, 'but this bunch of new registrars is purging all the people in the county who've been guilty of a misdemeanor since 1944. You know what that means. That means you and your brother won't get to vote.'

"That did it. At the next board meeting, first thing, one of the members, a friend of this bootlegger's, proposed an amendment. He wanted us to leave on all the names we'd already struck for misdemeanors but thereafter strike only those who'd been convicted since January 1946. He thought that way the bootlegger and his brother would be saved. It was outrageous, of course, but the whole business was fixed. There was no discussion after my usual protest, and his amendment passed. So they went right on with the purge. When they got to the name of this bootlegger, they got a little nervous and started to breeze right by. But I caught 'em short." The doctor's eyes twinkled. "I just said, 'Hold a minute,' and pointed to the court record. What they hadn't known was that this bootlegger and his brother had been fined twice since January 1946.

"Well, there was this long silence. And then one of the men, indignant-like, said, 'We been doing this all wrong. We ain't got no right to purge a man for a misdemeanor.' I just sat back and smiled. The only thing they knew to do, of course, was to reinstate all the names they'd struck for misdemeanors. They were that scared of the bootlegger.

"That didn't end it. A couple of them said they could purge anybody they pleased on the grounds of character— and would, by God. But I got really mean and stubborn. I said, 'Who's gonna judge if a man's character is good or bad? The law says a man's character is bad enough to keep him from voting only if he's been convicted of a felony. That's something for the courts to decide, not us.' Well, next thing they thought of was illiteracy. And that one almost beat me.

"They made up this list of questions, questions to ask the Negroes so hard I couldn't answer 'em myself. They planned to send out postcards to all the colored people who'd registered, telling 'em to report before the board on a certain day to show cause why they shouldn't be purged for illiteracy. But there was this long, drawn-out business of getting the postcards prepared. The man who'd been appointed to handle it first said he'd had trouble finding a mimeograph machine, and then he had trouble getting a girl to type the addresses, and next he'd temporarily misplaced the list. By the time I caught on, it was almost too late. What they'd hoped to do, understand, was to mail the postcards so late that none of the Negroes could possibly get them in time to show up for the tests. That way, they hoped to purge 'em all without having to test any of 'em. But three days before the meeting, I sat up most of the night with this board member and a stenographer, and the three of us managed to get all those postcards addressed—although, as you can imagine, this board member wasn't much help. Then, just to make sure nothing else went wrong, I called on the Negro preacher. I told him what the story was and asked him to make sure that every registered Negro in the county be at that meeting on time. And sure 'nough, an hour before the first board member got there, there was this line of Negroes two blocks long in front of the courthouse.

"Well, that just about floored 'em. One of the board members suggested we cut down the number of questions to one: 'What is due process of law?' And another one suggested we call 'em in groups of ten and give 'em tests at the same time. But I said no, and I wouldn't budge. When they tried to rush things up, I slowed 'em down. I made 'em give that examination to every Negro in turn, and the test was just too long and there were just too many Negroes. It was then only four days before the primary, and there wasn't enough time. I guess when it was all over the Negroes did pretty well. We got fifty Negroes for every fifty white men in this county. About twenty-four hundred of them stayed on the list and about sixteen hundred voted—some of 'em for Mr. Lovett. If you ask me, a lot more would have voted for Lovett if he hadn't been so high-handed about trying to keep 'em from voting at all."

He paused, as if that ended it.

"Was there any violence at the polls?" Jamie asked. "Any intimidation?"

"Some," he said. "No violence, I don't guess, but a lot of intimidation. I learned the day before the election that the chairman of the election committee—one of Lovett's boys— was planning to supervise the Negro precinct himself. But I squelched that by having two of my friends on the committee demand in open meeting that they be assigned to that precinct, and the committee went along with them. I understood later, too, that Lovett's friends marked the ballots for some of the Negroes, but I didn't learn it in time, and, anyway, they couldn't fix enough of them to matter much."

"What about yourself?" I asked. "Did they threaten you any?"

"No," he said. "They didn't like it much, and they had a lot to say, but they didn't try to beat me up or anything."

His receptionist, who must have slipped in while we were talking, spoke up at this. "What about the rope, doctor?"

"Oh yes, the rope." He smiled. "I woke up one morning and found a hangman's noose tied around the knob of my front door. They also hung me in effigy on the courthouse lawn, some of 'em. But they didn't hurt me any."

Herschel Lovett, state representative, Laurens County, interviewed in his office in Dublin, June 26

Mr. Lovett's use of power, we had been told more than once, is an example of how one man can control a Georgia county. He is owner and editor of the *Dublin Courier-Herald*, owner of much of the county's real estate, owner of the local cotton gin and the town's biggest hardware store. In addition, he engages in road contracting and has an oil distributorship. He is reputed to be a millionaire and to have an annual income of well over twenty-five thousand dollars.

Mr. Lovett was chairman of the House Ways and Means Committee during the last legislative session, in which capacity he pushed through the sales tax bill and forced the antilabor bills out of the Industrial Relations Committee. He voted for Herman and was a determined advocate of the white primary bill.

We had a hard time tracking down Mr. Lovett. We drove by his hardware store, where we were told he was out inspecting some new construction. We went by two construction sites, one on Dublin's main street and the other on the edge of town, and were told by carpenters that he had just left both places. Back at the office of the *Courier-Herald,* we were told that Mr. Lovett rarely visited the news offices and were advised to try his office in the Brantley Building. His secretary there said he was at home but was due in the office any minute. We called Mr. Lovett at his home. He told us that he was a terribly busy man but that if we would meet him at his office at quarter of ten, he could let us have perhaps twenty minutes of his time.

At his office Mr. Lovett greeted us much more cordially than we had expected. We remembered him from our observation of the legislature as a somewhat nervous man, usually petulant and peremptory and often choleric. Apparently, the time back from the capitol had done him good. He looked in good health and almost hearty. He is a big man, about sixty-two, with a mane of white hair and a round face that comes to a pointed chin (his hair parts in the middle, which gives his head the appearance of a valentine heart).

If we had had no prior knowledge of Lovett's political activities, we would have judged him merely as a man of the old school who continues to exert an influence on times to which he does not belong, a man, say, who acts by conviction but whose convictions have been converted to prejudices by time and social change. He said, as if he believed it, that no man had done more to advance the Negro in Laurens County than he but that he simply cannot approve of "social equality." Again, "Our young people are accepting ideas that are basically wrong. It used to be that the commonest kind of laborer took pains in his work and strove to do a better job every day. Now they're content just to get by. Why, a college man, with all his instruments and book learning, can't square up a joint today as well as a day laborer fifty years ago." (He commented on the need to check up on construction workers, something he had been doing early that morning when we had tried to catch up with him.) He then launched an attack against labor unions. Under unionization, he said, the sense of craftsmanship is lost and the personal relation between employer and employee destroyed, things that to businessmen of his tradition are all important. He said he had fought hard for the antilabor bills so that the Stephens Woolen Mills, which was then considering setting up a plant in Dublin and has since started construction, would have the chance to select its labor without interference. "Any employer ought to have the right to choose the men who work for him."

Mr. Lovett said that although he was not always for Eugene Talmadge, he's solidly behind Gene's son. "Herman has the broad perspective," he said. "He's one of the few men in the state who do. All the others are tools of special interest." He thinks Herman is a much finer person than his father and knows that his strength is growing throughout the state. He pooh-poohed Fred Hand as being too "temperamental" for a governor.

Mr. Lovett does not hope for much from Thompson's tax commission. "It's packed with special interest." He told "Fred" (Fred Wilson) that he had no business on the commission. From his knowledge of the other men on it, he doesn't expect the emergence of any serious recommendations for reform—that is, tax reform of benefit to the general welfare. "All you've got on the commission is a bunch of young lawyers. What we ought to have are men of long business experience."

He said he was still of the opinion that the legislature had the right to elect Herman governor, but he was "enough of a man" to abide by a decision of the state supreme court. "Lots of the boys didn't want to go along with the court," he said, "but I told 'em, the court had ruled and, right or wrong, we'd have to submit to it."

He thinks Rivers is telling Thompson what to do, that Herman will run against Thompson in 1948, and that the white primary will again be the issue. In response to our question about the validity of the *Journal's* disclosure of the election fraud in Telfair, he said he would like to see a careful investigation of all elections, that he was satisfied that such irregularities were common on both sides. He tends to think Herman got his votes honestly, since "he didn't have enough time to solicit 'em." He said he believes strongly in honest elections.

Jamie told him that as a young lawyer he had been trained to respect the law and consequently feared the impact of any effort to strip laws from the statute books, as was being proposed by the Talmadge forces. Instead, Jamie said, he would prefer to see an overhaul of all our election laws and some adjustment in registration requirements that would keep unqualified people—white and Negro both—from voting. Lovett said he would favor such a move, too, though we gathered from the way he said it that he didn't quite understand what Jamie's proposal involved.

About his race for the legislature last summer, Lovett said that he had a great many friends in the Negro community but that when a group of Negroes called on him and asked him to commit himself against Talmadge, he asked them out of his office. "You know where I stand," he told them. "I'm a friend of the Negro but don't believe in equality. I don't try to tell you how to vote, and I resent your trying to tell me. Get out of here and don't come back."

Reflecting on the extent of his political influence, Lovett said, "I've never told any of my hands to vote for me." He then said that he naturally attracted a lot of support from people because of his prominence as a businessman. "I had to go to work when I was fourteen. Every cent I've earned since then has come hard. People respect you for that."

He described briefly his attitude on the sales tax. When it was first proposed some years ago, he was a senator from

Johnson County and voted for it, despite the objections from merchants. His position was used against him when he ran for reelection. This time, he told voters that, though he still favored a sales tax, he would get instructions from them before he voted on it during the next session. When he called a public meeting at the courthouse to get his instructions, the people voted almost unanimously against the tax. He followed their instructions. The next time it came up, he got in a fistfight on the House floor with Henderson Lanham. Lanham, he felt, had double-crossed him by first promising to have a debate on the sales tax first thing one morning, then calling for a vote without a debate. "I leaned over to Lanham and said, 'You told me you'd call for a debate on this bill before a roll call, and now you're acting like a ———.' Next thing I knew Lanham had hit me on the cheek with his fist."

Lovett said he came up in the old days when he helped "niggers vote in droves." Now, the bad thing about the Negroes was that they used their churches for politics. The Negroes have some white men who work with them, particularly a Dr. Kittrell, chairman of the board of registrars, who "mixes and mingles" with them. Kittrell, he said, had lost all influence in the white community and was not likely to be reappointed.

Lewis Wilson, mayor-elect of Macon; state representative, Bibb County, interviewed in his campaign headquarters, June 27

Bibb County is almost evenly divided between Talmadge and anti-Talmadge sympathizers. Unless the issues are sharp, candidates try to avoid overt identification with either faction. Most campaigns are fought and won on the appeal of the dueling personalities. Wilson knows of no local race in which outside interests have actively intervened, although he suspects that the local agent for the Georgia Power Company may have been directed to work for his opponent in the race for mayor because of Wilson's vote in the assembly against the antilabor bills. "I would expect opposition from the Power Company because I've consistently favored measures in the legislature that would make it easy for municipalities to operate their own hydroelectric plants."

W. D. Anderson of the Bibb Manufacturing Company is a man of tremendous power in the county. It's a rule of life in Macon that local candidates seek the favor of the Bibb management—or at least do nothing that might arouse its disapproval. Wilson is especially proud of the fact that he won the mayoralty despite opposition from Anderson's Macon machine.

The Farm Bureau is active throughout the community, having its state headquarters here in the Bibb Building. Members didn't bother him much about the antilabor proposals, perhaps because "they knew only too well how I stood." (He thinks Wingate is a likable fellow but tends to distrust him "on political matters.") The Macon Merchants Association opposed the sales tax, as did the Macon delegation in the House. The white primary will, inevitably, be front and center in the next governor's race, but Wilson thinks it may not pull the weight it did in the last one. Should the courts declare the South Carolina white primary scheme unconstitutional, as Wilson hopes, "the Talmadge group will be hard pressed to find anything else." He believes that Thompson can beat Herman on the issue in a two-man race or if the race is decided in the general election. He looked surprised when we told him that we'd gathered from leaders in both factions that there would be only one primary and that Herman and Thompson would fight it out there.

Macon's labor leadership is altogether reasonable and responsible in Wilson's opinion. He told of a conversation he'd had with a foreman at the Bibb plant in which the foreman said the CIO would have a contract there today if management hadn't exploited the Negro issue so skillfully.

The Klan has made itself known in the county, although nobody seems to know how many members it may have. Wilson says that during the recent campaign for mayor Klan stickers suddenly appeared all over town.

Speaking of his mayoralty race, Wilson praised his opponent, Merritt, "the best man I ever ran against." He attributes his victory to long identification with the working people—labor and the Negro—as opposed to the "silk stocking crowd" and feels that with a lesser opponent he would have won by an even wider margin. Negroes voted for him in a bloc. As one Negro leader explained, "it would have been a catastrophic betrayal if Negroes had done otherwise" in view of Wilson's many years of loyalty to the Negro community. "No man running for office would ever again have any confidence in Negroes if they didn't vote for a man they knew to be their friend." Wilson also had a decisive white majority. "The Merritt crowd introduced the race issue about two weeks before the election and succeeded in winning over many white votes, more white votes than it lost Negro votes. The worst thing I did in the campaign was to let my picture appear in the Negro paper. Merritt leaped on that. He bought all the extra copies and circulated them through though mill town, in pool halls and beer joints—just about everywhere he thought there were voters who might fall for the nigger-nigger line."

Wilson is paralyzed in the neck and can't move his head without moving his body. He owns a chain of three grocery stores in Macon and apparently has prospered. He is a very friendly, kind man, with deep roots in the community. He has taught a Bible class in the mill community for many years. He says he "sticks to the lesson" and leaves it to the class to relate the lessons to the moral problems of daily living. He was a bit distressed, he said, to learn that many members of his Sunday school class had voted against him out of fear of the Negro.

Harry Lynwood Wingate, president, Georgia Farm Bureau, interviewed in his office in the Bibb Building, Macon, June 28

Mr. Wingate is an impressive stamp of a man. He's easily six feet three and must weigh close to 250 pounds, with no appearance of fat. He has massive shoulders and hands the size of peanut hams. His fingers are long and his nails well manicured. He has white, short-cropped hair. His eyes are deep set. They are not the sort of eyes that inspire trust. His face is the color of terra cotta, and I imagine to many people it suggests the permanent sunburn of a dirt farmer. I suspect, rather, that his ruddy complexion derives from some failure of the circulatory system; his cheeks are full of tiny, broken veins.

We didn't ask Mr. Wingate our routine questions. We went to him hoping to hear firsthand the things Alex Heard had reported and also to get his own story about the anti-labor bills he was instrumental in getting through the last assembly.[7] Mr. Wingate talked freely, almost too freely, and much of what he had to say had the sound of a memorized speech frequently delivered.

He began by telling us something of the Farm Bureau's growth. He repeated what he had told Alex—that membership now stood "better than fifty-two thousand," that there had been a sustained 47 percent increase in membership every year for the past several years, and that he hoped to hit a hundred thousand before the end of 1948. He said the bureau was active in all south Georgia counties and that only north Georgia remained to be organized extensively. He said that his relationship with the commissioner of agriculture had been entirely satisfactory and that he did not agree with Mr. Emmet in thinking the office should be abolished and its functions transferred to the Division of Agricultural Extension. To him, the two agencies represent two distinctly different and valuable services to farmers and should be kept separate.

Wingate said that the movement to push the antilabor bills started last October, when the AFL and the CIO announced plans to organize three million farm workers. According to him, the AFL said that any farm that hired more than two workers was a factory and should be organized. Jurisdictional strikes in Texas and California fruit orchards warned the Georgia farmers of what they could expect if the unions came to Georgia, so at the annual convention of the Georgia Farm Bureau in November 1946 he succeeded in getting the bureau to endorse the two bills that he later had introduced in the House. He insists that the bureau is a friend to the laborer and the unions, but in this instance their intent constituted a threat to the farmer, a direct threat, and the farmers' only salvation lay in protective legislation. He said he told his lawyers drafting the bill, "I won't stand for a bill that is discriminatory against labor; the only kind of bill I want will establish better regulation of both management and labor."

Wingate is enthusiastically for the sales tax. He views it as the only source of new revenue, which the state badly needs. When we ventured that such a tax might discriminate against the poor, he countered with this: "A lot of my friends in the legislature protested that it was unfair to make old-age pensioners pay a sales tax. I told them that in reality the tax would benefit the pensioners. Only forty cents out of a twenty-dollar pension would go for the sales tax. But with increased revenue the state could raise the pension to forty dollars. Wouldn't it be better to have pensioners pay eighty cents and get forty dollars a month than pay nothing and get only twenty dollars?"

He said "one of my men" is serving on Thompson's tax commission and he is going to have him push the sales tax. He is generally pessimistic about what may come out of the commission's work. "It has no outside experts, and no man in Georgia is qualified to recommend any overhauling of our tax structure."

Wingate was read off the House floor by Representative Stafford Brooke in the midst of one debate during the last session. He was indignant, but he refused to go back on the floor when some of his friends in the assembly invited him. Instead, he did all his work, very effectively, from the capitol corridors. Next morning, he persuaded the first man to answer roll call to get up and explain his vote: "I'm voting for these bills mainly for one reason. Some labor people read off H. L. Wingate yesterday, and I don't go for such high-handed tactics." The speech, he said, attracted a lot of other votes against labor.

Wingate denied that he held any personal ambitions for the governorship. He said last year many people approached him, some of them offering to contribute as much as five thousand dollars to a campaign fund if he would announce. He refused then, and insists he would refuse again, because the minute he got in the governor's chair, he could no longer serve the interests of the farmer.

He says he never takes partisan stands. As he had for Heard, he drew us a distinction between "business" and "politics." He says that if two candidates are running for office and one is against Farm Bureau policies, then it's "business" to see that the man is defeated. But if both men are in favor of these policies, then it's "politics" to favor one over the other, and this the bureau never does. He said that all Georgia's congressmen, save Henderson Lanham, went along with the bureau in voting to override the president's veto of the Taft-Hartley bill, and he has told his members, "All these men but Lanham are your friends. I don't care what they might have done in the past to displease you, they've proved themselves friends of the bureau by voting to override, and they deserve all the support we can give them."

Grover Byars, member of the Pardon and Parole Board and for twenty years chairman of the Floyd County Democratic Executive Committee, interviewed in his office at the state capitol, July 3

Byars says Herman Talmadge is dead politically. "At least he can't hope to carry more than two counties in the Seventh District. People realize that his election by the legislature was a pure steal, and they are not going to endorse this steal at the polls."

Byars recalled that during the 1946 campaign he told Ellis Arnall that he would vote for Ed Rivers out of personal loyalty and because he knew that Carmichael simply couldn't win any counties to speak of south of Atlanta. After the election, Arnall admitted that Byars was right.

The Democratic committee in Floyd County is elected by write-in votes. Byars says there is not much interest in the election of committeemen, but he thinks elections have been fairly run. "There never has been a real contest. But then that's true of almost all our elections. For the last several primaries a slate of candidates for the General Assembly has been offered without opposition. I have no knowledge of any irregularities at the polls."

Floyd uses the official numbered ballot. Byars stressed the fact that ballots were numbered on the back and that "this gives a maximum of privacy while permitting a contested ballot to be checked."

About twelve hundred Negroes voted in Floyd last summer. "The best way to handle this issue is to quit talking about it. If the Negroes are not prodded into voting by anti-Negro campaigning, they will not be a decisive factor."

Byars told us that Herman, Roy Harris, and others in the Talmadge machine promised him any job he wanted if he would use his influence to line up support for Herman. He said that Jim Page, Talmadge's campaign manager, was one of the men who high-pressured him at the Henry Grady. He considers it significant that Page has recently disavowed Herman and plans to accept a Thompson appointment.

Everett Millican, state senator, Fifty-second District (Atlanta), interviewed in his office (Gulf Oil Company) in the Hurt Building, July 3

Millican believes that the deceptive and illegal practices discovered in Telfair County were pretty general throughout the state, not only during the general election but during the primary as well. "What's important in Georgia politics," he says, "is not how the people vote but how the votes are counted." He says that not even voting machines guarantee an honest count.

Millican cited the election in Seminole County as reflective of a typical kind of fraud. In that county at one of the main precincts the first ballot box was filled by midday. The managers then removed the box to the rear of the polling place and substituted a new one. That night when the ballots were counted, the second box was counted first. Returns showed a wide margin for Carmichael. Then the returns from the first box were counted, showing a unanimous vote for Gene Talmadge.

In a lot of rural counties, he says, poll managers are usually, purposely, chosen from among the oldest adults in town, and these people are too physically tired by the end of an election day to be careful about the count. Their carelessness, their willingness to be used by the political bosses, and sometimes the out-and-out dishonesty of poll managers combine to make voting in most counties a fixed routine, in which the people are indulged the privilege of voting by bosses who have already counted the ballots.

He minimizes the prevalence of bribery in the legislature. He says there are only a handful of men in each session who can be had with cash, that in fact this last legislature was perhaps the finest in years in terms of the individual character worth of its members. He says special interest groups have a legitimate place in a legislature, that their importance in Georgia politics is determined almost entirely by the size of their campaign contributions, almost none by the number of votes they may be able to control. Most lobbyists are former members of the assembly, lawyers who served for the express purpose of developing sufficient know-how to develop a political practice later. He recalls one such lawyer who manages to make considerable sums each session by working both sides of a controversy. "A few years ago a group of Atlanta jewelers wanted to put a stop to the semiannual street auctions of Jewish jewelers, who were cutting heavily into their Christmas trade. This lawyer-lobbyist agreed to draft a bill for the merchants for a fee of three thousand dollars, which would not have to be paid if the bill did not pass. Then he went to the auctioneers, told them of the pending bill, and said he would work for its defeat for three thousand dollars, the fee to be paid only if the bill was killed. The auctioneers agreed. He couldn't lose."

Millican said that the biggest special interest fight that ever took place in the Georgia legislature was the pipelines versus the railroads in the 1941 session. He estimated that at least seventy lawyers in the assembly were on retainer for the railroads.

Gene Talmadge, he told us, always had the wealthy interests behind him, among them the Callaways and the Candlers. He knows Fred Wilson well and describes him as a "slick politician," perhaps "the closest man in the state to Senator George." In his opinion, however, Wilson did not deserve the editorial blast the *Journal* gave him. He does not consider Wilson "sinister" and says his appointment to the tax commission was thoroughly in order. "It brought him out in the open and puts him in a position so he can't fight the Thompson program behind the scenes."

Millican suggested that Herman Talmadge would not run in the 1958 primary if the South Carolina courts rule out his kind of white primary. He believes Thompson will lick Herman easily, provided no third man offers. In 1950 he expects Gene Cook to run. He likes Cook, whom he regards as a brilliant, personable, and honest man. Cook, he said, was the only man who kept Thompson in the fight after Herman's election by the assembly; it was his advice that convinced Thompson he had a chance to win.

Millican commented at length on his position as a Fulton County representative. The very fact that he comes from Fulton, he said, deprives him of any opportunity for real leadership. He's discriminated against in committee appointments, and it's virtually impossible for anybody from Fulton to be elected Speaker of the House or president pro tem of the Senate. He said several times that he's through with the legislature and does not intend to run again.

Joe Rabun, pastor, McRae Baptist Church, interviewed in the parsonage at McRae, July 7–8

Perhaps more than any other man in the state, Rabun has captured the imagination of those Georgians who hate Talmadge, accept Thompson only as the lesser of two evils, and are sufficiently aware of the state's needs to want to do something constructive and of the political realities to feel impotent.

Rabun surfaced as a statewide figure at last October's convention of Georgia Baptists when he forced through an amendment to a resolution that called for strong denunciation of groups thriving on race prejudice (the Columbians by name and the Klan by implication). Later, some of his sermons on prejudice were quoted in the press, and still later he testified against the white primary at a public hearing. His testimony was published in both Atlanta papers and given wide distribution through religious periodicals. Because of all this, he has emerged as the most articulate minister in the state on the race question and has been suggested as the one man who possibly could present the moral implications of the white primary from the campaign platform.

Rabun's family—his wife and two little girls, one nine, the other seven—were in Maine visiting relatives, and Rabun had invited us to spend the night with him in the parsonage. During the evening and at breakfast the next morning, we got a pretty clear idea of the man. Briefly, he is a man of God, genuinely. He takes himself and his religion very seriously and sincerely believes that he has a mission in a divine plan. "I take my orders from the Lord," he told us. He is a friendly man and a generous one, with a certain kind of nervous humor. Nevertheless, the overall impression is of an austere man who does not welcome contrary opinions. He is tall (more than six feet), lean, and muscular, and given a beard, he would look not unlike a picture of one of the Old Testament prophets in *Hurlbut's Stories from the Bible.* There is the stern face, the exhorting eyes, the same taut body. He is thoroughly self-absorbed, not offensively so, but in a way that makes you think twice before intruding on his thoughts. He is a man who long ago made up his mind as to what's right and what's wrong and is now devoting full time to putting his convictions into action. He is not a good listener. He rarely questioned what we had to say, never picked up on it, and to most of our stories merely responded, "I declare, I declare." Having thus made his polite acknowledgment, he would change the subject to one of his own choosing or bring up an entirely different angle to the subject Jamie or I had introduced. Our net impression was of an uncompromising man, with tremendous spiritual resources, great physical energy, and possessed of a profound sense of his own God-directed mission. We left him full of respect and perhaps a little awed, but we did not feel that we had made a friend. At supper in the McRae Café, Rabun talked of the county and of his congregation. He said Telfair County has been ruled by fear for so long that the people could not trace its source. When we suggested that perhaps the county might make a good laboratory for the study of group psychosis, he agreed. He said he couldn't explain why the people acted as they did. "I guess they're so concerned with making a living, any kind of living, and have been so accustomed to corrupt government." He spoke of the local reaction to the *Journal's* stories on irregularities in the general election in Telfair last November. "Most people didn't say anything at all. A few resented them. Maybe one or two wanted to do something about it. But you won't find anybody in the county who'll talk about those irregularities outside his own home. . . . The grand jury will meet this fall and deplore bootlegging and adjourn." He talked about the vindictiveness, "the just downright meanness," of so many of the people here. "They all use dynamite and seines on fish out of season. Especially the sheriff. Why, it's hard to find a fish in the creek now. Some time ago a man near here built himself a pond and posted his land and stocked the pond with fish. He had a lot of fish, too, and planned to have a lot more. But then some of the boys got mad about his posting his land, and they sneaked in at night and dumped lime in his pond. Wasn't a live fish next morning."

He told, too, of a particular nearby community of farmers—"just roughnecks, worse'n anything I saw overseas. The people are clannish. There's been a lot of intermarrying. They don't mind killing an outsider, and they don't seem to mind killing one of their own any less. They had a fine consolidated school out there. Really a fine school. Then one of the fathers got mad with the way one of the teachers was handling his son, and, next thing we knew, the school was burned down."

Back at the parsonage, Rabun showed us a copy of the June issue of the *Christian Herald* featuring a lead article about him and his fight against race prejudice in Talmadge country. "*Magazine Digest* wants to reprint it. They've asked me for some of my sermons and some more about my background. I'm going to send them what they want, because I think it's important that what I've got to say gets the widest kind of audience." From this article we learned some of the details about Rabun's curious background. He was born in Georgia but ran away from home at sixteen and joined the navy. Undecided on a career, he might have stayed in the navy for life if one thing hadn't happened. At gunnery practice one day the gun backfired, and he saw four friends die. The shock catapulted him into the ministry. When his hitch was up, he went straight to the University of Redlands in California, where he was an all-state athlete, excelling in track, and after four years enrolled in a Baptist seminary in New England, where for a while he roomed with a Negro. After graduation, he preached for several years in Florida, Georgia, and Alabama and then at the outbreak of war enlisted in the Marine Chaplains Corps. He went in with the first wave at Bougainville and Guam, and, all told, his war experiences made him even more conscious of the precious importance of life and dignity. After his discharge, he turned down several lucrative church offers on the west coast, choosing instead to come back to Georgia.

Rabun feels that his church is stronger now than when he came. A lot of the old members have stopped coming altogether (Miss Mitt and the rest of the Talmadge family came only once, on a Sunday when Rabun was preaching elsewhere and the guest preacher spoke comfortably of life hereafter), but his realistic sermons have attracted almost as many new members. He doesn't have the support of all his deacons, but those who are for him are more active in the church than ever before. "The church is more cohesive, more spirited, more aware now than it ever was."

Rabun saw Gene Talmadge twice before his death. The first time Gene was sick and couldn't talk. On the second visit, Gene talked for more than an hour. "I mostly listened," Rabun said. "He told me he thought I was sincere in my attitude toward the Negro, but he warned me against being drawn in by 'them Atlanta liberals.' He said there was a bunch of people in Atlanta who make their living out of agitating for reforms. 'They're a bunch of hypocrites,' he said. 'You watch out for 'em.'" Gene also told him that the Negro ranked fifth among the world's "five races—always had and always would—and nothing nobody can do will make them any better." When Rabun asked him to explain George Washington Carver, Gene said, "Hell, I happen to know that white men discovered all that stuff long before Carver thought about it." About Booker T. Washington: "A freak and a phony. Sonofabitch died a peeping tom."

Rabun did not come to McRae until last September, two months after the primary. It's his impression, however, that no Negroes voted in the McRae precinct, although a few may have voted elsewhere in the county. He said the people have a savage devotion to "Ole Gene" but generally do not think so much of Herman, who left the county as a small boy. The county is entirely run by Talmadge stalwarts—"the lawyer, Mann; Whaley, the state representative; Collins, the ordinary and commissioner; and Walker, the sheriff." Rabun went on to say that Talmadge poured a lot of money into the county when he was governor, and this, along with abundant and carefully directed patronage, has given him and his crowd a tenacious hold. "Walker the sheriff is a brother of the Walker of Millen who was one of the two illiterates in the state Senate this last session. The sheriff has a long record of sex offenses and bootlegging. His tie to the county underworld was brought out in court last fall when one of the bootleggers said, 'The only reason I'm being tried for bootlegging is that I stopped paying off Walker.'"

Rabun sees the South as the battleground for democracy. "America is the last strong democracy in the world," he explained. "Its enemies are not the communists or foreigners but our native fascists. When they seek to destroy America, they look for America's weakest spot, and our most vulnerable spot is the South. This last business, Herman's taking the governorship by force and the agitation for a white primary, was nothing but fascism. And the only way to beat it is through a moral militance on the part of the people. That's why the election next year is so terribly important. If we can't save democracy in Georgia, then democracy is lost in America."

Rabun is opposed to the closed shop and for that reason doesn't know how he would have stood on the antilabor bills that passed the 1947 assembly. "I don't like the closed shop because it restricts the worker's freedom of choice. I believe in unionization, though, and I recognize a general conspiracy to stop it in the South. . . . I guess I'm really opposed to pressure groups of any kind. What we've got to learn to do is to put the general welfare first and our own selfish interests last."

Rabun hasn't developed much confidence in Thompson yet. He didn't like his "pussyfooting" around with the white primary bill, and he doesn't like the Rivers influence. He feels strongly that the moral issues should be spelled out in the next campaign, and he doesn't believe Thompson is the man who will do it. We asked him if he'd thought about running as a third man in the race, even if his intent would be to pull out just before the primary and throw his support to Thompson. He said yes, he'd considered it. Several people had suggested it to him. "I'm no politician," he said. "But if I thought it was my duty to run for governor, I'd do it, the same way Jesus walked to Jerusalem, even though I knew it would mean suicide. I'd walk the plank if I thought the Lord wanted me to."

If he did run, he said further, he wouldn't mention personalities once. "They could say anything and ask everything they want to about me, but they wouldn't get any answers. I'd talk strictly about politics and the duty of Christians in politics. I'd talk about the things we need in Georgia and how we ought to go about getting them—like developing local markets for our cantaloupes. I wouldn't even mention Herman's name or Thompson's name." Nor would he make any promises of patronage. "I'd say very plainly that anybody who voted for me was voting because he thought I was the best man and because he wanted to see the Lord's work done in the capitol. I'd tell 'em that I wasn't promising anything to anybody, that state jobs would go to the people who could best do them and that road contracts would go to the lowest bidders, with no money to middle men."

At this point Rabun reminded us that politicians were not altogether unknown in his family. One of his ancestors was governor of Georgia back in the 1800s. A more recent relative is the only man who ever defeated Roy Harris for the state legislature before his dramatic repudiation in Augusta last year.

Rabun is a strong prohibitionist. He read us his rough manuscript for two articles he's doing for the *Christian Index,* in one of which he preaches against smoking and drinking as two of the things "that make us less able to do the Lord's work." Later he pointed to an ad in the local paper for the Brewers' Association, saying, "There ought to be a law against it." Although he was kind enough not to reproach me, he looked pained every time I lit a cigarette.

Clearly, were Rabun to run for governor, he could hardly expect to find favor with the liquor interests. Furthermore, he would probably be a severe, uncompromising man in the governor's chair, whose impatience with human frailty could hardly endear him to the average flawed citizen. At one point he said that if elected governor he would "take my orders from the Lord," which might make it rough indeed for his staff. He's adamantly opposed to fighting fire with fire and says he was worried about Thompson before he vetoed the white primary bill for fear that Thompson would sign it on grounds of political expediency. "It's like the Bible says—you've got to be wise as a serpent and gentle as a dove."

It's not to be assumed from this that Rabun is without personal magnetism. Having been born in Georgia and lived close to the earth, and sometimes close to the sea, he speaks simply and has a natural gift for imagery. He talks in phrases and in a cadence familiar to churchgoers; he would probably sound affected only were he to lose all identity with the ministry. At one point, when he thought we might be in danger of sinking into pessimism, he said that we should not be discouraged because things looked blackest now. "A mudflat always stinks worse when the tide is lowest. And yet the tide always comes back and the water covers the stench, and there's fresh fish to be caught." He is almost idolatrous of Franklin Roosevelt and calls Henry Wallace a great man. He speaks often of "fascists," "reactionaries," "special interest groups," "the people," sometimes as if he's dipped a bit too often into the pages of the *New Republic.* His appeal is likely to be stronger from the pulpit—or the platform—than from an easy chair in his living room.

Rabun spent more than an hour showing us his war souvenirs. As a chaplain he had ample opportunity to collect them—Japanese souvenirs in Guam and tourist items from the Mediterranean. Many of them—a Spanish revolver, a Samurai sword—had been recovered from dead marines, and sometimes his voice was heavy with sorrow. His war experiences have scarred him. He believes intensely that he must do everything he can personally to change the world into the sort of place the war dead would have wanted. Though he makes no attempt to hide his feelings, he never sounds maudlin or sentimental. Indeed, Rabun is something of a rarity—a man who can wear his heart on his sleeve as unself-consciously as a combat veteran wears a service stripe.

George L. Smith II, state representative, Emanuel County; Speaker pro tem of the House, interviewed in his law office in Swainsboro, July 8

The first time Smith ran for state representative, he spent about a thousand dollars and led the ticket by seven hundred votes. During this last campaign for the House and for Speaker pro tem, he spent more money than he received for his services. He says he has learned a lot about the mechanics of getting elected, but he remembers buying only one vote. On that occasion he got a drink of liquor for a boy of nineteen who had obtained the ballot of his father, who had passed out drunk.

Smith favors the white primary bill and a strong registration bill. He thinks the same issues will dominate the campaign next summer. He said several times that the county unit system "is mighty good for us country boys" and that it is idiotic to support any bill aimed at modifying it. He thinks that some representatives who oppose extending it into the general election—Alec Tuten of Appling, for instance—will be beaten.

Members of the county Democratic committee are elected from each militia district and from the county at large. Specific slates are offered, "and there is some competition." On Smith's recommendation, the county has adopted the real Australian ballot. Although he thinks it a good law and should be made uniform throughout the state, he has reservations about it. He doesn't see how you can eliminate the number "without making it easier to stuff the box." Elections in Emanuel are run pretty fairly, he told us. Later in our conversation, however, he said that in some militia districts it doesn't matter how the votes are cast "but how they're counted." In one of his early races, he said, he was told two weeks before the election that his opponent would get so many votes and he would get so many. When the returns were reported, this prediction turned out to be precisely correct. Since then, he's learned that you can always find out in advance what the count is going to be in that district.

About nine hundred Negroes voted in the primary, about twenty-five for Rivers and the rest for Carmichael. "There was no violence or intimidation. The people of Emanuel County believe in law and order." The Klan is unknown.

Smith spoke warmly and enthusiastically about Fred Hand as a prospect for governor; he has the ability and the personality. "Herman will be the candidate against Thompson in 1948 and will win." Roy Harris would make a fine governor and "would have been governor now had it not been for Arnall's double-dealing." When he first went to the legislature, he'd heard the usual talk about Harris and had watched him closely. He found him to be "a straight shooter" and the best-informed man about everything to do with state government. He thinks that Arnall's "brilliant program" was in fact Harris's brainchild.

Smith is about thirty-four, plump, baby faced, pug nosed, and amiable. He is close to Herman and has been present at most strategy meetings of the Talmadge high command. Some capitol observers have tagged him as the "payoff man" on the night of Herman's election.

A bit petulantly, Smith says that Thompson, Bill Dean, and Charlie Gowen were in on the planning of the white primary bill as well as the reregistration bill and that they approved both bills as drawn. "The two most obnoxious features of the reregistration bill—the registration fee and the biennial provision—were proposed by Thompson."

He described Fred Wilson as "a very slick guy—one of the most influential of the capitol lobbyists." Ed Rivers, he said, is on the Power Company payroll "at twelve thousand dollars a year."

He described a unique practice at one election in Johnson County a few years ago. It seems that the leaders of the strongest faction had come to suspect that in previous elections many of the voters they thought they'd bought had in fact double-crossed them at the polls. To guard against this in the future, and to make sure they got value received, they arranged with the election managers to require that, instead of marking his ballot, a voter cut out with a razor blade the name of his preference. "A voter who'd cut out the name of the machine candidate would drop his ballot in the box, then present 'the coupon' to a payoff man and receive his dollar. I know this was the approved practice during at least one election over there."

As evidence of occasional irregularities in his own county, Smith told us that he and several others had just enjoined one of the members of the county executive committee after finding that he had been falsifying returns. "Of course, you talk to some of my opposition and they'll tell you we're trying to get rid of him just so we can take over control of the committee."

Smith, who loves politics so much he says his only ambition is "to stay in the House as long as the people will send me," had sharp comments for some of his colleagues. He regards Dick Kenyon as something of a fanatic. "He takes himself too seriously. He'll beat Howard Overby next year only if a thousand niggers vote." He said that Tom Morgan, who ran against him for Speaker pro tem, lied lavishly about him. "For a man who likes to brag about his Christian upbringing and his career with the Boy Scouts, he pulled some of the dirtiest campaign tricks this side of Harlem." He considers Myer Goldberg totally insincere and Jake Joel something of a joke. "Why, we used to tell Charlie Gowen that the only thing we Talmadge people need to beat a bill was to get either Myer or Jake to speak for it." Bob Elliott, he says, is "very able" but indifferent to friendship. He does not believe that Walter Harrison could ever be elected Speaker but that Charlie Gowen might if Thompson were to win in 1948. He admires Herschel Lovett and believes he stands a good chance of being elected to Congress. "That guy Daniel [Senator R. G. Daniel, a strong Thompson man] is stupid, really stupid. You know what the sonofabitch is doing now? He's calling on all the contractors in the state—even Bull Blalock [a loyal Talmadge man]—and telling them that he can get them state business for a 10 percent commission."

Smith does not believe that the tax commission, of which he is a member, is going to recommend a sales tax. "There are too many people on it just stubbornly opposed, like Everett Millican." He's not confident that the commission will make recommendations of any kind. "It would have been fine if we could have brought in a few experts from the outside. But you let the boys know these tax recommendations were made by the Brookings Institute, they'd never pass 'em. They just don't like the sound or smell of outside interference."

Walter Harrison, state representative, Jenkins County, interviewed in his office in Millen, July 8

We found Walter Harrison in his real estate office. In this office he also works as mayor of Millen, lends money, sells property, makes bonds, manages a fertilizer plant, and transacts business for the Georgia Rural Electric Association, of which he is president. Across the street is the office of the *Millen News,* which he edits, and just down the street is the

bank, of which he is part owner. His secretary, who cataloged some of his activities for us while we waited, couldn't
"at the moment" remember what all else Mr. Harrison did
for a living, but she said his other enterprises were just
enough to match his almost inexhaustible energy.

Harrison talked with us only briefly. He greeted us
heartily, said he was very busy but that he didn't want to
leave in the rain and would be "delighted" to talk until it
stopped. It's not quite possible to describe Harrison to anyone who hasn't seen him in action. He's a giant of a man,
several inches taller than six feet, and must weigh close
to two hundred pounds. He's blond and bald. His skin is
a healthy pink; he looked as if he'd just stepped out of a
shower, still glowing from a towel rub. He talks loudly, in a
dialect so thick that if you closed your eyes it would be easy
to imagine him as an end man in a minstrel show. He called
us "big boys," referred to some of his clients as "yeller-
hammers," and in a telephone conversation told a man,
"Don't be scared to get a little dew on yo' feet." He never
halts for words. The words come fluently and sometimes
too easily. He impresses you as a man of tremendous self-
esteem (not necessarily egocentric), as a man enchanted
with the sound of his own voice and proud of the lungs that
can sustain it. He seems to have a ready opinion about everything. He very often talks nonsense, but whatever is on
his mind is conveyed so glibly and in tones of such fierce
conviction that most people find it hard to take exception
until they've had a chance to reflect.

Harrison is proud of Jenkins County. Politics are clean,
and the Democratic executive committee is made up of the
most respected and honest men in town. "If we ever get a
lemon on it, we don't waste any time giving him the boot."
Members are elected by write-in. No slate is offered, "but we
see to it that the best men are elected."

About the Negro: "People have got to realize that the
Negro ain't altogether responsible for what's happened to

him. During the war our government took 'em in the army and had to treat 'em like white men, because the constitution says it must. Then they sent 'em over to these foreign countries, where the people don't understand our southern ideals. Now they're back, and they want to be treated like equals. Couple a months ago a Negro soldier attacked two white women, and when they caught him they found in his wallet some pictures of him embracin' some English girls. Well, that's bad, and the nigger's got to understand that he can have opportunities and vote and go to school just like white people but that he can't go to bed with 'em." He pointed to a clipping from the *Charleston News and Courier,* sent him by an acquaintance—an editorial quoting the NAACP's new policy to break down school segregation. "That damn organization's its own worst enemy, coming out with all this damn foolishness."

He went on: "Our election laws are all right just like they are. They just need to be enforced. This white primary bill. That was an *iniquitous* bill. All we need is stronger educational qualifications for voting. You get stronger educational qualifications, and you'll disfranchise about 90 percent of your niggers and 25 percent of your whites. Matter of fact, I believe if you just cut out all this shouting about the nigger, you wouldn't have more'n a dozen of 'em voting in this county anyway—and not many more in the whole state. The Talmadge boys are shouting 'nigger, nigger' stronger and stronger in every issue of the *Statesman.* Now, that's a disgraceful paper. I don't see how any man who puts out that kind of trash can think he's making any contribution to Georgia. Some of the people in this county were pretty excited about me and my voting against the white primary bill. Now they're beginning to settle down, even the strongest Talmadge man in the county. He came in my office last week. Wanted to borrow some money. I said, 'Henry, didn't think you'd be speaking to me again, after what I did about the white primary.' He looked a little sheepish and said,

'Aw shucks, Walter, I know you'd have been for a white primary if Thompson had first crack at it.' I asked him, I said,
'Henry, you ever read that bill?' He said no, 'n I said, 'Well,
Henry, you come 'round some time this fall when it's talkin'
weather and we'll read that bill together.' Even old Henry's
coming 'round now. I lent him some money."

Harrison is convinced that the Georgia Power Company
has tried to run the state government, but he's "not all clear
how it does it." He believes the *Journal* was justified in its
editorial attack on Fred Wilson. "Wilson's doing for the
Power Company just what Shumacker used to do. He's very
valuable to the Power Company, havin' such a convenient
interest in the Henry Grady Hotel. He always sees that the
Speaker of the House gets his room free, usually takes care
of the president of the Senate, and I know last year he took
care of most of the committee chairmen—the important
committee chairmen, leastwise. Wilson, they say, usually
can name the Speaker of the House and the president of the
Senate. That's how strong he is." He repeated M. E. Thompson's rationale for putting Wilson on the tax commission.
"Thompson said, 'Walter, I want a man like Fred Wilson in
a spot where I can watch him.'

"One of the worst things I know about the Power Company
is its tie-in with the Georgia Municipal League through Zach
Arnold. Zach's been on retainer for the company for thirty-
five years, and just recently he got some kind of commen-
dation from them for his work with the league. A man can't
serve two masters. All Arnold's doing is using the league to
help the Power Company get so many city franchises that
when Clark Hill is built, it can tell the government it doesn't
need to build transmission lines." As evidence of the company's influence he cited the battle in 1945 to amend the
proposed constitution so that power-generating and gas-
distributing facilities would be included among the civic
projects for which revenue anticipation certificates could be
authorized. Roy Harris fought the amendment with every-

thing he had, "but we beat him to a pulp." He commented further that Arnold never once intervened on behalf of the municipalities but instead favored the Power Company's position.

Harrison said he didn't have much trouble with Wingate last session, but in 1945 Wingate got irked with him when he insisted on amending his bill to exempt farmers from the gasoline tax. "That gasoline tax is pretty big. You reduce it many places, and you won't have much revenue left. That's why I'm for taxing the airlines. That bill [to tax aviation gasoline] hurt me a little. I hated to have to vote for it, 'cause Wiley Moore is one of my best friends and I knew that, being a stockholder in Eastern Airlines, he wanted Eastern exempted." He paused and then added, as if the thought had occurred to him for the first time: "Might be a good thing, though, to reduce the gasoline tax if we had a real sales tax."

Harrison is a strong prohibitionist and hates the liquor industry. He told of a local election some time ago during the Civilian Conservation Corps (CCC) days when liquor agents paid CCC boys so much a head—"paid it right out of their overcoat pockets right there in front of the polls. I beat 'em by fourteen votes, though, by going over to a meeting of the Woman's Club, getting the floor, and tellin' those ladies that they were about to let the county go wet just because they were meeting too long."

Norman Chalker, editor, *Sylvania Telephone*, interviewed in his office in Sylvania, July 8

Screven County is traditionally pro-Talmadge, but factional lines are not too sharply drawn in the race for representative. Elliott Hagan, the current representative, is known to be anti-Talmadge but is generally popular. "He's pretty shrewd. He knows how to talk to people and butter 'em up."

Chalker thinks very few people in the county are aware of Hagan's record this past session; most of them don't know that he voted against the white primary bill. Chalker describes Hagan as "technically" a farmer, "but he's doing about what he's always done—as little as possible."

Chalker believes that elections in the county are held as orderly and as honestly as they can be. The executive committee is about evenly divided, or was last spring at the time of the Thompson convention. Thompson got certified by fourteen members, although later in a meeting, which only nine members attended, all but one voted to rule the delegation unauthorized. About four hundred Negroes voted in the primary. Screven's population is about 57 percent Negro. There were no incidents at the polls and no purging of the registration list.

Shortly after Herman had taken the governor's chair, some citizens met in a mass meeting—"not very mass"—and asked the legislature to adjourn. Herman's record this past winter, however, has lost him very few votes in Screven.

Chalker has seen no sign of Klan activity and no sign of outside interference in local elections. Screven uses the numbered ballot. The Farm Bureau is very active, but in farm matters only. The county has no organization devoted to political issues.

Leodel Coleman, Jim Coleman, and Worth MacDougald, interviewed in the office of the *Statesboro Herald*, July 8

Interest in the election of representatives is usually high in Bulloch County, but unless the issues are clearly drawn campaigns are likely to be fought out on the strength of personality. L. M. Mallard, the elder of the two representatives, is considered a wise politician who never clearly identifies himself with either faction. "He votes pretty much as he pleases and manages to make it all right with the people back home." He is now thought of as an anti-Talmadge man, having voted against Herman. According to Leodel, Johnson is "a young squirt." He's no more than twenty-eight, and his inexperience has worked against him. The story is that he went to the legislature pledged to carry out the wishes of twelve veterans who'd backed him, yet he voted against their expressed will by supporting Herman. Johnson did not go to Atlanta as a Talmadge man, but if he had not been so "bumptious" his vote for Herman might have been to his credit, for Gene carried Bulloch County by about four hundred votes. (The leading political figure here is the county ordinary, a respected Talmadge man.) As it is, practically everybody is displeased with him.

The Colemans do not think outside interests have ever had much to do with local elections. Leodel explained that the county is a relatively rich one. No one man has any dominant wealth or power, but, rather, there are about six rich farmers, each with an equal number of followers and about evenly divided in their political interests. If any corporation sought to use any one of the six to advance its interests, at least one of the other five could be depended on to expose him.

A League of Women Voters chapter has just been organized in Bulloch. It now has about fifty-two members, all anti-Talmadge. Leodel expects great things of the league, for women here have always taken a strong interest in politics. It was their votes and their work, he says, that threw the county to Ellis Arnall in 1942.

The Farm Bureau is also active politically, as might be expected in a county where farmers predominate. (Bulloch industries employ no more than eighty workers, most of them in a peanut-processing plant.) Not surprisingly, there has been no hint of unionization, although Jim Coleman "wished to hell the AFL or CIO would organize the farmers." He said that when he was in Washington recently, he was amazed to learn that some members of the Georgia congressional delegation took seriously the possibility that H. L. Wingate might be elected to succeed Senator Walter George.

Voters here have been generally passive toward the proposal for a sales tax. The white primary issue, all three agreed, had only served to strengthen factional lines; the Colemans do not believe that Herman's coup lost him a single vote. They say that "without doubt" the Georgia Power Company and other corporations in Atlanta run the state under the existing political system. Nevertheless, they maintain that "things would be much worse" if it were not for the county unit system, which they see as the only defense against "city machines."

The Democratic executive committee is elected informally by write-in. The county uses the numbered ballot. Bulloch County is small enough and cohesive enough for everybody to know everybody else. For this reason, the Colemans think it would be difficult for any small clique to manage elections to suit themselves. At the same time, they say, there is much informality about the counting of votes, the counters usually being recruited from "anybody who happens by."

Out of a total electorate of 8,000, about 960 Negroes voted in last July's primary. The Negro doctor in the area, a man named Van Buren, is understood to have "sold out to Talmadge."

R. W. Gadsden, Negro educator, interviewed at his home in Savannah, July 10

Dr. Gadsden was principal and superintendent of two Negro elementary schools in Savannah for more than twenty-five years. He's retired now and "a little undecided about what to do with my time." He serves on a local interracial commission and on a special committee set up by Mayor John Kennedy to advise him on Negro affairs.

Dr. Gadsden spoke mostly of the efforts taken to give Negroes a participating role in local politics. He said this effort began two years ago by a group of Negro leaders and white friends, in anticipation of the Primus King decision. Up until that time, since 1910, Negroes had the right to vote only in special elections and bond elections. Consequently, the Negro registration list never carried more than nine hundred names. But as the result of an intense registration campaign, the list had grown to nineteen thousand before last July's primary. Of these, only about nine thousand voted, the others being kept from the polls by the slowdown tactics of the election managers.

To build their registration list, Negroes first had to hurdle active opposition from the tax commissioner, an administration man. (In Savannah the "administration" is the name for the old-line political machine that was repudiated in the 1946 primary.) For a while, by making it inconvenient for Negroes to register generally, and requiring them to pay unlawful property taxes in particular, the tax commissioner was able to keep Negro registration at a standstill. The strongest Negro leader, however, John McGlockton of the NAACP, decided to bring suit against the commissioner, having as evidence the letters written to Negroes demanding that they pay certain illegal taxes before being allowed to register. This suit was filed in February with the federal district court before Judge Frank Scarlett, a man known to be friendly to the Negro. Although the suit was not settled until May, at which time the tax commissioner was ordered to return all taxes collected from Negroes, Scarlett forced the commissioner to open up all the books immediately, and from that time on the Negroes had no trouble. In fact, the commissioner proceeded to make it easier for them by setting up additional registration desks. When it was established that Negroes were registering "in droves," white people accelerated their own campaign to bring out the vote. As a result, the total registration list, which theretofore had never been more than sixteen thousand, soared to more than eighty thousand.

The Negroes were not entirely unanimous in their support of the Citizens' Progressive League (CPL). Many of them derived their living from the boledo (bug) racket and felt that their own interests lay with the administration. Curiously, some of the most vocal administration supporters—what few there were—were Negro ministers. This anti-CPL following, however, was so small by the time of the election as to be almost negligible. Those Negroes who did vote administration have since suffered reprisals from the hands of their former bosses—loss of jobs, one or two beatings. It seems that they had made lavish promises to their bosses to deliver the Negro vote and suffered badly when they did not. The only other violence connected with the election came when one of the disgruntled Negroes tried to beat up three other Negroes, one of them a Baptist preacher.

Gadsden said that on election day voting went with frustrating slowness at the Negro precincts. Part of this was due to the Negroes' unfamiliarity with the voting process, but most of it was attributable to the behavior of hostile election managers. The managers would refuse to pass out more than one ballot at a time and would keep pro-CPL Negroes in the polls as long as ten or fifteen minutes apiece. Some Negroes were at the polls as early as five o'clock in the morning and stayed until the polls closed, only to leave without having voted at all. Although some effort was made to get Judge Scarlett to demand that the election lines be sped up, it was too late to do anything effective. In a city election, held three or four months later, the Negroes were much more experienced and the election managers more tolerant, and Negroes voted almost as fast as whites.

Gadsden said that as soon as the nine thousand Negroes were registered, both the administration and the CPL began to make overtures for the Negro vote. The Negro majority was unsympathetic to the administration, their attitude being that the administration had had twenty-five years in office and if they hadn't been able to do anything for the Negroes in that length of time, they probably wouldn't be able to do anything for them if reelected. With the CPL, the Negroes bargained, principally for these things: twenty Negro policemen, Negro matrons in the city jail, paved roads through the Negro community, more streetlights, better schools, and better health facilities. On the whole the Negroes of Savannah are pleased with what the CPL has delivered—nine Negro policemen, two Negro matrons and a Negro jail attendant, a paved road to the cemetery. They have faith in the CPL. They believe that in time the other things will come.

Malberry Smith, state representative, Chatham County, interviewed in his office (Hutch, Morris, Harrison, & Smith) in Savannah, July 10

Smith is considered the most promising young man in Savannah politics. A graduate of Columbia College and the Columbia University Law School, one of a group of veterans who led the movement "to throw the rascals out," and the junior partner in the prestigious law firm from whose offices the Citizens' Progressive League was spawned, he led the ticket for the General Assembly in the last election.

Rather than leading with our usual questions, we asked Smith to tell us about the political picture in Savannah, especially as he found it when he came back from navy duty two years ago. He first gave us a bit of background. Savannah politics, he said, had been "a closed corporation" for many, many years. In all those years there had been only one serious threat to the supremacy of the "administration." That came in 1938 and grew out of a citizens' uprising that almost succeeded and proved valuable for what it taught leaders of last year's CPL victory.

For most of this century, certain identifiable economic interests in Savannah and Chatham County have worked through several agencies to maintain effective control of city and county politics. These interests are Union Bag, the world's largest pulp and paper company; the Citizens and Southern Bank; the Savannah Bank and Trust Company; and the Savannah Transit Company. These four, Smith said, work through the Industrial Council and the Chamber of Commerce and can pretty much determine whether any proposed industry can get under way. He cited several instances where new industries were blocked. Furthermore, these same economic interests have been able to control politics through a number of hired lawyers. John Bouhan of the firm of Abrahams, Bouhan, and Lawrence, chairman of the old Democratic executive committee, is the top lawyer for these interests and until last year had reigned over all aspects of city politics. His position has been such that he could almost make or break any lawyer in town by giving business or taking it away. Bouhan engineered many deals that proved costly to taxpayers and profitable for his clients.

Several factors led to the assault on the old guard.

First, the dissatisfaction that had been heating up for several years was brought to a boil after the war with the return of a number of idealistic, energetic, and "unencumbered" GIs; second, the law firm of Hutch, Morris, Harrison, and Smith had been in contention with the administration and lost business because of it; and third, the tremendous increase in voter registration among both Negroes and whites was interpreted as a heartening sign that the administration's control was slipping.

The first meetings were held in the library of the Hutch law firm and were attended by only a few men. Out of these meetings came organization of the Citizens' Progressive League and a statement of purpose: to overthrow the ad-

ministration and send a new slate of legislators to Atlanta.
A drive for supporters was launched at a series of public
meetings.

The CPL anticipated efforts by Bouhan to steal the election and prepared for them. Smith and his friends launched
a concerted training program for precinct captains; among
other things, captains were warned against accepting Coca-
Colas from the enemy's poll watchers, for in times past the
administration's agents had been known to slug Coca-Colas
with croton oil. (Smith also recalled that several years ago
one of the poll watchers had eaten enough of an opponent's
ballots to win a close count.) At the same time, they enjoined
Bouhan from packing the polls with managers of his own
choosing and also from holding a private count of the returns. (In the courtroom, when other words failed him, Bouhan told Judge Atkinson, a former law partner, "Hell, Judge,
I'm only trying to run things the way you used to." Atkinson
twirled his gavel; said, "Times have changed"; and issued
the restraining order.)

Smith said that they had been very careful to keep state
politics out of the Savannah elections. In fact, Bouhan was
ardently disliked by the Talmadge crowd, and much of
CPL's strength came from it. Toward the end of the campaign the administration, through the boledo racketeers,
spread the rumor in the Negro community that CPL was
endorsing Talmadge. CPL effectively squelched this rumor
by running half-page ads in the *Savannah Morning News and
Press* (papers, owned by the C&S Bank, that editorialized
against CPL) and over local radio.

Smith does not feel that the CPL position is secure yet and
won't be until it's won the county elections. At the moment
its strength is grounded in Savannah proper. Smith fears
that the Chatham County delegation to the General Assembly may have lost favor in outlying precincts. It introduced
a bill to extend the city limits but failed to get it passed,
thanks to the lobbying against it by agents of the repudiated

administration. The big industrial interests will continue to fight CPL, "knowing that we tried to bring them within the city's tax limits." Also, somewhat perversely, "the average guy may now be a bit less impressed with our know-how, figuring that if we'd been smarter and more experienced— as experienced, say, as the men we licked—we could have got the bill passed."

Captain Frank Spencer, master pilot of the Savannah Bar Pilots Association, interviewed at lunch in the Savannah Hotel, July 10

Captain Spencer is perhaps the best white friend Savannah Negroes have. He meets with them and advises them and has done much to help them increase voter registration from nine hundred to nineteen thousand in the past two years. His view is that the Negro will have to wield real political power if he is to get the police protection, the schools, and the paved streets he wants. This view has been vindicated, he says, by the fact that both factions courted the Negro vote in the last two elections.

He is delighted with the nine Negro policemen and thinks they will prove an asset to the entire community.

Spencer said there were two really outstanding Negro leaders: Gibson, the Baptist preacher, and Gadsden, a scholar and recently retired schoolteacher. McGlockton, the man mostly responsible for getting Negroes out to register, has a record for receiving stolen goods or some such charge. The Talmadge people are exploiting this fact, and Spencer has urged the Negroes to remove him from his position with the Citizens' Progressive League. So far this has not been done.

He deplored the fact that not a single white minister except for George Clary Sr. will meet with Negro groups. And it has been exceedingly difficult to bring young people together for interracial meetings. At the one meeting held, not one of the twenty white youths present had any suggestion, whereas half a dozen Negro youths came up with valuable suggestions.

Spencer said he never went to college but got a good education during his seventeen years at sea before settling down at his pilot job. He spoke warmly of Denmark as a truly Christian, cooperative democracy and described conditions in Savannah as lamentable by contrast. "Savannah's slums are the worst in the world," he said. We are an ignorant people, he thinks, "because the trinity of church, school, and home has failed its educational job." The best thing that can be done in the immediate situation is to get superior men to offer for public service, but the long-range job must be centered on education.

Although he gets terribly put out with the Rotarians, he maintains his interest because they have good speakers occasionally. Some of his former friends consider him a "nigger lover." It's no secret, he said, that he cares about Negroes and wants to see their lot improved. It was with real pride that he told how fine the Negroes were who worked with his towing company and how he had managed to pay them wages equal to those paid whites for the same kind of work.

John J. Sullivan, Savannah city alderman, CPL leader, interviewed in his office in Savannah, July 10

Sullivan says the CPL is now suffering from a few "honest mistakes" but is confident it can redeem itself before the next election. Among these mistakes is the purchase of seven hundred parking meters at $80 apiece, a figure Savannah people think too high, knowing that other vendors offered meters at $70. He explained that the city council bought these higher-priced meters because "it was a better business proposition." That particular company was alone in offering to set up meters with no initial cost to the city other than the cost of installation, the meters themselves to be paid for out of the revenue as it was earned. That company also was the only bidder to agree to make free repairs for the first year. "Installation cost only $1.50 per meter, and I figure the city will get about $50,000 in increased revenue from the meters this year. The average guy doesn't understand or appreciate this, though."

The CPL may have made another mistake in revoking a certain whiskey license without cause. "We did revoke it without cause," Sullivan said. "Maybe the mistake we made was that we revoked it without explanation. The license was revoked because we learned that this particular dealer was operating as both wholesaler and retailer and consequently underselling independent package stores. The council interpreted the law as giving us the right to revoke without cause, something the whiskey dealer challenged in superior court, which granted him a restraining order." The case is soon to be decided by the state supreme court, and Sullivan feels that the high court will reverse the ruling. He said further that when the council explains why the license was revoked—"as we will at the proper time"—the people will accept it.

Chatham uses the secret ballot—perforated number and all—but Sullivan knows that it has been abused in times past. It's possible, as Smith had pointed out to us earlier, for one man to drop in a blank sheet of paper instead of his ballot (provided he has a careless election manager who's not looking) and sell his blank ballot on the outside. The man on the outside can then mark the ballot as he likes and bargain with another voter to substitute it for his own. The second voter then deposits the marked ballot, returns to the payoff man, and gives him his blank ballot in exchange for cash. The process can thus go on indefinitely, and, except for the first ballot, which was replaced by a blank sheet of paper, there can be no check on how many ballots were bought all told.

Sullivan repeated what we had heard before, that Union Bag had spent fifty thousand dollars in lobbying fees getting the local extension bill defeated in the General Assembly.

Sullivan thinks people are generally pleased with the nine Negroes on the police force. He's now trying to increase the number to twelve.

Charles Gowen, state representative, Glynn County, interviewed in his office in Brunswick, July 11

Gowen believes that "the people with the money" control Georgia, and since the money is in Atlanta, this means that, county unit system or no county unit system, Atlanta and its corporate wealth run the state government. He mentioned "the powerful few"—Georgia Power, the railroads (though not so much as formerly), Coca-Cola, and the pipelines. He said there was no doubt that Fred Wilson was fixer for the Power Company but that Wilson had been so careful to stay in the background, and to cover his tracks, that perhaps nobody but Wilson himself knew how strong his influence was or in what directions he applied it. He recalled that during his first term in the legislature in 1939, when the Power Company was being investigated by the Securities and Exchange Commission (SEC), the Henry Grady Hotel gave free rooms to many state legislators, but it was never clearly established that the hotel management did so for political purposes, since it also regularly provided free rooms to all manner of visiting celebrities, "including Mae West." Gowen suggested that the Wilson legend may have been cultivated by Wilson himself. "If Wilson gets on the phone and calls a representative, the mention of his name may be enough. The representative automatically thinks, 'Hell, I'm talking with the most powerful man in Georgia. I better do what he says.'"

Gowen said that Wilson patently was one of the most effective lobbyists in the business, even though he almost never showed "hand or head" around the state capitol. Others who also worked offstage and were nearly as influential, he said, are Henry Troutman and Hughes Spalding. The most visible lobbyists—"Hamp McWhorter, Rembert Marshall, Phil Alston"—aren't so effective. He doesn't believe lowering the registration fee for lobbyists would materially help things; "the best ones never work around the legislature anyway." Reflecting a moment, he added that Ted Forbes of the Cotton Manufacturers Association "is very effective," but he neglected to tell us whether Forbes should be grouped with the visible or invisible hands.

Gowen estimates total costs of all three campaigns last summer at $450,000. "If you consider the money spent at the local level that didn't come through campaign headquarters, the figure would probably be nearer $750,000," he said. "That kind of money doesn't come from preachers, either."

Glynn County voted fourteen hundred Negroes in the last primary. After the Primus King decision, and with the anticipation of an enlarged Negro vote, registration in the county had shot from thirty-five hundred to nearly twelve thousand just before the last primary. About fourteen hundred Negroes turned out at the polls, without incident. Gowen believes that Talmadge will cry "nigger, nigger" as long as he can, even if the Supreme Court should rule the South Carolina white primary law unconstitutional. Glynn County, though, will stay anti-Talmadge. Gowen looks to the Negro vote for constructive reforms in political alliances and campaign rhetoric. "Once these local boys get convinced Negroes are going to vote, they'll be mighty careful to be friendly with Negroes. They won't be so likely to take orders from Herman on statewide elections, for fear of jeopardizing their standing in the colored communities. More than that, you can expect increased participation in county elections—for instance, more Negroes voted in a county election a couple of months before the state primary last year—and this will make it harder and harder for the corporations in Atlanta to control the county votes. That way, we may be able to break this present system." He is optimistic that after the Supreme Court decision on the South Carolina case, Thompson will be encouraged to make "a healthy sort of statement, something to the effect that 'the federal government has ruled that Negroes can vote in our primaries, and I intend to see that they do without discrimination.'"

Gowen has certain reservations about the wisdom of a sales tax or the need for one. "But if we do have one, I hope we have one without exemptions. A sales tax is not a tax based on ability to pay, not intended to be. I think if we put a tax on any article, we ought to put it on all. The only justification for a sales tax is to increase revenue."

Although Walter Harrison has fought the Power Company, the liquor interests, and the Coca-Cola people, all three would support him in a gubernatorial race if they thought he could win. "They'd have to," Gowen said.

If he could draft a platform for the state, he would include the usual things—schools, roads, better health facilities, and so on—and add a civil service system for state employees, improvements in the institutional buildings, and much more revenue. He also thinks that some governor—although he probably would be wise not to announce his intent during a campaign—should abolish the county road gangs and put them under state supervision. He recognizes the political barriers, however, and says he is at a loss to know where best to begin. "If we could have only eight years of good government in Georgia, we'd never go back to Talmadgeism. At the moment poor Thompson doesn't have a chance to do a job. He's already embroiled in next year's campaign, and he isn't a free agent. He's got too many men around him whose political fortunes are dependent on him."

Although Glynn County uses neither the numbered nor the official ballot, Gowen thinks it's as secret as the official ballot. "There are tricks that can be used to violate any kind of ballot you can devise." He recalled that several years ago in a local election there was much buying of votes on both sides, but generally he thinks voting in the county now is honest and clean.

Bernard Nightingale, state representative, Glynn County, interviewed in his office, July 11

Interest in last summer's race for the assembly was unusually high throughout the county, Nightingale told us. Both he and Gowen were opposed. "My opponent moved in on the Negroes and made big promises. He slapped them on the back and worked hard on their leadership." Nightingale then asked the Negroes for an opportunity to speak to them, a meeting was arranged, "and I was asked a lot of penetrating questions." His audience wanted to know how he felt about the Klan, the white primary, the schools, the police, and other issues. He believes that by the time he'd finished, he had won over many votes, and as a result "the Negro vote was pretty well split."

About a fourth of those voting last summer were Negroes. The polls were not segregated. Nightingale saw no evidence of threats or intimidation, and he's satisfied that the count was accurate.

The people also showed more than usual interest in what went on in the legislature, as best Nightingale can judge from his correspondence and personal contacts when he

and Gowen came home on weekends. There was vocal opposition to the sales tax, the white primary bill, and the antilabor bills. (Nightingale voted against the anti–mass picketing bill and for the anti–closed shop bill.) "Still, when we
had a public meeting here to protest Herman's election, only
about twenty or thirty people showed up."

People in the county seem to be pleased with Thompson's
administration. "They're especially glad that he's not making any move to raise taxes." His own feeling is that the
Thompson tax commission, of which he is a member, is doing a disappointing job. He doesn't feel that he's in a position
"to push" but hopes that it will soon become apparent to
members that "we'll have to bring in some top-flight spe-
cialists." Fred Wilson has had little to say so far.

Jack R. Williams, state representative, Ware County; editor, *Waycross Journal-Herald*, interviewed in his office, July 12

Mr. Williams is a kind, generous man of sixty-odd who has
won a reputation *as* a character (he's white haired and wears
flowing black ties) and *for* his character. He's been honored
several times by the Kiwanis Club as Waycross's most valuable citizen.

Mr. Williams, we gather, is—or considers himself—something of a benevolent dictator. He loves Ware County, and
apparently the people love him. Through his paper and his
radio station, he has tremendous influence and has consistently used it, he says, for constructive purposes. He rarely
has any trouble getting elected to the legislature. This last
time, neither he nor his colleague, Wayne Hinson, had opposition, so public interest was centered largely on the
gubernatorial election. Ware County went for Carmichael,
whom Williams endorsed.

Mr. Williams says that Georgia has no big-city political machines, thanks to the county unit system. He believes in the system for this reason, although he thinks the bigger counties, particularly Fulton, should have more representation in the assembly. Several times in past sessions he has considered introducing bills to accomplish this, but he hasn't had enough support to get his proposals on the floor. He says he knows nothing about corporate interference, since he's seen no signs of it in Ware County and has had no experience with campaigns except at the local level. He's inclined to believe that Fred Wilson can get just about anything he wants out of Georgia politics simply because he's in such a strategic position to do favors. He recalled that Wilson got a room at the Henry Grady for a friend of his daughter's after the room clerk, "and everybody else I talked to, said the hotel was full." He recalled, too, that a few years back a "Big Businessman" offered to pay his entry fee. He refused. He does not think this practice—that of corporations paying entry fees—is as general as the public believes. Nor does he think bribery is very prevalent. Only once has he ever heard of a lobbyist offering to pay a representative for a promise to withdraw an undesirable bill.

Ware County's population is composed of about three whites to every one Negro. Before the First World War the percentage of Negroes was closer to 45 percent, but the exodus to the East during and after the war and an increase in the birthrate among whites brought the percentage down to its present 35 percent. About fifteen hundred Negroes voted last summer, almost all of them for Carmichael, despite efforts on the part of the Rivers forces to "confuse them." There was some intimidation of Negroes, but it was generally ineffective.

The county Democratic executive committee is self-perpetuating and has wide latitude. "We don't always follow the books," he said.

Lawson Neel, state representative, Thomas County, interviewed at his desk on the mezzanine of Neel Brothers' department store in Thomasville, July 12

Personalities, not issues, determine the outcome of elections in Thomas County, as they do in most local elections, and Neel feels that he got a lot of votes merely because he's a member of a prominent family. "A lot of people who voted for me didn't know which Neel they were voting for."

Neel feels that he's alienated most of his constituents. He voted against Talmadge and the white primary, which made the Talmadge element mad; against the veterans' bonus, which angered the organized veterans' groups; and for the sales tax, which angered most of the merchants. He said he felt little pressure from lobbyists—a circumstance that Jamie and I think may be because of his reputation as an outspoken man with conviction, a trait that lobbyists don't quite know how to deal with.

No one man runs Thomas County, according to Neel, but there are several powerful men who have a big hand in which way the county goes. Fred Scott—contractor, Rivers man, and a former candidate for governor—is influential. Nat Williams is a big supporter of Congressman Eugene Cox, as is Claud Rountree, who uses his office as postmaster for political purposes. Frank Forrester is pro-Thompson and "a political lawyer" of a fairly high type. J. N. Pilcher of Meigs, currently the state purchasing agent, is pro-Thompson and has a lot to say about how the county goes. Haywood Vann is a young lawyer that Neel hopes will run for the legislature next time if Neel doesn't. Mrs. W. W. Jarrell is leader of the League of Women Voters. Neel says she "has one of the keenest minds in town," is the best informed on national and international affairs, and "is becoming the best informed on state affairs."

The white primary will always be a popular issue with "the unthinking Talmadge crowd," but Neel doesn't believe it can carry Thomas County if properly presented. The sales tax was vigorously opposed by the merchants, including some members of Neel's own family. The veterans are organized and working through chapters of the American Legion and the Veterans of Foreign Wars. The legion formally condemned Neel's position on the veterans' bonus, but the resolution passed by only a narrow margin.

There was considerable feeling against Eugene Cox in the Second District, as evidenced by the large vote piled up for Neely Peacock, a generally unpopular man. Neel is aware of the need for better representation in Congress and perhaps more aware of the urgency of the international situation than any other state legislator we've talked with. While he was in the hospital overseas, he thought about coming home and running for Congress, but his family preferred that if he did anything at all in politics (which they'd rather he didn't), he should take a stab first at the state assembly. Neel says his experience so far has made him realize just how inadequately his education had trained him for "representing the people." At times he thinks he would like to quit work and go back to school in an effort to prepare himself for a run for Congress. At the moment, he said, he was reading Arnold Toynbee, and from Toynbee's analysis he doesn't think Western civilization can survive much longer.

Neel says seriously that he may never offer again for the state legislature, partly because he thinks he might not win and partly because his seventy days away from the department store resulted in a marked drop in sales volume. We asked if this might have had anything to do with his voting record. He said no, he didn't think so, that many customers had commended him for his positions even though they disagreed with him. He suggested that an annual session of thirty days might be better; he lost so much time last winter that he's had to forgo a summer vacation.

Mr. and Mrs. Tom Cottingham, Coffee County, civic leaders, interviewed in their home, July 13

Sometime before the last city election, veterans got together and decided that something should be done to activate citizens in Coffee County and Douglas, the county seat. The group, which came to be known as "Citizens Desiring More Progressive Government," decided not to offer a slate or start a new political party but rather to talk about issues and to increase the number of registrants. Perhaps the most effective thing the group did was to publish the entire registration list, some 107 voters. Many people who thought they were registered were surprised to discover that they were not, and the discovery embarrassed them into registering. As a result of this and other efforts, registration in the county went up to two thousand, of whom more than seventeen hundred went to the polls.

The veterans felt that all their energies should be directed toward saving the town and county from a man named Francis Stubbs, commonly referred to as "Boss Stubbs." They were extraordinarily encouraged when one of their number ran against Stubbs for council and beat him. Until the local situation further improves, they do not want to divert attention to state issues. Other than occasional noises from "the usual Talmadge faction," there has been little said about the white primary.

We talked with Tom and his wife at length, and on Saturday night they had a group of young men in with their wives to talk with us. One of them had been an employee of the Georgia Power Company. He said that most of his time was spent in the courthouse checking records of men in office and men who were likely to be candidates for office. He expressed the conviction that the Power Company was thoroughly informed about every officeholder in the areas where they operate.

Last summer Negroes were purged without cause from the voter registration lists. A courageous lawyer in Dublin took the case to federal court and obtained an order of reinstatement. The county officials, however, said the order could not be carried out because the registration lists had been destroyed. As a consequence, only about eighty-seven Negroes voted in the Douglas precinct. This illegal purging is a matter of record now, the FBI has a complete file on the matter, and Tom said he thought the fear of God had been put into county officials.

Tom pointed out the difficulty opposing a man with really great economic power in the county. He spoke of one young veteran who resigned from the group "with tears in his eyes" because he was convinced that to oppose Stubbs would cost his family's insurance agency a five-thousand-dollar premium that they couldn't afford to lose. Tom went on to say that his own leadership in the movement had undoubtedly lost his firm the sale of three or four trucks.

The conversation about affairs in Coffee County confirmed the impression we've received in most rural counties—that for the most part Talmadge people read the *Statesman* and little else and that they will not debate anything on which "the leader" has given them an opinion. "There can be no righteousness on the state level," Tom said as the meeting broke up, "until we achieve it at the local level."

Clyde Cooper, president, Pelham National Bank, interviewed in his office, July 14

A 1909 graduate of Emory University, Mr. Cooper settled in Pelham in 1914 when a new bank was founded here. At that time Mr. J. L. Hand, founder of the Hand Trading Company, was lord and master of Mitchell County. Just prior to the opening of Mr. Cooper's bank, "old man" Hand, who wanted no competition, had driven another bank out of business. Since then times have changed a great deal, and Mr. Cooper's bank has had a long and pleasant association with the Hands. "Although they're still a family to reckon with, the Hands can no longer dictate what goes on in this county," Mr. Cooper said. "In fact, if Fred Hand ever had a man of consequence running against him, he'd be defeated."

Both Hand and Frank Twitty ran unopposed in the last election. Twitty has intimated that he won't run again, even though people don't feel any bitterness toward him for his record in the legislature. On the other hand, people *are* bitter about Hand's prominent identification with Herman Talmadge, and they also think he was too ready to do the bidding of Roy Harris.

In Mr. Cooper's view, people's willingness to be swayed by personalities and appeals to prejudice is a severe indictment of our schools. Nowhere, he says, is an adequate job being done educating people to the nature of government and the responsibilities of citizenship. "People are facing an acid test now. They're having to decide whether the people shall support the government or the government support the people." As evidence that they would prefer the latter, he says there are too many Negroes in Mitchell County on relief who'd rather stay there than go to work, "even though they've been offered jobs that would pay them much better." His attitude toward Negroes seems to be mixed. At one point he said, "Negroes have come a long way, and it's unfortunate that when they've come up in the world, there's no place for them in south Georgia." He told us of a young Negro who had caddied for him and impressed him with his intelligence and potential. He arranged for the boy to go to college in Albany. When the boy finished college, he was "a well-developed man with good training," but there was no place for him in Pelham. So Mr. Cooper got him a job with the NC & St. L. working in the diner. "Every time he and his wife come through Pelham now, they look me up."

Mr. Cooper said he can't understand "the wool-hat mind that will accept without questioning anything endorsed by a Talmadge." Although he favors strong procedures to eliminate unqualified voters, he thinks the white primary bill dangerous. How, he asked us, can educated men like Frank Twitty and Fred Hand go along with such a proposal? Hand, he says, is a great personal friend, and so is Twitty, but he simply cannot go along with their politics.

There are undoubtedly election irregularities, he said. When he went to the poll in his precinct last year, he asked the poll manager for whom he should vote for chairman of the Democratic executive committee. The manager told him to vote for John Collins, the incumbent. When asked why, the manager said that Collins had been in first thing that morning and written his own name in for chairman on a hundred or so ballots. When Mr. Cooper asked if this were not out of order, the manager replied that since Mr. Collins had charge of the elections, he supposed that it would be all right for him to do anything he wanted to do.

I asked Mr. Cooper why we couldn't get better men to offer for public office. His reply was that the same amount of energy applied to private affairs would be much more rewarding and, further, that good men did not want to suffer the vilification heaped on candidates.

As for organized labor, Mr. Cooper expressed his conviction that workers should be protected in their right to organize, but it worried him that they were so often exploited by their own leaders.

He considers H. L. Wingate "a good man" who would make a good governor if elected. He has made trips to Washington with Wingate and thinks him an able lobbyist who knows how to get his points across. "But he positively will not run for governor. That's what he says, and I believe him."

Mr. Cooper described M. E. Thompson as a man of integrity but "not astute" and sorely handicapped as a chief ex-

ecutive. He praised Ellis Arnall's first three years but thinks
his pursuit of national recognition had destroyed much of
his effectiveness in Georgia.

Fred Hand, Speaker of the House of Representatives, president of the Hand Trading Company, interviewed in his office in Pelham, July 14

Hand does not dismiss the possibility of a second party:
"Everything will depend on this next election." He did not
go on to speculate whether the second party might be organized before or after the election but instead volunteered
two hints to the course of Talmadge strategy to reclaim the
Democratic Party. "When we have our own convention—
and we're gonna call one—I'm gonna call names and ask
that Thompson crowd to prove that they haven't bolted.
They're the bolters, not Herman." And, "What do you think
the national Democratic Party would do if Georgia's congressional delegation were to vote to recognize Herman as
head of the party in Georgia?"

Asked whether Herman could win in the event two primaries were held and the decisive vote was in the general
election, he said, "I just don't know. Certainly we can win
the primary." He went on to say that Herman's strength was
growing and that everyone who worked with him considered him extremely competent. Meanwhile, Thompson is
steadily losing support; "a lot of people around here who
never voted for Gene Talmadge in their lives tell me that
if they have to choose between Herman and M.E., they'll
vote for Herman." He said he'd known nothing about Herman Talmadge before the legislature met and that he was
surprised and immensely pleased with the way Herman
handled himself as governor. He said he recognized Her-

man's love for drink but that Zack Cravey had assured him that Herman hadn't touched a drop since the Supreme Court decision.

Hand said that he voted for Herman for only one reason. "I felt the law required me to." That was the way he interprets the state constitution, and he told us so in a tone of sincerity that is hard to discount. He said that he'd called Jimmy Carmichael to ask if he would accept the governorship if the legislature named him and felt that when Carmichael said no, he, Hand, had no choice but to vote for Herman.

He plainly distrusts M. E. Thompson. He pulled out a telegram he'd received from Thompson just before the legislature convened in which M.E. said he was for the white primary bill and would support it, along with everything else adopted at Gene's Macon convention. Telling us what we'd earlier heard from George Smith, he added that it was Thompson who insisted on a registration fee. Thompson wanted the fee to be two dollars, and it was only with much persuasion that Hand and Roy Harris got him to lower it to a dollar. "It wouldn't surprise me if Thompson was forced out of the party," he said. We waited for him to elaborate, but he moved on to what we gather is one of his favorite subjects. "One thing I've never gotten you newspaper people to understand is that we don't want a white primary just to keep the niggers from voting. Hell, they've been voting in the general election in this country for years. What we don't want 'em to do is to get in a position in our party so they can be manipulated. I say, let 'em have their own party, a black Democratic Party if they want." Here, too, Hand sounded sincere.

He doesn't know what Herman might do if the Supreme Court sustains the South Carolina decision, but he would advise him to keep preaching the white primary right through the next election, on the grounds that the South Carolina test suits were for South Carolina only and that such suits would have to be tested in Georgia before they would have any effect here. "That would at least carry us through the next election."

Hand minimizes the political influence of the Power Company. "I've been in the legislature since 1931—the only time I got beat it was by five votes—and not once has Fred Wilson or any other Power Company man come to me asking my support for or against any bill." He knows Wilson and likes him and feels that the *Journal* editorial was uncalled for.

Nor does Hand believe that there are as many as forty counties that are one-man controlled. "Maybe two," he conceded. He spoke of neighboring Baker County, where the people brag of the fact that they have neither a railroad nor a preacher. "Family over there named Hall. They own a lot of property, and they've intermarried so much you'd think they could win any election they wanted to. Yet they've never been able to carry the county against Talmadge. They're bitterly anti-Talmadge." Even Judge "Red" Townsend isn't as strong as people give him credit for being. "He couldn't carry Dade against Gene when Judge Pittman was running against him."

Hand said he might be for a uniform ballot law, "but that would depend on what ballot they wanted to make uniform." He said they used the "really secret" ballot in Mitchell County but that nobody bothered to tear the number off. He acknowledges that this ballot can be abused, since somebody can stuff the box and "the managers would have no way of knowing which ballots were fraudulent, even if they knew the box had been stuffed." He said Mitchell had consistently clean elections. He recognizes, though, that other counties frequently doctored the counts. He deplored the Telfair irregularities but thought the *Journal* was most unfair in its report of them. He said that such irregularities were pretty general throughout the state in the general election but not so common in primaries. He named one man in one

militia district who could control the vote in that district
simply because he did so many favors throughout the year,
"like driving them to the doctor's and arranging to pay their
hospital bills, that sort of thing. The people 'round here, they
don't think they're selling their votes. But just try to get 'em
to go to the polls on election day. You go up to a group—
say they're packing peanuts. You ask 'em to go down to the
polls with you. They shake their heads. You offer 'em a ride.
They say they're too dirty to go to town. You say you'll wait
till they take a bath. They say they're getting paid for doing
a job, and it'd cost 'em money to leave peanuts for the afternoon. So what do you do? You end up payin' 'em the
equivalent of their wages. Of course, when you have to do
this, you'd be a fool to take anybody to the polls who you
know isn't gonna vote for your man."

Hand admits that white people have failed to care for the
educational needs of the Negro. "But just because we made
a mistake not educating 'em, does that mean we now got to
let 'em vote and take over the state? What we need is an
educational qualifications bill." He likes the Weaver bill,
which would establish literacy criteria for voter registration,
and insisted that we study it.

Exactly 106 Mitchell County Negroes voted in the last primary, "all for Carmichael." Hand was "very disturbed"
about their bloc vote and also by the Negroes' use of sample
ballots. He said he got hold of one of their sample ballots and
had them reprinted and dropped by airplane over Mitchell
County. "We wanted to give them wide distribution."

Georgia has two basic needs, Hand says: "better schools
and better economic opportunities." When I deplored the
injection of race into the campaign, he said he deplored it
too but that the way things are it's necessary.

Hand is forthright and clearly lives by his own honor
code. When he decided to support Ellis Arnall, he wrote Eugene Talmadge a letter telling him so. "I didn't want him to
hear it from anybody else." He described "Ole Gene" as a

person of great personal magnetism but "the stubbornest man in the world when he wanted to be."

He thinks that if anybody runs Georgia, it's Roy Harris. "Roy knows Georgia and government better than anybody else in the state. Worst mistake M. E. ever made was to tell Roy, 'I dedicate the rest of my life to getting you out of politics.' There's nobody I'd rather have on my side than Roy."

Asked if he would ever run for governor, he said no. "I've got a job like nobody else in the country. I've got a million-dollar business in a town of three thousand people." He thinks Harris can still run and that he would be a competent governor. "Roy's getting old, though."

Delacey Allen, state commander, American Legion; lawyer; politician, interviewed in his office in Albany, July 15

In 1936 Mr. Allen ran in the Democratic primary for the then nonexistent office of lieutenant governor. He did so on two presumptions: (1) that the office would be authorized by a constitutional amendment to be ratified at the coming general election; and (2) that Ed Rivers would do as he'd promised and support the amendment. Allen won the primary, but Rivers "double-crossed" him by having the amendment defeated. Allen swore to spend the rest of his political life getting back.

Recalling this today, Mr. Allen quoted the Bible: "'Vengeance is mine, saith the Lord,' and I don't think the Lord will mind if I help him a little." He said he had been tempted to oppose Rivers in the gubernatorial primary; he had been offered President Roosevelt's personal endorsement and campaign funds from the national Democratic Party. He had turned the offers down, thinking that to accept would mean breaking his pledge to Rivers, whom he had confidently expected to support the amendment that would have made

him, Allen, lieutenant governor. Reflecting on his sacrifice
and what he considers Rivers's betrayal has made him all the
more vindictive. He says now that if the only choice next
year is Thompson or Herman, he'll have to vote for Herman,
simply because he cannot take Thompson with Rivers. Although he campaigned for Carmichael in the district last
summer, on two previous occasions he supported Eugene
Talmadge.

Allen referred several times to Rivers as "the lying bas-
tard" and cited several instances of his corruption. "Why,
just recently Thompson tried to give Rivers the bootlegging
franchise in Dougherty County. You know how it works.
The favored bootlegger sets up his warehouse in a wet
county, and the word goes out to the neighboring dry counties that this warehouse has the governor's protection. Well,
Rivers didn't get away with it here. The other liquor dealers
got so mad they scared Thompson out of it."

Allen says he has no doubt that Fred Wilson kept Rivers
in the race on a sacrifice play last summer. As an example of
how smart the Power Company is, he reminded us of the
1942 election, when Wilson was plugging for Gene. After
the election, he said, it was discovered that all the while
Power Company people elsewhere in the state had been
working for Arnall. "They play both sides and always manage to buy their way back if they have to." He said too that
although the rural counties may elect a governor, it's Atlanta
that runs him. Pressed, he admitted that maybe if Atlanta
was given more of a voice in state government, the big corporations couldn't wield such heavy influence.

"Though we tend to forget it, Georgia's still predominantly an agrarian state," Allen said when we asked him to
identify our most pressing needs. "First thing we ought to
do is get better markets for our farm products. We ought
to send marketing agents everywhere there's a big market—
Chicago, Boston, Baltimore, New York. Sure, it'd cost money
getting it started, but it'd pay for itself in a while and prob-

ably increase income to farmers by 50 percent." He said that if it weren't for his bad stomach, he might run for governor on such a platform.

Henry McIntosh, editor emeritus, *Albany Herald,* interviewed in his office in Albany, July 15

Politics in Dougherty County, according to editor McIntosh (with a few emendations, as noted, by Leland Ferrell, a merchant and landowner whom we visited later):

People here are not exceptionally active politically, and their participation never divides along factional lines. Representatives Durden and Sabados were unopposed, having been selected in caucus by "the politicians." The county has a tradition for electing "high-type men" to local office and sending good men to the state legislature. Some people, however, resented Sabados's voting for Herman and are likely to oppose him should he offer again next year.

F. R. Champion, a fertilizer producer and "the man of most authority in the county," is chairman of the Democratic executive committee. The committee submits a slate of nominees that is routinely confirmed by voters in the primary. About twelve hundred Negroes voted last year. No violence, no noteworthy intimidation.

The League of Women Voters is active and "has done a good job." The Farm Bureau also is strong. McIntosh thinks well of Wingate but regrets that he thinks so exclusively in terms of the farmer.

Nobody got very excited about the sales tax, one way or another (Ferrell). Nevertheless, Sabados was one of the strongest opponents of the tax, testifying against it before the Senate committee even after it had cleared the House. McIntosh is proud of his editorials against the white primary bill and would welcome a Supreme Court decision declaring it unconstitutional. He believes that registration laws should be changed so that "unqualified" voters—white and colored—would be barred from the polls. He is sympathetic to "courtroom challenges" to the county unit system because he's convinced that it can never be legislated out of existence. "It's like the old man of the sea—it's ours, and we're stuck with it."

The chamber of commerce has granted "almost every concession in the books" to get outside industry located here, and the policy has paid off handsomely. Clark Thread Company (J. P. Coats) has recently set up a plant, along with a subsidiary in Pelham, and several candy factories have started up. A hide factory is coming to the county this fall. Any efforts to unionize workers "would be bitterly resisted" not only by management but by the people in general (Ferrell).

Congressman Cox has lost popularity steadily and won last time only because of weak opposition; Neely Peacock, who ran against him, is universally disliked. Cox was unanimously opposed by the county's Negroes, who cannot forget his attack on the Fair Employment Practices Commission.

Of additional interest: McIntosh said that when his father came to Dougherty County in 1873, 53 percent of the population was made up of Negroes. It was the custom then for one Negro and one white man to be sent to the General Assembly. But after the census of 1880 Dougherty lost one of its two representatives, and the next election was a hot one between his father and a Negro. "My father won, and no Negro has ever been in the legislature from this county since." He spoke warmly of his friends and neighbors. "We're pretty prosperous here and above average in education. We've had a tradition of decent government, and we've usually been above petty political quarrels. Our county board of education and our city board, for instance, work right together. Not like that in most counties, not even Fulton. If a good man is in office, we're inclined to keep him there." He can't keep track of the *Journal's* editorial policy and deplores the apparent rivalry between the *Journal* and the *Constitution.* He thinks Ralph McGill's endorsement of Herman and his "light excuse" of the Telfair election frauds were "the most unfortunate thing that could have happened to the mind and soul of Georgia."

Robert Elliott, state representative, Muscogee County; floor leader for Herman Talmadge, interviewed in his law office (Smith, Elliott, & Swinson) in Columbus, July 16

Elliott said he didn't see prospects for a second party. "Not any time soon, anyway. I wish we could have a second party, but labor's too weak, and the Negro wants to join the white man's party. The Negro always wants to do that. He doesn't want anything for himself. He wants what the white man's got."

I suggested that there might be a sizable number of white folks in urban centers dissatisfied with both factions who might get behind a second-party movement. He smiled very slyly. (It is, I think, Elliott's peculiar smile that makes many hearers feel that he's being less than candid and more than a little duplicitous.) "It's against my own political interests to defend the county unit system," he said, a statement of dubious accuracy, since he is rumored to have ambitions for Congress. "But I defend it every chance I get. It's our only protection against city machines." When he suggested that my next question might be whether he favored the rural philosophy over the urban philosophy, I said no, my next question was whether or not "city machines" did exist, operating as liaison between moneyed interests and politicians. He shook his head and proceeded to downplay the influence of corporations. "The Georgia Power Company doesn't have the influence it's credited with," he said. "You suppose they control Senator Russell?" I said maybe not, but there seemed to be some evidence that they controlled Senator George. "Hell, a lot of people control George," he said, and he then moved on to another point. "You take most of your small counties. They don't care about the Power Company or the railroads. They're not even aware of them. They push a button, and the lights go on. A train passes through their town and leaves off passengers and freight. That's about the sum of it. Only thing the Power Company and the railroads mean to them is the chance for their towns or counties to collect some more taxes." I ventured that, granted that most people in rural counties may not be aware of the link between the corporations and their local governments, certainly legislators like himself and the county bosses must be. He said in reply, "Well, that's something I couldn't say without a lot more facts." Asked if he thought the *Journal* was justified in its editorial denouncing Fred Wilson, he said, "No. I know Fred Wilson socially. He's a grand person. Of course he has political influence. That's his job—public relations."

I asked Elliott next if he thought politics in Georgia was any worse than in any other state in the union. "No—if anything, better. Only reason people think our politics is worse is that we take our politics seriously and because our newspapers print so much of the bad side. Hell, looks like every newspaperman in the state writes with the idea of getting quoted in *Time* magazine. You can just see 'em sitting before a typewriter, saying, 'Now, what can I write about that'll be picked up by *Time*?' *Time*'s a good magazine, but it's not interested in printing anything good about the South."

He went on: "North Carolina is considered the most progressive state in the South. Well, compare North Carolina and Georgia. North Carolina has a much lower income tax rate than Georgia. But North Carolina has a sales tax. That's how they get the revenue for all those fine things, through a sales tax." I suggested that maybe North Carolina had achieved its ends through an economic oligarchy. He nodded and smiled, again slyly. "There's no conspiracy among the moneyed interests in this state to keep people so confused they won't ask for higher corporate taxes or more revenue. The corporations haven't put any pressure on us for a sales tax. Why, last session not a single corporation executive asked me to push the sales tax. Matter of fact, some merchants asked me not to. Another thing—even after I said we'd introduce a bill to raise the income tax rate, once the Senate passed the sales tax, nobody seemed interested, one way or another. No corporation agent tried to discourage a hike in the income tax."

He said there's been no active unionization in Muscogee County. "General sentiment here is antiunion. Everybody applauded the antilabor bills."

About the Telfair County election frauds: "I'm not convinced that there *were* any frauds. I don't string along with the *Atlanta Journal,* you know. But I suspect such irregularities may be pretty common in at least fifty counties. Through carelessness, mostly."

"What's Herman Talmadge going to do if the Supreme Court upholds the South Carolina decision?"

"Be elected governor of Georgia."

"How? On what grounds?"

"On the grounds that he would have given us the white primary if he could."

"Then what?"

"Then he'll think up something else to keep the niggers from the polls, and if two years later the Supreme Court decides that's unconstitutional, then he'll think of something else."

A young lady came to the door to announce the arrival of a client. Our conversation was over. As I got up to leave,

Elliott said again, "I wish the niggers and the unions and those white folks you talk about *would* start another party. I'd like especially to see the niggers have their own party."

The Reverend Mac Anthony, pastor, First Methodist Church, Columbus, interviewed in the parsonage, July 16

Since 1930 Mr. Anthony has held pastorates in Thomasville, Macon, and Columbus. He is commonly considered to be one of the most popular and influential ministers in the South Georgia Conference.

Anthony expressed grave concern over what happened last summer. He said he had told the chairman of his board of stewards that he was ready to move out of Georgia if Talmadge was elected. When the legislature met in January, he was equally troubled by the attack on the ballot. "The white primary is contrary to the Kingdom of God."

There are many paradoxes in Georgia politics, Anthony observed. For example, the wool-hat Talmadge crowd includes some "pretty good men." Abbott Turner, son-in-law of W. C. Bradley and one of the wealthiest men in town, is a Talmadge man. Why? "Talmadge called out the national guard and broke the textile strike, and since then all the mill owners have been loyal to him." These men are not wicked, he said, "just conservative." He deplores their stand in politics but says they are loyal and generous to their church. He said he had to walk "a tightrope" with his congregation. Still, he did speak out unequivocally against the white primary "because ethics were so clearly involved."

Although not much interest was shown in the election of legislators (Anthony voted for Bob Elliott) and the candidates did not run on issues, the public was keenly aware of the struggle that ensued later in the General Assembly. Anytime you wanted to start a fight, he said, you could do so by getting out on the street and arguing one side or the other.

There was talk pro and con on the sales tax, and there was much talk in favor of the antilabor bills. He was not aware of extensive Negro participation in the primary, but he did know that some Negroes were not permitted to register. "Mr. Dudley, the registrar, told me that many white people were also struck from the registration list."

Theo McGee he considers the best-informed man on politics in Columbus. A former member of the county Democratic executive committee who abetted the Primus King case, McGee is a genuine friend of the Negro. Among other "good men" in Columbus he named Quentin Davidson, lawyer; Bob Arnold, head of the school board; Albert Stubbs, lawyer; and Roscoe Thompson. He has little regard for Judge T. Hicks Fort. "He left the Methodist Church during unification. Now he teaches a Bible class at the Presbyterian church." He added that although Judge Fort was "very indiscreet" on the Talmadge-Thompson question, he remains a solid influence in the community. He suggested that the publisher of the Columbus newspapers, Maynard Ashworth, might make a suitable candidate for governor because he is the most "broad-gauged" man in the county. Parson Jack Johnston is unquestionably subsidized by the mills, one of which is owned by the chairman of Anthony's board of stewards. Johnston is tolerated "and used" because of his violently antilabor sermons, he said.

Parson Jack Johnston, interviewed in his study at the Baptist Tabernacle, Columbus, July 17

The Baptist Tabernacle was founded as the Columbus Roberts Memorial. It was named without the knowledge of Mr. Roberts, and it may have displeased him. Parson Jack says it was named without his knowledge too.[8] In fact, he says he didn't like the name. "I don't think it's fittin' to name a memorial for a man who's still living." Just why the name was changed—whether at the request of Mr. Roberts or on the initiative of Parson Jack—we don't know.

The tabernacle is made up of two low and wide buildings, the newer and smaller of which houses Parson Jack's printing plant. In the larger and more public building there is an auditorium, a kitchen, the Sunday school rooms, and an office or two. Construction on an addition to the Sunday school seems to have been started some time ago but interrupted; the wood framing is turning dark from exposure, only the subflooring is down and only a few walls up, studs are rusting, and windows without panes are open to the weather. Completion apparently is having to wait until the Parson can float another loan or find a new patron.

We talked with the Parson in what we take to be his study. He sat behind a desk littered with pamphlets, letters, paste pots, and pencils, his back to two windows that came down almost to street level. On one wall was a reproduction on newsprint of the picture of Father Divine and his white wife, the same picture that *Life* magazine carried some months ago as its photo of the week. At the top of the picture was an overprinted message: "This is what we don't like about the Negro." A stack of cartoon art lay atop a small table. The top one showed a spotlight labeled "The South" turned on a monkey labeled "Rape" that cast a shadow of a servile Negro. To the right of the Parson's desk was another table, on which sat a typewriter. Beside it was a mailing list, and in the typewriter was a roll of address labels, one end spilling onto the floor. Throughout the room were piles of the *Trumpet*.

Parson Jack Johnston is a dark-skinned, slightly built man who could be anywhere from fifty to sixty-five. He has thick white hair dirty with printer's ink. He talks in the idiom of the rural South and with an air of intimacy more appropriate to a locker room than a church study.

We explained that we were making an informal survey of political conditions in Georgia. "We'd like to know how you expect the 1948 governor's election to turn out and whether or not we're going to restore the white primary."

Mention of the white primary started him off. "Niggers say they want to vote," he said. "What they really want is to mix the blood. They want to have our women and wipe out the white race." He paused dramatically, waiting for his point to sink in. "Mongrelization. That's what they want." He paused again. "And there you are."

He thought for a moment. "I don't mind them voting. I think they ought to vote." (This may seem hard to believe in the light of his writings in the *Trumpet* and in view of his intense loyalty to Herman Talmadge, but that's what he said.) "But we aren't gonna have peace in Georgia till niggers stop raping white women. Take that recent case in Chicago or somewhere. You boys know about that one? Well, there were these two white boys and two white girls parked near a lake, and three niggers came up and beat up the two white boys. Chased 'em away. One of the girls ran, too, and swam all the way across the lake. Then these three niggers jumped that one white girl. Took turns. Why it didn't kill her I don't know." He gestured, raising his hands and showing his palms. "And there you are."

"I know, Parson," Jamie said, "but our white men have been doing a little raping, too. It looks like our white men in Atlanta have gotten out of hand, don't you think?"

The Parson shook his head sadly. "Yeah, that was bad, wasn't it. That poor Refoule girl."[9]

Jamie ventured again. "This business of mongrelization. I don't think it's come from Negro men and white women. Seems to me the reason we've got so many mulattoes is that white men have taken advantage of Negro women."

"Yes, that's true," the Parson conceded. "But there's not so much of that as there used to be. You know why? Our white girls are a lot freer now. These little fourteen-year-old girls. They know how to take care of themselves now. Way it is, white boys don't have to go over to niggertown."

Two men passed by the window on their way to the print shop. I started.

"That was Homer Loomis," I said.[10]

The Parson was silent for a moment. "You know Homer?"

"I interviewed him once."

"It's a shame and a sin what they did to that boy. He can't get anybody in Atlanta to publish his side of the story. I told him I'd publish it in the *Trumpet*. You just wait for our next issue. It's going to tell the truth about what happened, what the police did to him."

"When does he go to court?" I asked.

The Parson ignored my question. "See that boy with him? He's going to turn state's evidence. He'll perjure himself, sure, but he'll have his say. He's a real brave boy, that one."

"The Columbians made a mistake," Jamie said. "Loomis took on the Atlanta police force. He shouldn't have done that. He shouldn't have said the police weren't doing their jobs. And when he put his own men to patrolling the streets, why that gave the chief a ready-made case. He could have gotten away with almost everything else, maybe even gotten some policemen to join up, but he was done for the minute he tried to usurp police authority."

The Parson nodded. "That wasn't smart, was it?"

"They made another mistake," I volunteered. "They put too much emphasis on the Jews. Nobody's worried about the Jews in Atlanta."

The Parson showed a new interest. "You know, it's always a mistake to take on the Jews. They're real sensitive. Year or so ago I said something about 'em in the *Trumpet*, and first thing I knew old Simon Schwab had me on the carpet." The Parson caught himself and blushed. "Well, he didn't call me on the carpet exactly. He asked me to come up to his office

for a talk. He had this young rabbi with him—Rabbi Wal-
ler, I think his name is, a real shrewd boy. Schwab told
me, polite-like, to lay off the kikes, and this rabbi, he had
some real fine things to say about what Jews had done for
America. I didn't argue. I just told 'em frankly that I hadn't
meant any harm. I told 'em I wouldn't take on the Jews because I know better. History shows that anybody who starts
fightin' the Jews always gets whipped. . . . There are some
real fine Jews, you know, but you have to watch 'em. They
want to take over the country."

"What about the Catholics, Parson?"

. . . . . . people are fighting the Catholics just
as a smoke screen for communism. On the other hand, the
Catholics are fighting the communists as a smoke screen
for spreading Catholicism. Catholics work termitically"—
he paused again and gestured—"like termites. They want to
take over the country, too. My, they're slick. They came into
Columbus not so long ago and wanted to build a hospital.
They even talked Mr. ——, an Episcopalian, mind you,
into serving as chairman of the committee to raise money. I
don't see any reason why us Protestants should help the
Catholics build a hospital. We need hospitals of our own.
Anyway, before this Mr. —— started his drive, he called
me in his office. He said, 'Parson, I know how you feel about
Catholics, but I want you to lay off the Catholics during this
drive. They're going to build a fine hospital for the town, and
we need it.' Well, I didn't say anythin'. I just went back home
and picked up a copy of the *Christian Century* and opened it
up to this article, 'Can Catholics Take Over America,' and I
marched right back to Mr. ——'s office. I put it on his desk
in front of him and told him to kiss my ass."

He paused. "These Catholics"—and again he shook his
head—"well, there you are."

"Around Atlanta," Jamie said, "we hear stories that the

Klan is growing stronger. You think that's true all over the state?"

"It sure is." The Parson thought awhile. "Understand, I'm not a member of the Ku Kluck [*sic*]. I was a member of the old Klan, but I haven't joined this new one. They tell me, though, that chapters are starting up all over Georgia. The boys have the idea that if they can't keep niggers from votin' any other way, they'll have to use force."

"What do you think about Herman's chances next year?"

"Herman's smart," said the Parson. "A real smart boy. Lots of smart young men in Georgia—like yourselves. Take my friend Bob Elliott. Smart as they come. Might be governor himself some day."

"You really think so?" asked Jamie. "People we've talked with say Elliott wouldn't do so well on the stump. He lacks the common touch."

The Parson leaned forward and smiled. "Yeah, you're right. No matter how hard he tries, somehow Bob can't help being a pretty boy, can he?"

"Do you know Herman personally, Parson?"

"We're real good friends," said Parson Jack. "He came in to see me not so long ago. Said he was real pleased with the *Trumpet*. He told me he liked what I had to say about the CIO and the nigger and told me to keep it up. He said he couldn't print stuff like that in the *Statesman* but that he wanted me to be sure to keep on printing it in the *Trumpet*. He even gave me a couple of suggestions for stories." He smiled from the memory. "That's how it is with Herman and me." Pause. "And there you are."

"What about Mr. Tom Linder? You know him, too?"

"Oh yes. Tom's a great Bible scholar, one of the best. He's sent me a copy of his book. I haven't had time to read it, but I gave him a nice little story in last week's *Trumpet*."

"What do you think about his prediction the world's coming to an end in two thousand four?"

The Parson frowned. "Now I don't understand why Tom would say a thing like that. It violates all the rules. It's against the rules of good Bible prophecy to name dates like that. Course he may be right—this atomic bomb and everything."

He started to get up. All of a sudden, he looked wary. "You boys aren't trying to trick me, are you?"

"Trick you?" Jamie said. "We don't believe in tricking people."

"Somebody tried to trick me not long ago. A kike. From New York, I think. I had to have him thrown off the grounds." He paused again. "You know who you boys ought to talk with? Frank Norris. He's the smartest man I ever knew in my [Norris is the Baptist preacher who recently filed a libel against Ralph McGill.)

"I'd like to take a look around the tabernacle before we go, Parson," I suggested, rising. "I understand you've got quite a plant."

"Well, it's not as good as it will be." Parson Jack moved toward the door. "Come on this way. I'll show you the print shop first. He took us across a short alleyway and through a door into the adjoining building. We didn't get a look at his printing equipment. We saw a man standing over a composing stone, making up what appeared to be an A&P circular. We got a glimpse of a flatbed press. But the Parson rushed us back to the Linotype. "Want you to meet my son. He's the smart one. Works here with me during the day and goes to law school at night. Married, too." At the Linotype a small, black-haired boy about twenty raised himself to a half-standing posture and smiled weakly. He shook hands with us without saying a word. He appeared highly nervous and embarrassed and quite relieved when we left him.

"Now come this way," the Parson directed. We walked back across the alley into the church proper, down a corridor and into the auditorium. "It's not finished yet, but it's really gonna be grand. Look at that." He pointed to the font. We saw three tiers, the first a pulpit, the second a choir section, and the third a stage. What the Parson wanted us to see was the backdrop. It was impressive, all right. Flanking the stage up front, reaching up to the proscenium, were two panels, each about six feet wide. On each was painted a palm tree. Across the back of the stage stretched another scene. It was painted on cloth in bright greens, yellows, and blues of billboard art, and it resembled the sort of curtain that rolled down in old-time vaudeville acts when the comic came out to crack jokes while the prop men changed the set and the girls their costumes. At first we took the scene to represent a south Georgia landscape, but no, we agreed later, it must have been the Parson's idea of the River Jordan. There were swaying palm trees and a waterfall and a big full moon.

"You boys wait here a minute," the Parson told us, indicating a spot about halfway back from the stage. "I got something special to show you." And he ran up front and disappeared. In a minute we heard a series of clicks. The whole scene lit up. "It's painted on velour cloth, and it illuminates from behind," the Parson yelled. "Now watch." There was another click, and lo and behold, the moon lit up.

"That's swell Parson," we yelled back. "That's really swell."

"Don't go 'way," he shouted. "That ain't all."

Then we heard a knob turn and after that the sound of running water. We looked hard. From behind the backdrop, as if originating from the painted waterfall, flowed real water. Our eyes followed it as it moved in a stream down what must have been a concealed trough and spilled—you guessed it—into the baptismal font.

The Parson let it run and came trotting back to where we were standing. He was clapping his hands and smiling proudly. "It takes a lot of water to run a Baptist church, you know."

And there you are.

Theodore J. McGee, member, Muscogee County
Democratic Executive Committee; former law
partner of Bob Elliott, interviewed in
his office in Columbus, July 17

I asked Mr. McGee to tell me something about the composition and character of Negro leadership in Columbus,
commenting that several persons I'd talked with had described it as weak and corruptible. He immediately de-
murred. "There are many upright Negroes in Columbus,"
one of them a Baptist minister named Smith and another a
medical doctor, T. H. Brewer Sr., "the smartest of them all."
Dr. Brewer, he said, has done well in his "profession," as
well as in several business enterprises, including ownership
of a couple of liquor stores. "Brewer may not be completely
honest, but there's no evidence that he is a scoundrel, and
he's a fearless fighter for his people." It was rumored last
summer that he had sold out 25 percent of the Negro vote to
Talmadge. McGee says "this proved to be false."

McGee is deeply and "conscientiously" interested in the
plight of the Negro and has done what he could to help. This
has brought down a lot of criticism on his head, but he is
willing to accept it. He welcomed the Primus King case and
urged the state and county committees to accede to the Negro petition. He felt that a voluntary act would do "so much
more to create understanding and good will" than a court
decision. In a letter to Arnall he urged that be the course
taken, but Arnall said no, the Supreme Court should decide.

McGee managed the Negro polling place in last summer's
primary. Some three thousand Negroes voted, nearly every
one against Talmadge. What impressed McGee was the orderliness and seriousness of the Negroes as they came to the
polls. They had dressed for the occasion, and they handled
themselves with "great dignity." Almost none voted for
M. E. Thompson for lieutenant governor. Instead they voted

in a bloc for a relatively obscure candidate, L. N. Huff, because he was the only man in the race to say flatly that the Negro ought to have the right to vote—a valid reason, McGee thought. "When Negroes vote in a bloc, it usually *is* for a valid reason."

Parson Jack Johnston is a "pimp," McGee said. "Any time he gets out of line, the boys who pay him off can tell him where to stop and go."

McGee practiced law with Bob Elliott for five years and parted with him for reasons he did not care to state. "Bob knows better," he said. When Elliott returned from the legislature, McGee reproached him mildly: "Bob, you weren't sincere in the positions you took in Atlanta." In reply, Elliott only gave him "that smile."

James V. Carmichael, chief executive offficer, Scripto Manufacturing Company; candidate for governor, 1946, interviewed in his office at the Atlanta Scripto plant, July 23

Carmichael says that he feels more relieved than embittered by his defeat. He's glad that he is not having to serve as governor and in a position where he'd "have to fight the pressures from all the groups that supported me."

He is profoundly dissatisfied with the character of Georgia politics but, like so many others, is at a loss to know what might be done to raise it above the level of smear and name-calling and tawdry bargaining and degrading campaigns. He deplores the situation that dissuades good men of proven ability from offering for governor ("No man who's earned the respect of his community wants to subject himself to the slander of a campaign. Any man competent enough to be governor can earn much more money in private business.") And he especially deplores the county unit

system. ("That's the crux of our problem. Of course, I defended it last summer. I had to. But it's bad, bad, bad—the
worst barrier to good government. I don't know how you're
going to get rid of it, either. No legislature is going to vote to
abolish it. Hell, few men are going to vote for something
that'll abolish their jobs.") He believes that what's needed in
Georgia is a two-party system ("Call 'em Democrats and Re-
publicans, Democrats and Loyal Democrats, or anything
you please"), under which two distinct primaries would be
held and the decisive vote would be in the general election.
"It looks as if through a series of lucky breaks we might
have two primaries next summer. 'Course the last thing
Talmadge wants is two primaries, but if he can't get into
Thompson's primary. . . ." (When we told him that we had
been told by almost everybody in the Thompson camp that
Herman would be admitted into the Thompson primary, he
shook his head and said, "Well, that answers it. We won't
have two primaries.") He likes Thompson personally, considers him a man of dignity and character, but is worried
that the Rivers influence may destroy him politically. "I'm
afraid it really doesn't make much of a damn with me. I can't
see enough difference between M. E. Thompson with Ed
Rivers and Herman Talmadge with Roy Harris. I'd support
Thompson, of course, but I can't be very happy about it as
long as he's got Ed Rivers hovering over his shoulder." He
would like to see Cason Callaway as governor but doesn't
think anything in the world could persuade him to run. He
also mentioned Lon Duckworth—"a politically ambitious
man, and a good one, but he lives in Fulton County and he
stands no chance of being elected."

Carmichael speaks readily and firsthand about the political role of the Georgia Power Company. "It's not an influence that works for greed, and it never initiates any legislation, for good or for bad. To my knowledge it has never
sought to get a bill passed that would grant it special privileges. But the Power Company must always maintain such

a favored position that if the time ever comes when a higher
tax rate is threatened on kilowatts or whenever a bill is introduced that might single it out, it can kill it through its influence with the assembly, and that failing, through its influence with the governor. . . . The Power Company does have
an interest in local elections, but it exhibits it so quietly and
so skillfully that the public never knows. . . . The company,
as such, never supports any candidate. But its executives do,
and the executive in charge of politics is Fred Wilson. I'm in
business with Fred. I like him personally. But he didn't support me last year. He was very pleasant about it. He told
me he wouldn't go along with me, because he knew that I
wasn't a safe man. He knew from having worked with me
that I would decide an issue on its merits and not on the
basis of special interest. There's not a doubt in my mind that
Fred kept Ed Rivers in the race last summer to split the unit
vote or that at the same time he contributed to the Talmadge
campaign. Wilson is smart. He doesn't talk politics except
when politics is business. He operates on the theory that
every man has his price, and that the price isn't always
money. He always manages to control at least fifty men in
every assembly—the fifty so-called key men—by just making friends with them or doing them favors. He does this
often long before they get to the legislature. He buys a gun
for the man's son—simply as a friendly gesture. Or he'll
lend a man some money. . . . He never extracts a promise,
but he always knows that if the time comes when the Power
Company is under fire, he can count on these men to do
what he wants done. . . . Fred is a good businessman. He's
made a lot of money honestly. He bought the Henry Grady
Hotel with Cecil Cannon when hotels could be had for almost nothing, and in hardly any time at all the hotel business was booming. He's invested wisely, and he's made piles
of money in real estate. I don't think anybody will tell you
Wilson is a crook, and I'm not sure he's a sinister influence,
either. Certainly he has the power, but whether he uses it for

sinister purposes is something else again. . . . It's a baneful situation, though, when any one man can control a legislature. . . . Wilson became active with the Power Company and in Georgia politics sometime in the early thirties. Somehow or other he became the fair-haired boy to Wendell Willkie when Willkie was head of Commonwealth and Southern. Willkie liked him and made him his chief political adviser in Georgia on Power Company policies. For a time Wilson answered only to Willkie himself. He could act as if Preston Arkwright didn't exist. Now that Willkie's out of the picture, Fred answers only to Whiting, and it'll be the same set-up under this new Southern Power Company. . . . It's through the Henry Grady that Fred can exert his strongest influence. He's in an ideal spot to do almost every kind of favor for a politician. And he can do 'em without ever implicating the Power Company."

Carmichael said he didn't know how many counties could be bought. "Certainly it's true that there is one group of counties that can be bought with cash and another group so venal they can be controlled by the right man. That man, of course, is Roy Harris."

He said that he had tried purposely not to know the exact cost of his own campaign. "A lot of money was spent through campaign headquarters, and a lot more was spent on my behalf that I didn't know about. I made it very clear every time I accepted anybody's contribution that I was taking it as their investment in good government and that I did not commit myself to do their bidding. Some people took their contributions back, rather than give on those terms, too. . . . You add up everything it takes to run a campaign— radio time, full-page ads, workers to plaster the state with posters, automobiles, all that—and I'd say it takes a quarter of a million dollars to run anybody's campaign. The bad thing, of course, is that people don't invest fifteen or twenty thousand dollars just for good government. If they tell you they do, it's ————."

Roy Harris, former Speaker of the House, interviewed in his room at the Henry Grady Hotel, July 29

We caught Mr. Harris finishing breakfast. He appeared to us to be an extraordinarily gregarious man, comfortably opinionated, and generous with comments and stories about anything that occurs to him or is asked of him. It's obvious that he loves to talk politics, and he began talking almost before we opened our mouths to explain our purpose. The words came as if shot from a Gatling gun. He talked almost without pause. He stopped momentarily when the phone rang, murmured briefly to the caller, and picked up where he left off, hardly missing a beat. When nature called, he merely raised his voice and left the bathroom door ajar. It taxed every brain cell in my head to absorb and retain what he told us. To reconstruct, from my few notes and immediate recollection:

"We haven't had two parties in Georgia because of prejudice and the Negro. [He meant prejudice against the Republican Party.] Prejudice doesn't have much to do with it now. It's mostly the Negro question.

"If we have two parties in Georgia, of course the second party will be Republican. That's the only one, unless you want to go along with the Henry Wallace pinks. I don't know whether the niggers will go Republican or not. I do know we're going to have a white man's party in Georgia. . . . It won't make any difference what the Supreme Court decides on the South Carolina primary. The Negro is going to motivate Georgia politics for years to come. Under a two-party system the Negro would be the balance of power. The Negro always goes to the highest bidder. I'm not sure if it would be at all healthy for Georgia to have two parties.

"Labor doesn't make a damn in a state election. Their strength is only in eight counties: Fulton, Floyd, Bibb, Chatham, Richmond, Muscogee, Whitfield, and Greene. The CIO can deliver Whitfield and Greene, but the AFL is strong in all the rest and the AFL doesn't stick like the CIO. 'Course, if you start treading on labor, the AFL and CIO will vote together. But it's very rare that they do get together, and usually in a campaign I forget about labor. The anti–closed shop bill could conceivably bind the AFL and the CIO together next year, but it won't. Who've they got to choose between? Only Thompson and Herman. They could put in a third man, but they wouldn't get to first base. It'd amount only to a protest. I predict that they won't even try to back a third man. I predict instead that next year the CIO will go for Thompson and the AFL for Herman.

"The Georgia Power Company doesn't have much influence outside Atlanta. I usually work through their attorneys, though. You get Abit Nix in Athens, Inman Curry in Augusta, John Bouhan in Savannah, and Frank Foley in Columbus—you get those four on your side and you can usually count on their delivering. Mr. Arkwright could always deliver a big block of votes in Atlanta. Mostly from labor. He was always good to labor—always paid 'em a little more than they could have earned anywhere else. He could talk to his people in Atlanta, and they'd vote for the man he said vote for. But that isn't true anymore and never was very true out in the state.

"The Power Company has had no real influence since Dick Russell beat their man Crisp in 1932. The Power Company backed Rivers in 1946. Fred Wilson was smart. He's a business partner of Carmichael's, and he knew that he could have Carmichael's ear if he should go in. [Harris implied that Wilson could also have Talmadge's ear.] . . . Rivers didn't hurt us any. He baited the hell out of Jim Cox and the *Atlanta Journal* and left Gene free to talk about the nigger. But Rivers didn't decide the election for Gene. If he'd stayed out of the race, Gene would have got ten more counties than he did.

"The Coca-Cola Company has been the biggest corporation for the last ten years. Backed Carmichael last year. Coca-Cola people are scared to death of a soft-drinks tax, and they dish out big money to campaigns—$25,000 or more. But the Coca-Cola Company, and all the other corporations for that matter, are important only as a source of campaign funds. They aren't able to deliver many votes.

"It cost Rivers and Carmichael $125,000 apiece to run for governor last year. It cost Talmadge only $100,000. Rivers got better than $60,000 from one liquor man in Atlanta, Horace Bowen, and the rest from contractors. Carmichael raised only $50,000 for actual campaign expenses, and when it was all over, Talmadge Dobbs and Wiley Moore were stuck with a note for $75,000. They got it paid off by having Ellis Arnall hand out state insurance to Wiley's firm. . . . Most of Talmadge's funds came from people all over the state in small contributions. We were getting $1,000 a day in unsolicited contributions right up to the day of the primary. A lot of small businessmen gave, too—$250 or $500. But there were no promises, tacit or otherwise. That's the beauty of a Talmadge campaign. In good times Talmadge never had any trouble raising money, and he always had scads of people around wanting to work free. He never got any big money, either, so he wasn't beholden to the Big Boys.

"There's no tricks to Georgia politics. Ralph McGill thinks so. There's nobody in the state knows less about politics than Ralph McGill. He's like a schoolgirl who gets so involved in geometry and algebra she thinks there must be some great mystery to it. Hell, there's no mystery. Georgia politics are simple when you understand them. To win in Georgia you've got to be a smart organizer and work hard. That's all. You've got to know how the counties line up, what counties are in the bag, what counties to work on, and what counties to forget about. Last spring [1946], right after that special session, I wrote letters to six friends in every county in the state. I asked them which of the three candidates [Rivers,

Talmadge, and Carmichael] was likely to carry that county. When I got my answers, I studied them for awhile and told Gene that he had seventy-five counties in the bag; we had to worry about only twenty-five more. 'Course you have to know how to read 'em. Some replies you can just discount entirely, depending on the source. But if you've been around as long as I have, you know who to believe and who not to believe.

"If you're going to win in Georgia, you got to know the counties. They differ, you know, almost as much as the forty-eight states. You got to know how the people think and what they want. The history and background of a county is important, too. Effingham County was settled by German Salzburgers. Ben Hill County—the county Fitzgerald's in— was settled by a colony of Yankee soldiers. Never went for Talmadge until 1946, when they got scared of the niggers.

"I never get worried when people tell me somebody's try-ing to buy a county. You can't buy a county. Hell, there are some counties in Georgia that'd go against you if you tried so much as to hire an automobile to carry voters to the polls. You can buy an election only in the sense that you're sure to lose it if you can't match your opposition, penny for penny, in spending on newspaper and radio publicity. I wouldn't try to buy a county. I don't believe you can buy a county and get it delivered. Only time I get worried is when they tell me the opponent's sewed up the election committee and plans to steal the election. But there isn't much of that. We have open elections in Georgia, public counting. How can one side steal an election if the other side's watching? I know I'm always damned sure to get watchers at the polls. I get people who are hot for my man, just as hot as I am. They see that there's no funny business.

"You know how that thing happened in Telfair, don't you? The election managers didn't understand what the strategy was. They got dismayed when they saw all those write-in votes for Herman and figured the old man wouldn't like it, so they voted so many for Gene. That's how the voting list got alphabetized. They just took the last thirty-four on the registration list and voted 'em for Gene. Nobody ever pays any attention to the general election anyway. It's never amounted to anything before. Usually you can get good poll managers for a primary, but hell, nobody wants to work a poll during the general election. You usually have to get old people, who're just naturally slow and careless. Sort of thing doesn't go on during a primary count. Our primaries are honest and fair.

"There are no tricks in Georgia politics. You pull one and you're through.

"Ed Rivers had the biggest radio audience last summer anybody ever built up in a Georgia campaign, and he still pulled only seventy thousand votes. He's the best stump speaker in the state. Nobody can beat him on the stump. But they won't vote for him. They listened to him last year 'cause they liked what he had to say abut Jim Cox and the *Atlanta Journal*. Same people voted for Gene.

"Now Gene wasn't the best man on the stump. But he knew how to handle his audiences—spotting questions, organizing claques. The audience made the show. . . . Ellis Arnall's campaign in 1942 cost twenty-five thousand dollars. Most expensive campaign in the history of Georgia. And if the campaign had run two more weeks, he'd have been licked. . . . But in 1942 and in 1946 the campaign never changed from the beginning. Arnall had it in his pocket in 1942 and Gene in 1946.

"We can't let the niggers run Georgia. They'll do it, though, if Thompson gets elected next year. Hell, Thompson got elected lieutenant governor on the strength of Ed Rivers's seventy thousand votes and the niggers' one hundred thousand votes. . . . I *know* a hundred thousand niggers voted last year because I had my men in every county count the nigger ballots before they were consolidated. . . . If the election was held tomorrow, Herman would win in a walk. Why, within a week after the Supreme Court decision his strength increased 20 percent. I took a poll and I know.

"But if five hundred thousand niggers register—and that many could, you know—we might as well go fishing."

Notes

1. In 1939 the Citizens' Fact-Finding Movement commissioned Georgia scholars in the fields of education, economics, and public welfare to annotate the President's Report on Economic Conditions of the South. The result was a graphic statistical profile of the state, based on the then most reliable data. Among the disclosures: 50,000 Georgia families (188,804 persons) were on relief. Annual per capita income was $253. The state ranked forty-third in literacy; 9.04 percent of the population over ten years of age could not sign their names. Only 40 percent of children from five to seventeen were in school. More than 8,500 Georgians had tuberculosis. More than 300 died from malaria every year. In rural areas there was 1 physician for every 1,800 persons, in urban areas 1 per 1,100, in the state as a whole 1 per 1,560. Two counties (Chattahoochee and Webster) had neither physician nor dentist. It may be assumed that for most Georgians conditions improved during and after World War II, but the average black had considerably less to be encouraged about. To give but one example: in 1946 there were only 44 noncharity hospital beds and only 25 physicians available to the 100,000 blacks in segregated Atlanta.

2. Ulrich B. Phillips, *Life of Robert Toombs* (1913), quoted by C. Vann Woodward, *Tom Watson, Agrarian Rebel* (New York: Macmillan, 1938), 55.

3. Thomas E. Watson (1856–1922), a lawyer and landowner from Thomson, began his political career as a champion of the farmer and the poor of both races. Coming to maturity during the crucial years of Reconstruction, he saw the rising industrialism of the North as an agent of destruction and spent most of his unhappy life trying to defend a declining agrarian society against it.

Watson was a fiercely independent politician, quick to move in and out of the Democratic Party as issues and conscience directed him. He was a young and fiery leader of the Farmers' Alliance in the 1890s. He ran for vice president on the ticket with William Jennings Bryan in 1896 and was the Populist Party's candidate for president in 1904. His successive defeats only served to strengthen his resolve and to personalize—indeed, to demonize—the forces of eastern capitalism that he saw "conspiring" to make a colony of the South.

He was elected to one term in Congress, during which his main achievement was the law that created rural free mail delivery. He lost his bid for reelection in 1892, mainly because neither his supporters nor the U.S. marshals in attendance were able to prevent wholesale bribery, intimidation, and ballot-box stuffing at the polls. Until he returned to Washington as a senator thirty years later, that was his last elective office.

Nevertheless, throughout his long and turbulent career Watson retained a large and loyal "wool-hat" constituency. During the period of his so-called political inactivity, his influence was so powerful among rural voters that no candidate for governor who had earned his disapproval could expect to be elected, and few governors were elected without his endorsement.

His influence was nourished by a form of personal journalism that he practically invented (he founded and edited a forerunner of the *Statesman*) and also by a remarkable talent for oratory, which one biographer has described as a powerful blend of "robust metaphor and Gargantuan simile struck off with spontaneity in the genuine rural idiom" (Woodward, *Tom Watson*, 47–48). (Speaking of his opponent in an early campaign: "I presume from what he says that he could with all ease tell you the sex of the hog merely by smelling the gravy" [ibid., 48].) To his rural countrymen, most of whom had reason to feel perpetually hard done by and were grateful for any free entertainment, his colorful invective was irresistible. During the panic of 1893, sensing their anger at the impotence of the statehouse, he called the scholarly Governor William Northen "a long-whiskered imbecile" whose "brains are chronically stagnant" (James F. Cook, *The Governors of Georgia, 1754–1995* [Macon: Mercer University Press, 1996], 180).

He learned early to satisfy his followers' need for a scapegoat. But as he grew older, he came to feel thwarted "in all deepest desires" (Woodward, *Tom Watson*, 460), and he found more and more scapegoats on which to blame his frustration. Embittered and disappointed, he aimed his venom variously and recklessly at Yankees, Negroes, Catholics, and Jews. Woodrow Wilson, he once charged, had "kow-towed to the Roman hierarch" and was "ravenously fond of the negro" (ibid., 426).

Regrettably, his rhetoric never lost its power to wound and incite, no matter how irrational he became. His editorials are widely believed to have motivated the 1915 lynching of Leo Frank ("the Sodomite," "a libertine Jew," "a lascivious pervert.") "Rise! People of Georgia," his headlines exhorted. "When 'Mobs' Are No Longer Possible," he wrote, "Liberty Will Be Dead." He exceeded himself by defending lynch law as the ultimate expression of democracy: "The Voice of the People Is the Voice of God" (ibid., 439, 445).

To many historians of the South, Tom Watson appears as a tragic figure in whom legitimate grievance turned into paranoia and whose resistance to corrupting new economic forces was itself corrupted by an unreasoning commitment to the past. True enough. But most political scientists today think him worthy of study primarily as a model of the stereotypical demagogue. Apparently, in his student days at the University of Georgia, Eugene Talmadge also thought him a model for study. According to a college roommate, young Gene used to tramp up and down the dormitory floor reciting Watson's speeches, with gestures. "I once walked ten miles to hear him speak," Talmadge himself recalled years later (*Atlanta Constitution*, December 22, 1946, as quoted by Ralph McGill).

For a superb biography, see Woodward, *Tom Watson*.

4. In some rudimentary form, the county unit system may date from 1757, when, with approval of the Crown, the Georgia colony elected its first House of Commons. As best one can tell from surviving records, the number of representatives a parish had in the lower house was based on the number of people living in the parish, and voting in the House was on the basis of one representative, one vote. The whole arrangement could hardly pass for self-government. To vote for representatives (and other officials not appointed by the king's governor), a resident had to qualify as a male tax-paying property owner, and laws passed by the assembly were subject to veto by the king or the governor. Still, in the beginning—if one can believe early accounts—apportionment was fairly equitable, and the number of "unit" votes cast, while not necessarily reflective of citizen preference, was close to the ratio of representatives to constituents.

But the population grew, parishes became counties after the Revolution, and more and more counties were added. This inevitably skewed composition of the House in favor of the least populous counties, as each county, no matter how small in population, still had at least one representative. By 1843, the number of House members had increased to more than a hundred, whereupon an act was passed to limit thirty-seven of the more populous counties to two representatives and the remaining fifty counties to one. The same act gave each county twice the number of unit votes as it had representatives. With that, the pattern was set.

In concession to population growth and political pressures, the size of House membership changed over the years, as did the number of representatives (and unit votes) to which each county is entitled. Even so, population has had very little to do with the weight of suffrage. The constitution of 1868 fixed membership in the lower house at 175, granting 3 representatives each to the six most populous counties, 2 each to the thirty-one next in population, and 1 each to the remaining ninety-five. Again, each county was accorded twice as many unit votes as it had representatives. With slight alterations, this formula held for the next ninety-five years.

In 1876 the unit system was adopted as the basis for electing delegates to the state convention of the Democratic Party. And, with the introduction of statewide primaries in 1898, the system was extended to nominations for the governorship and most other state offices. After that, the most significant change occurred in 1917 with passage of the Neill Primary Act, which brought the system, theretofore mandated by party custom, under the imprimatur of Georgia law. Although Georgia was to remain a one-party state for another fifty years, the Neill Act (named for its sponsor, W. Cecil Neill, of Columbus, then president of the state Senate) theoretically made the system applicable to all political parties. This was a provision that was to acquire unexpected significance in the early forties when the U.S. Supreme Court began applying the Constitution to the conduct of party primaries.

By the time of the 1946 primary, several political realities were making the county unit system an increasingly contentious public issue. By then almost 50 percent of the people lived in the more populous urban counties, so that the system's discriminatory effect was being felt by a near majority of voters. The disparities in voting privilege were so magnified as to defy belief: for example, the 18,635 people who lived in Bryan, Camden, and Clinch Counties had as much weight at the polls as the half million residents of Atlanta's Fulton County. The disproportion was more than twenty-five to one.

More dramatically, returns from the 1946 primary gave long-frustrated opponents of the system the specific grievance they needed for a court challenge. Twice before, once in 1934 and once in 1936, candidates with popular majorities had been defeated by men who had won more unit votes, but these anomalies had occurred in congressional races of relatively little statewide interest. Now, for the first time, the unit vote had defeated a gubernatorial candidate with an impressive following: James V. Carmichael had polled 314,000 votes to Eugene Talmadge's 297,000. Moreover, this time a congressional candidate with a popular majority had been defeated under such egregiously unfair conditions as to inflame feminists and lowercase democrats everywhere. Helen Douglas Mankin, a liberal, no-nonsense Atlanta lawyer, had won the Fifth District seat in a special election earlier that year. She had won it, however, because of a peculiar circumstance. The Neill Act had made the unit system optional in the nomination of U.S. representatives, and in 1932 the Fifth District Democratic Executive Committee had abandoned its use in congressional races. Now, clearly to block her reelection, a district committee dominated by the reactionary DeKalb and Rockdale Counties reinstated unit rule. The rule prevailed in the July primary, and Mrs. Mankin lost. She won 53,611 votes to her opponent's 42,482. She lost anyway.

Almost immediately, an aroused group in Atlanta filed two suits—one on behalf of Fulton County residents, the other on behalf of those in DeKalb—asking the U.S. Supreme Court to declare the system a violation of the Fourteenth Amendment's equal-rights clause. The justices refused to hear this first petition, and it took, all told, six suits and seventeen years for the Court to act. But on March 18, 1963, Justice William O. Douglas spoke for the majority: "Once the geographical unit . . . is designated, all who participate in the election are to have an equal vote. . . . The conception of political equality from the Declaration of Independence to Lincoln's Gettysburg Address, to the 15th, 17th, and 19th Amendments, can mean only one thing—one person, one vote" (*Gray v. Sanders*, 372 U.S. 368). So ended the county unit system.

5. Dr. Philip Weltner had been chancellor of the University System of Georgia. Blanton Fortson was a judge of the Superior Court of Clarke County. Both were men of impeccable character, united in contempt for Eugene Talmadge and enthusiasm for Franklin Roosevelt. Both were outraged by Talmadge's savage attacks on the New Deal, which were expected to continue in the 1936 primary through the campaign of Talmadge's would-be successor, Charles D. Redwine. Fearful that no likely candidate for governor would adequately represent the president, Dr. Weltner organized an impressive number of Georgia New Dealers and with their backing persuaded Judge Fortson to run. As a "best-element" candidate, Judge Fortson did a commendable job stating the case for himself and the president. But somewhat to his and Dr. Weltner's surprise, another candidate, E. D. Rivers, a man who only a few months before had been a prominent Talmadge partisan, turned out to be an even more effective spokesman for Roosevelt. Fortson lost gallantly.

6. Ellis Arnall's enemies faulted him for accomplishments that struck them as a mite too liberal, among them the creation of a merit system for state employees, repeal of the poll tax, abolition of the chain gang, and a modernized state constitution. Even more, they disliked him for the way he courted the national media; he was too quick, they said, to talk about Georgia's problems with outsiders, to enhance his own image at the expense of the state's. But what really infuriated his opponents—white-collar and wool-hat alike—was simply that he could outsmart them. Too late, they came to appreciate his very real political skills. He looked stream-washed, young, and innocent—pink and almost cherubic. He was, however, neither without guile nor, as necessity called, above using dubiously ethical means to reach a worthy end. For instance, in the immediate aftermath of the legislature's election of Herman Talmadge, he did not hesitate to suborn the chief justice of the state supreme court. Almost forty years later (May 29, 1986) in a video-taped interview for the University of West Georgia's oral history project, he described what only he and a few of his closest associ-

ates knew at the time: "I'd said I would never surrender the office of governor to a pretender, but I wanted to be sure [of the constitutional issue]. So I spoke to the chief justice of the supreme court of Georgia. He was my close friend, we had been assistant attorneys general together . . . and I told him to go talk to the court, canvass the other justices, and then tell me whether I was right in making this fight. And he came back and said, 'You have a majority of the court that will support you.' So I knew what I was doing. . . . I violated all the legal principles, all the ethics and everything else for the greatest good. I talked with the supreme court because I could not subject Georgia to a banana republic kind of war and I did not want to prolong the controversy unless I knew the ground I was standing on. . . . I tried to get the court to announce it without a court case but they said no, we have a procedure we have to get through. Judges will be judges, I guess."

For a good account of Arnall's term as governor (1943–47) and his rise to national prominence, see Harold Paulk Henderson, *The Politics of Change in Georgia: A Political Biography of Ellis Arnall* (Athens: University of Georgia Press, 1991).

7. For those of us in our teens when Eugene Talmadge was first elected governor, it is hard to believe that he was only sixty-two when he died. We always thought of him as an old man. He was "turkey-necked," as *Time* magazine was prone to describe him, and even in a tuxedo he looked as if he'd been "drove hard and put up wet." Not too long after the July primary, he had been taken to Atlanta's Piedmont Hospital after a stomach hemorrhage. On a diet of poached eggs, he began to recover. Then, in character, he rebelled, left the hospital, drove two hundred miles home to McRae, and over the Thanksgiving holidays ate fried chicken, ham, and hot biscuits with gravy. He drove back to Atlanta, collapsed, and got terribly ill. He was diagnosed with hemolytic jaundice and cirrhosis of the liver. No number of transfusions could save him. He died three weeks before he was to go back to the governor's mansion for the fourth time.

Talmadge left the University of Georgia in 1907 with a Phi Beta Kappa key. He built his political career on ignorance and bigotry. During his three terms as governor, he fought the New Deal, opposed higher wages and labor unions, and brought Georgia into national disgrace with witch hunts on schoolteachers. He was for keeping "the nigger" in his place. He made "white supremacy" a theology and preached it with all the scary passion of an old-time evangelist. Shortly after his body was brought to lie in state under the capitol dome, a large floral wreath was delivered and placed nearby. The inscription read "K.K.K."

A great many Georgians thought he could do no wrong. Others thought he could, and would, do anything. However they regarded him, almost all of them long ago learned never to underestimate him. He authorized three-dollar license tags even though the advisers he most respected told him that to do so would bankrupt the state. (It didn't.) He sent in the militia to break up textile strikes even though he'd sworn not to. He dismissed the Board of Regents even though he knew he was breaking the law. According to a joke circulating during his last campaign, if Eugene Talmadge were to announce that he planned to move Stone Mountain, the average Georgian would say, without batting an eye, "Where's he gonna put it?"

"What did he do for Georgians?" Jamie and I asked a country-weekly editor. The reply: "He gave us a three-dollar tag. And a dern good show."

8. To justify Herman's election by the legislature, Talmadge lawyers drew on an ambiguous provision in the new state constitution, one carried over from the old: "If no person should have [a] majority (of the total votes cast) then from the two persons having the highest number of votes who shall be in life and shall not decline an election . . . the General Assembly shall immediately elect a governor *viva voce*." From this, the assembly inferred no obligation to call a special election but, rather, the authority to name as governor one of "the two men" who had received the highest number of write-in votes at the November 5 general election. To make sure that Herman would be one of these two, the Talmadge leadership contrived to produce 675 write-ins, 6 more than the number recorded for James V. Carmichael. Fifty-eight of these write-ins were later discovered to have been tallied fraudulently, 34 of them in the names of voters as they appeared in alphabetical order on the registration list. But never mind. In a raucous joint session on the night of January 15, the assembly put thirty-three-year-old Herman in his father's place. The vote was 161 to 87.

With the dramatic support of incumbent governor Ellis Arnall, the legislature's action was promptly contested by M. E. Thompson, whose election as lieutenant governor had been indisputably verified in the November general election. For rationale, Thompson cited another paragraph in the same article in the 1945 constitution: "The executive power shall be vested in a governor who shall hold office for four years and until his successor shall be chosen and qualified. . . . In case of the death, disability, or resignation of the governor, the lieutenant governor shall exercise the executive power." There then ensued a series of court appeals, ending in a five-to-two ruling by the state supreme court on March 19. According to the majority opinion written by Presiding Justice W. H. Duckworth: "In 1824 by constitutional provision the General Assembly was divested of its general power to elect a governor, and the power was retained by the people, where it remains today. . . . The death of the Hon. Eugene Talmadge after his election by the people . . . did not change the duty of [the General Assembly] to declare his election nor authorize the General Assembly to declare by resolution that because of this death no person had a majority of the votes and to elect a governor." The decision came down shortly after 11 A.M. Less than two hours later, Herman Talmadge was out of the governor's mansion.

9. As passed by the House, the sales tax bill provided that goods costing under nine cents would go tax free, and those costing between ten and thirty cents would be taxed a penny. This provision was inserted ostensibly to avoid the use of tokens.

10. Another expert, however, told us that there was no tax man outside the Georgia Power's own staff qualified or sufficiently informed to appraise its property accurately.

11. *Time*, January 27, 1947, 21. This same piece positions Roy Harris in a suite on the fourteenth floor of the Henry Grady Hotel plying legislators "with bourbon, cigars, veiled threats and glittering promises."

12. Having lobbied successfully for abolition of the closed shop for labor unions, shortly before the assembly adjourned, Mr. Wingate drafted a bill that in effect would set up a closed shop for peanut processors. His proposal never made it to the floor.

13. *Atlanta Journal*, May 4, 1947.

14. Whatever reputation the Power Company has for meddling

in politics comes from the activities of its officials and employees, not from any stated policy of the corporation. (In 1946 the chairman of the board was a staunch Talmadge supporter, while its president publicly endorsed Carmichael. Mr. Wilson did not declare himself but is presumed to have backed Ed Rivers.) The risk is much too great for the company to authorize campaign contributions in ways that can be traced. Its books are open to inspection at any time by the Securities Exchange Commission (SEC), the Federal Power Commission, and the State Power Commission. In 1938, after the campaign in which Senator Walter George defeated President Roosevelt's choice, Lawrence Camp, the SEC sent three men to examine the company's books. In the course of their investigation, helped by FBI men, they talked with virtually every politician in Georgia of any prominence and also combed the books of the Henry Grady Hotel. After a year and a half they could find no violation of the Public Utility Holding Act of 1935, under which the inquiry was made. Their findings were never published.

15. We tried three times to arrange for an interview with Fred Wilson. Once we actually got inside his office. Our visit was brief, however, for as soon as we gave the purpose of our visit, he remembered other business. He asked that we phone him the following week. When we did, he told us politely that he was so busy he didn't know when he could find time to talk with us; he promised to phone us soon and make a definite appointment. He has never phoned. One of his working acquaintances told us why: "Fred talks politics only when it's *his* business."

16. "A Shocking Appointment," *Atlanta Journal*, May 4, 1947.

17. OC GA47–1001; see also Constitution of the State of Georgia, art. 1, sec. 2, para. 5.

18. Ibid.

19. Ibid.

20. It is possible, of course, that a Negro bloc could win in the thirty-nine counties where potential Negro voters outnumber potential white voters. It was in these counties, however, that the heaviest purges of Negro registrants took place, and therefore the 1946 primary offers no key to what might happen if elections were free. Georgia's cultural history being what it is, this is likely to remain a purely academic question for years to come.

21. In an effort to preserve its own white primary, South Carolina legislators had voted to remove all references to primaries from the statute books, hoping thereby to "privatize" political-party business and thereby exempt primaries from federal intervention. A state court declared the move a subterfuge, and for much of the summer of 1947 politicians throughout the South were hoping the Supreme Court would rule otherwise. It didn't.

22. The *Journal's* survey was admittedly incomplete, since at least three counties gave no figures at all and in Fulton the books were still open. That the survey was far short can be assumed from the fact that at the time the *Journal* story was written total registration stood at 897,117; two weeks later the secretary of state officially reported it at 1,077,949.

23. Constitution of the State of Georgia, art. 2, sec. 1, para. 4, 2.

24. About 5,000 Negroes voted in the Alabama primary, 2,500 in Mississippi, 10,000 in Virginia, 50,000 in North Carolina, and between 36,000 and 40,000 in Tennessee.

25. In Taylor County, one day after the primary, Marceo Snipes was called out from supper by four white men. Sometime later he stumbled back, clutching his belly, trying to catch the blood that spurted from bullet wounds, and died. Marceo Snipes had been the only Negro to vote in Taylor County.

PART 2

1. Gerald L. K. Smith was a rabble-rousing leader of the radical right. During the thirties, while a preacher for the Disciples of Christ in Shreveport, he had become a loyal accomplice of the Louisiana boss, Huey Long. After Long's assassination in 1935, he picked up his mentor's crusade against the New Deal, took to the radio, began publishing a newspaper called *The Cross and the Flag*, and for the next ten years preached a frightening dogma of Christian fundamentalism, isolationism, and racism. In 1936, as part of his campaign to unseat President Franklin Roosevelt, he staged a "Grass Roots Convention" in Macon, for which one of his proud sponsors was Eugene Talmadge. His enthusiastic and perhaps unsolicited endorsement of Talmadge became an issue in the 1946 gubernatorial race.

2. In the summer of 1936 I worked for the Power Company as a "petty cash boy," my job being to hold a range pole for one of the surveyors. I remember that displayed on bulletin boards at the Atlanta headquarters were poster-size messages urging employees to vote for Ed Rivers, the candidate for governor best qualified "to serve the interests of your company." The messages were signed by Preston Arkwright, the company president. CK.

3. It may be regrettable that Jamie and I had this interview when we did. Both Mr. Bryan and Mr. McGill were showing wear from a long winter of discontent, and Mr. McGill was under extraordinary personal stress. Nevertheless, no summary of events in Georgia of this period can ignore the fact that for much of this time Mr. McGill's condition was the subject of public speculation. While Malcolm Bryan may have been only one of a few friends close enough to observe the behavioral shift, no literate Georgian was unaware of the startling change that had begun to show up in Mr. McGill's daily column in the fall of 1946. The change was evident both in attitude (once aggressively anti-Talmadge, he was now writing as a Talmadge apologist) and in style (customarily friendly, anecdotal, and understandably indignant, his tone was now petulant, angry, defensive). As we made our way through the counties, Jamie and I heard different reactions to this apparent turnaround. The more tolerant among Mr. McGill's readers were dismayed; those less forgiving felt betrayed; the Talmadge-minded were disbelieving, even as they welcomed his favor. They all asked the same question: "What in the world has come over Ralph McGill?"

McGill had given some of his Atlanta admirers cause for worry as early as spring. In April, after the Supreme Court decision outlawing the white primary, Talmadge had proposed that as a way to save it the Neill Primary Act be repealed. By so doing, he argued, the party primary would revert to its old status as a private affair and blacks could be barred again. McGill's response, ostensibly to repudiate Talmadge in the eyes of his rural following, was to write a series of columns in which he pointed out that abolition of the Neill Primary Act might lead to abolition of the county unit system. In a line of expediency that many readers found hard to accept, he argued that although the white primary would have to

go, preservation of the unit vote under the Neill Act would remain as "an effectual check on the influence of large city popula-
tions . . . and the aggressive politics . . . of the CIO." As a clincher,
he added that it would also be the "most effective means" for keeping "the Democratic primary in white hands" (*Atlanta Constitution*,
March 4, 1946, column, Ralph McGill). This did not sound like the
Ralph McGill his readers thought they knew.

His obituary of Eugene Talmadge in December (ibid., December 22, 1946, 1) confused them even more. He called his old enemy
"a political miracle," likened him to Ishmael, and left many feeling
that he was being excessively sympathetic. It was an impression,
however, that his text did not truly support. In his bridge paragraph, McGill was careful to say, "It is of him as a politician, and
not the issues, I want now to write," and throughout some thirty-
four hundred words he confined the adjectives to Talmadge's per-
formance and personality. But it was a case of volume triumphing
over both content and style. The obituary occupied the bottom
of the fold on page 1 and occupied the equivalent of six columns
on page 2 before jumping and ending after two more columns on
page 6. In fact, in the Sunday edition that featured McGill's qualified eulogy, the first section of sixteen pages was almost entirely
devoted to Talmadge's life and death. No wonder, then, that it
looked as if the paper was out to canonize him and that the decision to do so was McGill's. In readers' minds, the *Constitution* and
Ralph McGill were one and the same.

A few days later, citing the opinion of a former "Superior
Judge," McGill argued that the General Assembly had the authority to name a governor and in succeeding columns developed the
case for Herman. "The Talmadge people," he wrote, "more alert
than others, noted the presence in the new State Constitution of a
provision brought over from the old one. . . . It gave them a legal
leg to stand on" (all quotations are from McGill columns, *Atlanta
Constitution*, January 5, 12, 17, 26, and 27, 1947). He thought it only
smart for the Talmadges, anticipating old Gene's death, to manage
775 write-ins for Herman in the general election, and dismissed as
so much "pious whooping" protests from those who looked on it
as shady politics.

He refined his theme in column after column: "The average citi-

zen believes the intent of the Constitution was to have the Lieutenant Governor serve in such a situation. . . . But the Constitution
does not say so. The Constitution contradicts itself." "The chief
persons to blame for the immediate controversy are the writers of
the new Constitution, who left in the fatal defect of legal doubt and
contradiction." "The Talmadge forces have kept carefully within
the law." "Herman Talmadge may be the legal governor."

Equally worrisome to his friends was McGill's readiness to enter
the confessional. "Whatever I am," he wrote, "I am not a hypocrite,
and when the other fellow gets caught I can never quite bring myself to come out calling for the constabulary. . . . Put me down as a
strong exponent of clean elections. But if my man, on whom I have
pinned the flag of moral right, needs a box to win . . . and it can be
stuffed or erased or changed, I would unhesitatingly look the other
way—if that is what it took to get my man in." Stooping to an
argument that demeaned him, he justified the Talmadges' corruption by saying "everybody does it." Apparently peeved by a scold-
ing letter from some follower of M. E. Thompson, he wrote: "The
slot-machine and black-market-liquor ranks of the coastal counties . . . produced plug-uglies and corruptionists [for Thompson]
to match any marshaled behind the Talmadge campaign." In this
same column, he described Roy Harris as "the ablest state politician of the century. . . . I always respect champions, and Mr. Harris
is a champ" (McGill column, January 20, 1947).

He assured readers that he had not been "sulking in my tent,"
but he had to admit to "a certain new cynicism." He lamented that
people rarely get aroused until it is too late. "The average citizen
is too busy to consider his government. He prefers to ignore it until it pinches him. Then he squalls loudly and virtuously and de-
nounces the politicians who have him by the throat. He rarely deserves any better" (ibid., February 29, 1947).

More and more, his columns had the mark of a man besieged. "I
had been writing against the white primary bill, and I was being
cussed for that. I had said that in my opinion the Legislature, being
the elected representatives of the people, had a right to choose a
governor, and was being cuffed around right heartily for that. . . .
To try and answer the many questions about his condition, I had
got into the hospital to see the late Eugene Talmadge and found

him looking good. He thereafter failed to obey his doctor's orders, being a restless, stubborn man, and had died, and I was getting a brisk going over by the second-guessers. So I was at the time doing a daily routine of fast, verbal footwork" (ibid., January 4, 1947).

Throughout the period of the three governors, McGill in print held to what his biographer, Harold H. Martin, described as a "strangely detached, non-partisan attitude" (*Ralph McGill, Reporter* [Boston: Little, Brown, 1973], 120). To members of his staff, however, McGill seemed to be leaning toward Herman Talmadge, and the fear that he might endorse Talmadge editorially was enough to cause a serious rift. The breach was healed only after his associate, Jack Tarver, confronted him in an uncharacteristically emotional appeal that left them both weeping.

In retrospect, McGill's behavior and state of mind—beginning with Eugene Talmadge's election in the 1946 primary and continuing through the spring of 1947—have to be seen as an aberration in a life otherwise noteworthy for courage, generosity of spirit, and a journalist's respect for objectivity. (He once said of himself, "I have been cursed all my life with being able to see both sides of things" [*Newsweek*, June 25, 1973, 88].) Considering the wounding events of the time, the remarkable thing is not that he sank into fits of depression but that he survived without irreparable harm to his health and reputation.

During the 1946 campaign he had fought against Eugene Talmadge's race-baiting with all his heart and soul. For his efforts, he had been called "Rastus" and "Red Ralph," a traitor to his southern heritage, and a tool of eastern interests. Moreover, as Martin reminds us, right up until the returns were in, "he had hoped, even prophesied," that World War II would put an end to the race issue in politics (*Ralph McGill*, 117). "Now, the old Wild Man from Sugar Creek, sounding his war cry of white supremacy, was heading for the statehouse again," and the prospect was almost too much for McGill to bear.

He chastised himself for his naïveté and at the same time had cause to feel that he was fighting the good, lost cause all alone. The *Constitution* was running in the red; because of his editorial views the paper was said to be losing circulation, maybe as much as 3 percent a year. He had risked the wrath of the Klan all by himself.

He was the target for libel suits while the *Constitution*'s lawyers were counseling the news department to avoid any controversy that might bring on more. Clark Howell, the owner, may not have been telling him what to write and not write, but it would not be until 1949, when the paper was sold to James Cox, a proud and liberal Ohio Democrat, that he could be confident of his boss's support.

Of Welsh ancestry, McGill was an emotional man, given to swings between optimism and melancholy, but with a steady undercurrent of idealism. Professionally, however, he prided himself on his pragmatism. "He was leading the thinking of his region," Martin said of him, but he would go "only so far and so fast as his instincts told him he could go without losing his audience" (*Newsweek*, June 25, 1973, 88). It is likely that, reacting to Eugene Talmadge's victory, McGill came to believe that his instincts had failed him. Bleeding and brooding, he now felt obliged to scramble backward and to the right to retrieve his audience.

But it should be noted that despite his new and surprising embrace of the Talmadges, during this period of bitter disaffection McGill rarely wavered in his advocacy of civil rights, in his moral outrage at racial injustice, or in his conviction that whites should welcome blacks as full civic partners. In the same column that first defended the legislature's right to elect Herman governor, he wrote: "If we fail to go ahead with . . . political justice for the Negro citizen, there will be more and more chickens come home to roost. It simply is not possible always to uphold a moral wrong. And that is what we have been doing."

In full context, McGill deserves to be remembered as his former colleagues remember him and as he is typically represented in contemporary histories: "Journalism's last angry man." "A rock in a weary land." "The conscience of the South."

4. Tom Linder's first term as commissioner of agriculture ran from 1935 to 1937. One of his predecessors in that office was Eugene Talmadge, whom he claimed to have discovered in 1925 at a time when Talmadge had no thought of getting into politics. As Linder told the story proudly and repeatedly in later years, he caught Talmadge in the fields at Sugar Creek, called him to a fence, and there persuaded him to run against the incumbent

commissioner, J. J. Brown, whose army of inspectors had come to be a growing nuisance to farmers in the wiregrass country. Once elected, Talmadge made Linder his assistant in the Department of Agriculture. Six years later, when he became governor, Talmadge made Linder his executive secretary and in 1934 supported him in his successful race for commissioner. Defeated for reelection in 1936, Linder defected from the Talmadge camp and did not return until ten years later, lured by the white primary issue. Meanwhile, in 1941 he won back his position as agriculture commissioner. He served uninterruptedly thereafter until 1951.

Throughout most of his career Linder preached a strange admixture of religion, racism, and ruralism. Openly anti-Semitic, he told his followers that "the money-changers in the Temple were the internationalists of today" and insisted that the Roosevelts were originally "Jews in Germany named Rosenfelt who immigrated to Holland in search of asylum" (*Georgia Market Bulletin*, July 15, 1942; *Atlanta Journal*, March 23, 1947). At some point during his last years in office he became addicted to astrology and various forms of mysticism, including a few of his own creation. The *Market Bulletin*, which he edited, began to carry fewer and fewer items about weather, crops, and price supports and more and more ideas about God and Armageddon. On Christmas Eve, 1947, he told his followers to get ready for the end of the world. "According to the timetable of prophecy . . . the hour of cock crowing, or dawn, will be the year 2007 A.D." (*Atlanta Journal*, March 23, 1948).

5. Iowa-born Walter Cocking was dean of the College of Education at the University of Georgia. Governor Eugene Talmadge fired him in 1941 partly because he was "a foreigner" and partly because he was reported to have expressed the hope that white and Negro teachers might study together at a proposed graduate school. This, Talmadge said, was "racial co-education" and could not be tolerated. At the governor's insistence, the Board of Regents dismissed Cocking and another able educator. Almost immediately thereafter, the Southern University Conference issued a reprimand, declaring the action "a clear case of political interference with academic freedom." When it looked as if the university might lose its accreditation, students and alumni rallied in suffi-

cient numbers to send Talmadge packing in 1942 and to elect the young Ellis Arnall governor (*Life*, October 17, 1941, 43; also Cook, *Governors of Georgia*, 232).

6. In Greenville in May a jury had acquitted thirty-one white men, all but three of them taxi drivers, for the lynching of a Negro named Willie Earle. The twenty-four-year-old black had been accused of killing a cab driver and was in jail awaiting trial when a mob of about fifty, mostly friends and fellow cab drivers of the victim, snatched him from his cell after overpowering the jailer. Shortly thereafter Earle's mutilated body was found in a rural slaughter pen; he had been beaten, stabbed, and shot in the head. When Williams refers to "sensational" coverage in the New York press, he may have had in mind "Opera in Greenville," an unusually long report by the English writer Rebecca West that ran in the *New Yorker* only a week before our interview. A classic example of literary journalism, the piece treated the trial as social drama in which defendants and attorneys played out as a metaphor for the human condition. In hardly more than a week, Dame West's report had become the subject for vigorous discussion among lawyers, criminologists, and psychiatrists all over the country.

7. Dr. Alexander Heard. In 1947, a young political scientist not too long graduated from the University of North Carolina, he was working as a researcher for V. O. Key, author of the monumental *Southern Politics.* During the spring and summer of that year, our paths crossed frequently. After a distinguished teaching career, Alex became chancellor of Vanderbilt University and president of the Ford Foundation.

8. A journeyman printer and an ordained Baptist minister, Jack Johnston arrived in Columbus in 1930. He is said to have left Lynette, Alabama, on the edge of disgrace, for he had borrowed various amounts of money from his deacons, and his deacons were beginning to show an un-Christian spirit about wanting it back. He chose Columbus apparently because its mill villages offered the most receptive audience for his particular kind of evangelism. The Parson was of the school of fundamentalists who concentrated on the hereafter, and he had learned early in his ministry that the prospects of Heaven could be powerfully comforting to mill workers dissatisfied with the here.

Oddly enough, it was the AFL that first embraced Parson Jack when he pitched his tent in Columbus. In the midst of the depression, local union leaders put him on their payroll to preach about the sins of management. That arrangement, however, proved to be unprofitably short lived, because the AFL suffered a retrenchment and had to drop him. The Parson then turned to management. By 1932 he had started publishing irregularly a small opinion sheet called the *Trumpet*, which the masthead defined as an "orthodox, fundamental, pre-millennial, missionary" religious organ. With his first issue the Parson took aim at unionization and kept up a relentless fire—first against labor in general, then against the CIO in particular. Every time a union organizer showed up around Columbus's textile mills, copies of the *Trumpet* mysteriously appeared in workers' mail boxes. The message was that the CIO was communistic and un-American and that "no man could join a labor union and remain a Christian."

Thereafter Parson Jack did very well indeed. He established himself in his own Baptist Tabernacle, strategically located on Columbus's Second Avenue at Sixteenth Street, between the town proper and the old residential area, in the heart of the factory district and not too far from workers' homes. At the time we saw him in 1946, his sermons were attracting no fewer than a thousand persons every Sunday, drawing the faithful not only from the Columbus mills but also from those across the river in Phoenix City, Alabama. To augment receipts from the collection plate, he was soliciting contributions from wealthy uptown Columbus. Though little was said publicly, it was generally known in the white-collar community that both the Bradley and Bibb mills were subsidizing the *Trumpet* and giving him lucrative printing jobs.

Perhaps because mill executives preferred that he confine the *Trumpet* to antilabor and semireligious subjects, sometime in 1946 the Parson launched a second publication, the *Georgia Tribune,* to accommodate his expanding sociopolitical views. It was mainly through the *Tribune* that he emerged as a shrill advocate of white supremacy and Herman Talmadge. Circulation may have been at one time as much as thirty thousand, as he claimed. Street sales in Atlanta, however, ceased abruptly when a prominent Jewish citizen discovered the Parson's affection for the hate-mongering Columbians and wrote personal letters to *Tribune* advertisers. The result was twofold: indignant screams from Parson Jack ("Jews Attempt to Gag Freedom of the Press." "Jews Make Trouble for Themselves; Let the Anglo-Saxon Giant Awake") and such a marked decrease in advertising revenue that to fill space the Parson was obliged to run full-page public service ads, half-page pictures of the tabernacle, and quarter-page pictures of himself.

9. Parson Jack is referring to Peggy Alston Refoulé, member of a prominent Atlanta family who had been found murdered in her home on May 14, two months before our interview. It was widely held that Mrs. Refoulé had been raped, although there was little or no supporting evidence. The chief suspect died before he could be charged. The case was never solved.

10. Homer Loomis Jr. was the thirty-two-year-old organizer of the Columbians, a Nazi-like hate group that blossomed fearsomely in Atlanta in the fall of 1946 and died ignominiously six months later. A graduate of Princeton, he was the son of a wealthy Manhattan admiralty lawyer. To a newspaper interviewer, he explained himself as someone who had come to hate Jews growing up in New York on Park Avenue and to admire the Nazis while in Germany with the Second Armored Division during World War II. A reading of *Mein Kampf* had convinced him that Hitler's methods could yet make the world safe for Aryans, and on his return to the States he targeted the South as the most promising place to begin his mission. He arrived in Atlanta shortly before the July primary in time to canvass for Eugene Talmadge.

Loomis called himself "founder and executive director" of the Columbians. He gave the title of president to his chief lieutenant, a former railroad draftsman named Emory Burke, a native of Alabama who had sat out the war in New York City writing diatribes for the German-American Bund.

During their brief flurry in Atlanta, the pair garnered a lot of publicity but only a relatively small following. Loomis had a theatrical flair. He designed a lightning-flash symbol for a flag and worked the same symbol into shoulder patches on surplus U.S. Army shirts. He drilled a small cadre of rabble-rousers into the menacing image of crew-cut, ramrod-straight storm troopers. He rented a meeting hall and, inspired by Hitler's burning of the

Reichstag, arranged to have a smoke bomb thrown through a window just as Burke was winding up a harangue against Negroes, Jews, communists, and the Atlanta newspapers. ("The communists and the niggers did it," Burke shouted, seemingly on cue. "Now we're sure to win!") A series of similar incidents kept the Columbians on the front pages and brought notices in *Life* and *Time* magazines for several months thereafter.

At most, the Columbians never numbered more than a couple of hundred—all, in Loomis's words, "white trash from the slums." Prospective members were asked only three questions: (1) Do you hate Negroes? (2) Do you hate Jews? (3) Have you got three dollars (the inititation fee)? Although dues were negligible, the operating fund was known to rise appreciably after Loomis's trips to New York and Washington. The organization also got dollar contributions and useful, though camouflaged, moral support from a few Georgia politicians. The most conspicuous of these was Judge James C. Davis, a onetime Klansman then running for Congress against incumbent Helen Douglas Mankin. Davis's attorney, John A. Dunaway, wrote the Columbians' bylaws, and his advertising agency funneled as much as thirty thousand dollars into its treasury. After receiving Burke at his headquarters, Davis wrote a letter thanking him for his "real, tangible, and down-to-earth work."

The movement's goal was nothing less than to take over America and set up a dictatorship. As an example of the kind of dictatorship it had in mind, it zoned sections of Atlanta "permissible" for Negroes to occupy and set up patrols in white neighborhoods from which Negroes were "banned." The patrols ended after police caught three Columbians beating on a young Negro man with a blackjack. Loomis, Burke, and several others were indicted for assault, inciting to riot, illegal possession of dynamite, and usurpation of police authority. During the trial that followed, defecting members reported that Loomis and Burke were planning to dynamite Atlanta's city hall and the home of *Constitution* editor Ralph McGill. The two were convicted and imprisoned. Leaderless, the Columbians collapsed.

Index